Did David think for a minute that what ı
in to God's Word for his congregation d
still be part of his daily routine nearly a yeı
David and his wife, Joy, have become firm   ...privileged to
enjoy the rare opportunities we get to catch up. David's ability to
understand and communicate how the Bible, the truth of scripture, can
relate to everyone's everyday life is remarkable and demonstrates both a
lifetime of faithful study and an ear to hear. For this I'm grateful and I
know these brief studies will bring encouragement, challenge and
comfort, and will be useful in training us in righteousness. An old-
fashioned word but well worth investing in!

Derek Thomas MP

I'm so glad to commend this collection of lockdown reflections from my
old friend David Flanders. There's plenty of wit and wisdom in these
pages as David draws on personal experience and anecdotes as well as
scripture to provide encouragement and 'daily bread' for us. This is the
work of a pastor for his flock, but also a resource to draw on for anyone
in the joys and trials of life beyond this pandemic. But be warned, you
will be challenged as well as inspired by what you read. Enjoy!

David Mitchell
Senior Pastor
Woodlands Church, Bristol

David Flanders was fourteen years old when he attended one of our
missions in Tintagel, Cornwall. I was very aware that the hand of the
Lord was upon him as I prayed with him to receive the Holy Spirit. Over
the years David has gone from strength to strength and I am delighted
and honoured to have the privilege of writing this short endorsement for
his lockdown talks. I find these talks inspiring, enlightening and
empowering. It is obvious that these talks are anointed and God-
honouring; they are full of the Word and very relevant for these times
and seasons we are now currently experiencing. I highly recommend
these talks to anyone who really desires God's best and who has a vision
to reach their destiny and fulfil God's purpose for their life in these
challenging times.

Dr Cecil Stewart OBE

About the Author

David Flanders has travelled over a million miles with the gospel. He has been in full time ministry for forty years and started preaching when he was fourteen years old.

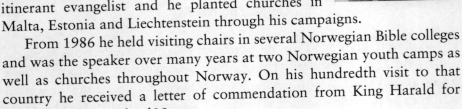

God's call on his life saw him ministering all over Europe, the UK and the United States as an itinerant evangelist and he planted churches in Malta, Estonia and Liechtenstein through his campaigns.

From 1986 he held visiting chairs in several Norwegian Bible colleges and was the speaker over many years at two Norwegian youth camps as well as churches throughout Norway. On his hundredth visit to that country he received a letter of commendation from King Harald for services to the youth of Norway.

In 1987, while still travelling extensively, David and his wife Joy were led by God to plant Souls Harbour Church in his hometown of Camelford, Cornwall where he remains the senior pastor today.

Other positions David has held for the Assemblies of God are West of England Church Planting Director, Director of Missions (The Americas) and leader of the AOG in Cornwall.

David was founder of The Malta Mission and co-founder of Agape Christian Training and the iSpeak Training course for preachers.

Since the coronavirus pandemic David's 'Daily Talks' on Facebook have garnered an international following with up to four hundred people watching each day.

David is also an accomplished watercolour artist and actor, and enjoys reading, films and the county of Cornwall!

To contact the author, please send an email to:

david@soulsharbour.com

More information about the author can be found
on the book's web page:

www.onwardsandupwards.org/lockdown-talks

Lockdown Talks

David Flanders

O&U
Onwards & Upwards

Onwards and Upwards Publishers

4 The Old Smithy, London Road, Rockbeare, EX5 2EA, United Kingdom
www.onwardsandupwards.org

First edition, published in the United Kingdom by Onwards and Upwards Publishers (2021).

ISBN: 978-1-78815-578-6
Typeface: Sabon LT

The views and opinions expressed in this book are the author's own, and do not necessarily represent the views and opinions of Onwards and Upwards Publishers or its staff.

Preface

When Prime Minister Boris Johnson announced the first Covid-19 lockdown in March 2020 my immediate thought was that my ministry would be suspended for twelve weeks. My second thought was, *could this be an opportunity?* I immediately set up my iPhone on a tripod and began to record a message to my church members. I heard myself saying, "…and I am going to record a message of encouragement and send it to you every day." The die was cast!

For the next year I recorded a three-minute message every morning; first writing it and then filming it, sometimes indoors, sometimes in my garden and sometimes 'on location'. It became a helpful habit and would help me through lockdown. What I discovered, though, was that it was helping many others too. People were listening every day from such diverse places as Cairo, Romania, the Philippines and Texas! The audience grew, and although I had only planned to do it for twelve weeks, neither the audience not the pandemic diminished!

At one point the Lord reminded me of something that I had spoken to Him about in 2019. I had sensed Him ask me what I would most like to do. I had replied, "Preach every day." So that was it! My prayer was answered in the most unexpected way.

After a year of writing and recording, the thought occurred to me that someone might like to publish the talks as a devotional book. I contacted Upwards and Onwards on the recommendation of a friend and the result is what you have in your hands.

I am profoundly grateful to God for His faithfulness and the inspiration of the Holy Spirit and to Onwards and Upwards for not hesitating.

David Flanders
Camelford, Cornwall
June 2021

1

…when he looks at it, [he] shall live.

Numbers 21:8 (NKJV)

There's a story in the Old Testament about how the people of Israel complained when God brought them out of Egypt and they were in the wilderness. They said, "Why have you brought us out to die? There's nothing to eat, nothing to drink, no toilet paper and we are fed up with the manna you send!" God was so annoyed that He released a load of snakes among them that started to bite them.

Moses their leader prayed for help and God said, "Make a bronze snake and lift it up on a pole and tell the people to look at it – when they do they will be healed."

You see, you can never be healed, you can never be saved, you can never be helped while you are looking at yourself. You always have to get your eyes off yourself and your situation.

When Peter and John met a lame man begging they told him, "Look at us." He had to take his eyes off himself. He couldn't be healed unless he did.

In Hebrews 12 we are told to fix our eyes on Jesus, the author and finisher of our faith. And that's the ultimate place to focus. The story in the Old Testament was an illustration of the story of Jesus on the cross. "When he looks at it he shall live."

In these days of self-isolation and social distancing it is tempting to look at ourselves and our plight. Nothing could be worse. We need to get our eyes off ourselves – look at Him and we shall live in every sense of the word.

God bless you – why not phone a neighbour today and check on them?

2

Idle hands are the devil's workshop.

Proverbs 16:27 (TLB)

My dear pastor and mentor, Rev. Arthur Neil, was once speaking at the AOG Home Missions Conference, and afterwards Stan Hyde and Keith Monument came up to me and said how refreshing it was that he had used the word 'indolent' instead of 'lazy'. That's how he was!

When I looked out at a confinement of twelve weeks stretching in front of me, my first thought was of laziness: *wow, a twelve-week holiday!* My second thought was, how quickly would I go mad?! I sat down with my iPad and started to work out what I could fill my time with for the Lord.

Idleness, laziness, indolence is something that is a result of the fall of man. It is like a sinful response to God's judgement that we should have to feed ourselves by the sweat of our brow. It is something that God hates because He knows what it produces; hence our text, "Idle hands are the devil's workshop," or, the devil finds work for idle hands. I think we all know this to be true.

Colossians 3:23 tells us Christians should "work with all your heart as though you were working for the Lord" (GNB). The work ethic is something that runs deeply though our faith. The Bible even says that lazy people are not going to get into heaven.

There is another side of the coin: boredom. Creative people will know that boredom actually sparks creativity. Professor Heather Lench at Texas A&M University, who has studied boredom, tells us it is a positive thing. Children with nothing to do will eventually invent something to do. Psychologists are worried that as we try to eliminate boredom with smartphones and gaming, we will be shutting down the creative side of our brains.

So I'm looking forward to being bored – my paintings might improve…

3

Rise up and walk.

Acts 3:6 (KJV)

On Wednesday I was talking about the lame man begging at the gate of the temple. Peter told him to "look at us" – to get his eyes off himself and look at the answer rather than the problem. When he did, Peter said, "In the name of Jesus Christ of Nazareth, rise up and walk." And he did. In fact, he started jumping around like a spring lamb and praising God.

I have found by personal experience that 'rising up' is a big part of healing. When I was extremely ill with water poisoning in Romania, Pastor Cornel prayed for me and then unceremoniously pulled me out of bed. "Get up, get up!" he shouted. As soon as my feet touched the floor, I was completely healed.

I felt God saying the other day that there is more to this 'rising up' than we have seen. We usually associate rising up with 'uprisings' – rebellion, revolution – but what about rising up in a good way? What about rising up for Jesus? Yesterday I mentioned two of my heroes: Arthur Neil and Stan Hyde. When they went to heaven I heard God say to me, "Rise up."

Some of us have been putting off rising up for years. We have used every excuse in the book. Now is the time! Rise up and walk! Stand up and be counted, step up and fill the gap!

To some today, God is saying it's time to rise up into new life – give your life to Jesus, rise up and walk with Him.

I'll leave you with the words of William Merrill's poem:

Rise up, O men of God!
Have done with lesser things;
Give heart and soul and mind and strength,
To serve the King of Kings.

Why not make contact today with someone you haven't spoken to for ages?

4

Rejoice always, pray continually, give thanks in all circumstances; for this is God's will for you in Christ Jesus.

1 Thessalonians 5:16-18 (NIV)

When I pulled back the curtains this morning and saw the sun rising over the horizon, it made me feel glad. I said, "Thank you, Jesus!"

Now, I know you all know this, but it's good to be reminded: *give thanks in all things.* Gratitude is amazing; it helps us keep things in perspective and therefore helps us to stay positive. It is also important to keep a balance in our relationship with God. Thanksgiving should be present in every prayer so that we remember how good God is and so that our prayers aren't just full of moans and groans!

Give thanks in all circumstances... Well, most of us have never had a circumstance like this lockdown before, but the Word says "in *all* circumstances".

We have got so much to be grateful for: the sun shining today, spring beginning to show itself, the hot meal we are eating, people who love us – the list goes on – but most of all that we are saved, that we know God, that we can talk to Him, that He gives us hope and peace and joy.

In this verse we are told to *keep rejoicing, keep praying* and *keep thanking.* Now, I'm no psychologist, but what a perfect recipe for good mental health that is! Let this be our slogan for the coming days: *keep rejoicing, keep praying* and *keep thanking!*

Hey, here's a good idea: write down twenty things that you are thankful for – and yes, you can put chocolate.

5

Joseph's master took him and put him in prison, (the place where the king's prisoners were confined). But while Joseph was there in the prison, the LORD was with him; he showed him kindness and granted him favour in the eyes of the prison warden. So the warden put Joseph in charge of all those held in the prison, and he was made responsible for all that was done there. The warden paid no attention to anything under Joseph's care, because the LORD was with Joseph and gave him success in whatever he did.

Genesis 39:20-23 (NIV)

I did think of dressing up in some prison garb for one of these talks but Joy wouldn't let me. Nevertheless, as we now have a lockdown in the UK for three weeks, some of us are going to feel like we are in prison. I promise you that your home is not like any prison that I have ever been in – and I've been in a few!

Even worse is that some of us are isolated alone – that is hard – so again, I ask you to call people or, better still, to Facetime them for a more personal touch.

I love the story of Joseph (he of the multicoloured dream-coat), though in our verses today we read about his prison experience. Twice in these verses it says that "the LORD was with him". I want you to remember that; *the Lord is with you* in your lockdown situation. And actually, the Lord is more with you than He was with Joseph because His Spirit lives in us.

There are two things I want you to see from Joseph's imprisonment:

- *His attitude was always right.* All the things that that guy went through – hated by his brothers, sold into slavery, falsely accused of rape, thrown into prison for years – and yet his attitude was always sweet. He never complained and never blamed God. I am sure that is why God stuck by him.
- *He made good use of his time.* Many jailbirds give up, languish in miserable boredom, but Joseph took it upon himself to revamp the jail. He sorted out their systems, took care of the other prisoners and soon became the guy running the place! So much so that the warders paid no attention to anything he had charge of.

What a great example for us in our temporary confinement – keep a sweet attitude and make good use of your time. If you do, God is going to bless you and use you in ways that you never expected.

6

Then the Philistines seized him, gouged out his eyes, and brought him down to Gaza, where he was bound with bronze shackles and forced to grind grain in the prison. However, the hair of his head began to grow back after it had been shaved.

Judges 16:21 (NLT)

Another well-known Bible hero who was in prison was Samson. You might know that the secret of his incredible strength was his hair. He had taken the vow of the Nazarite, which was to show his devotion to God by not having his hair cut (among other things). His girlfriend Delilah deceived him into letting her into his secret and his enemies came in by night, cut off his hair and captured him.

We don't know how long he was in prison for but we do know that it was long enough for his hair to grow again and his strength return. This set him up for his final victory. I am more and more convinced that this time of forced isolation is going to have the same effect on God's people. It is going to do us good. If we use our time wisely, as I said yesterday, we are going to grow in God, we are going to renew our strength, we will emerge stronger than we have ever been before! There are wonderful days ahead for the people of God! Let's believe it and let's get to it. If you have a study project or a prayer target that you have kept putting off, do it now. Oh, by the way, your hair is growing too.

7

While Jeremiah was still confined in the courtyard of the guard, the word of the LORD came to him a second time.

Jeremiah 33:1 (NIV)

A less well-known prison story from the Bible involves the prophet Jeremiah. Jeremiah was in and out of prison for most of his life. He was a young man, just a teenager when he started prophesying the messages that God gave him for the king and the people of Jerusalem. This kept getting him into trouble as his messages from God were not very popular. He warned the people that the Babylonians would capture Jerusalem and burn it to the ground. On one occasion he was put in stocks for a day; on another he was lowered into an empty water cistern where he sank into the deep mud at the bottom. Usually, though, it was a more conventional prison.

When I was reading about Jeremiah yesterday, Jeremiah 33:1 was the verse that jumped out at me. When Jeremiah was confined, the Lord spoke to him. Now, Jeremiah was a prophet – it was his gift, his calling and his job to hear God's voice – but God speaks to all of us.

What better time than a time of confinement to hear God speak? To hear God speak, you have to be quiet. Joy and I are actually enjoying the quiet at the moment. We are not putting the TV on as much. We are not listening to music as much. The quiet is very therapeutic. And in the silence you can hear God's voice.

My question is, what is the Lord saying to you? Listen for His voice today – you'll hear it.

8

I, John, both your brother and companion in the tribulation and kingdom and patience of Jesus Christ, was on the island that is called Patmos for the word of God and for the testimony of Jesus Christ. I was in the Spirit on the Lord's Day, and I heard behind me a loud voice, as of a trumpet...

Revelation 1:9-10 (NKJV)

Because we are in lockdown, we are looking this week at some of the things that happened to people in the Bible when they were in prison. There's quite a few of them! Today we go to the last book in the Bible – the book of Revelation, which was written by John the disciple of Jesus. More than fifty years after Jesus had died, risen and ascended into heaven, John was on the Roman prison island of Patmos. He had been sent there for preaching the gospel.

So John was confined, and what happened? God spoke to him in a vision – he had a revelation, probably the most significant revelation in history.

In the 1660s John Bunyan was confined in Bedford Jail. He was there for twelve years. But during that time he had a revelation – it was his book *Pilgrim's Progress* – and he wrote it there in the prison. It wasn't just one of the greatest Christian books of all time; it was the first ever novel in the English language.

Not many people get a revelation like that, but there is one revelation that everybody can have and that is a revelation of who Jesus is. You cannot become a Christian without that revelation. That is why I pray the same prayer every time before I preach the gospel: "Lord, open people's eyes to who you are." The Bible tells us that we are blind to who Jesus is and that we need a revelation – an eye-opening experience to see it.

I'm praying that anyone reading this who has not had that revelation will have it while they are in confinement! Why don't you pray it too? It could happen today!

9

Suddenly an angel of the Lord appeared and a light shone in the cell. He tapped Peter on the side and woke him up, saying, "Get up quickly." And the chains fell off his wrists.

Acts 12:7 (BSB)

Today Peter is our subject – Peter the disciple of Jesus who had been a fisherman. Soon after Jesus had ascended into heaven, the authorities made preaching about Him illegal. Peter didn't stop and so was arrested. He was chained by day between two soldiers with more soldiers guarding the cell. The church there in Jerusalem started to pray earnestly for his release. Then in the night an angel appeared in the cell, it was flooded with light and his chains fell off. The angel told him to get up and get dressed and follow him. He led him out of the prison to freedom.

Two things struck me when I read this today. Firstly, the confinement of Peter triggered earnest prayer. How wonderful if the confinement of all the Christians in our church / your church triggered earnest prayer! This situation should bring people to their knees. We had an online prayer meeting this week with Zoom. It was brilliant and we had more than double the number of participants than usual. A great use of your time is to pray – and pray for each other.

The second thing that struck me was that in response to their prayers Peter's chains fell off and he was free. Now, of course we are not manacled in chains in our confinement, but some of us are in bondage of a different sort. We have bad habits, wrong ways of talking and thinking, addictions which hold us captive. This period of forced isolation could be the time when our chains fall off. It would be great to surrender our faults and addictions to the Lord at this time and ask Him, in prayer, to deal with them and set us free. We could pray that the same would happen to others as well.

10

Then the LORD spoke to Jonah a second time: "Get up and go to the great city of Nineveh, and deliver the message of judgment I have given you." This time Jonah obeyed the LORD's command.

Jonah 3:1-3 (NLT)

This week I thought we would look at other people in the Bible who were isolated – not in prison this time, but for other reasons. The first one that came to mind was Jonah, of 'Jonah and the Whale' fame. Now, some people say it wasn't a whale but a fish – well, in ancient Hebrew there wasn't a word for 'whale' so they called it a great fish.

God had told Jonah to go to Ninevah to tell them to repent and turn to Him, but Jonah promptly got onto a boat and sailed off in the opposite direction. God sent a storm and the sailors threw him overboard as he advised them to. He was then swallowed by a whale and lived in its belly for three days.

It was there in isolation that he had time to reflect. He realised that he was going in the wrong direction and so he prayed and told God he was sorry. The whale then spat him out on a beach heading toward Ninevah.

So what happened to our friend Jonah when he was in isolation? Answer: he had time to consider the direction he was heading in and changed course. I wonder if there is anyone reading this today who needs to change course. You might need to repent and start walking with the Lord. You might have been disobedient, like Jonah, and know that what you are doing isn't God's will for your life. You might, when given time to seek God in isolation, find that God has something new for you to do – a new direction in ministry.

It's a great time to consider these things.

11

"Do not fear; go and do as you have said, but make me a small cake from it first, and bring it to me; and afterward make some for yourself and your son. For thus says the LORD God of Israel: 'The bin of flour shall not be used up, nor shall the jar of oil run dry, until the day the LORD sends rain on the earth.'"

1 Kings 17:13 (NKJV)

The story of Elijah has three people in isolation: Elijah himself, the widow of Zarephath and her son. Elijah had delivered a shocking message from God to King Ahab and his wife Jezebel: because of their idolatry, there would be no more rain. Then God told Elijah to get out of there fast! He went and hid by the stream called Cherith near where he came from in Gilead. There was no way to feed himself there, in hiding, but God sent ravens each morning and evening that brought him bread and meat, and of course he could drink from the stream. But after a while the stream dried up.

So God told him to go to Zarephath, about a hundred miles north on the Mediterranean coast, where a widow would feed him. When he got there the famine situation was desperate. The widow told him that she and her son were about to eat their last meal!

Elijah knew that God had promised to provide and he made a declaration of faith based on that promise. And what he said is exactly what happened: the flour and oil miraculously replenished each day.

In this coronavirus crisis many are worried about their ongoing situation. Will things run out? Will I be able to take care of my family? Will eighty percent of my wage be enough?

God has promised those that trust in Him that they will have all they need and will never be in want. But this doesn't just happen automatically. You have to do something. If Elijah had said to the widow, "Well, we'll just see what happens, shall we?" the miraculous provision would not have come. He had to make a declaration of faith. He had to say it out loud: "Thus says the Lord – the bin of flour will not be used up!"

Faith is activated by words. That's how it works. So, let us declare the promises of God over our family and see Him work. That's why I recommended saying Psalm 91 out loud each day. Do that and find other promises to declare too.

12

So when the woman saw that the tree was good for food, that it was pleasant to the eyes, and a tree desirable to make one wise, she took of its fruit and ate. She also gave to her husband with her, and he ate.

Genesis 3:6 (NKJV)

It's April Fools' Day! Did you know that the biggest fool that ever lived was someone in isolation? And that he and his wife were also the most isolated people that ever lived? Have you guessed yet?

Yes, Adam and Eve, our original progenitors. The only people in the world. God had made a perfect world. There was no death, no disease, no hard work, nothing to fear or worry about, and wonderful face-to-face fellowship with their creator. There was only one rule: don't eat the fruit of one tree. It was a real tree with real fruit. God told them that if they did, they would surely die. And guess what? Adam was a fool. Everything bad in the world started there. Thanks a lot…

My message today is, *don't be a fool.* Isolation, if we let it, can be a real tool in the devil's hands. Boredom, hopelessness and just being fed-up can make us susceptible to temptation. I have read of several states that have banned the sale of alcohol during the crisis; there have already been cases of domestic violence; others will be tempted to binge on pornography…

Psalm 101:2-3 (NLT) says, "I will be careful to live a blameless life – when will you come to help me? I will lead a life of integrity in my own home. I will refuse to look at anything vile and vulgar." What a wonderful statement for a time like this – "I will lead a life of integrity in my own home." So, don't be a fool today or any other day. We want to regenerate not degenerate! Let your relationship with God deepen in isolation, not be threatened by foolishness like Adam and Eve.

13

So Samuel took the horn of oil and anointed him in the presence of his brothers, and from that day on the Spirit of the LORD came powerfully upon David.

1 Samuel 16:13 (NIV)

You know, some people's jobs take them into isolation – I immediately think of lighthouse keepers, although there aren't many of them any more.

In the Bible we have one well known example of this – David the shepherd boy. He would spend many days in a row completely alone on the Bethlehem hillsides tending his father's sheep. One day one of his brothers came to fetch him. "There's somebody back at the farm who wants to see you," he said. David hurried back to the homestead where the prophet Samuel was on a mission from God to find the next king.

Farmer Jesse brought out seven of his sons but the Lord said no to each of them.

"Are these all the sons you have?" asked Samuel. Jesse told him there was the youngest, David, who was out tending the sheep. He was sent for, and when he came, God said, "This is the one!"

And what happened next? David went back to tending the sheep. But it wasn't the same David. The Spirit of the Lord was now upon him and in his isolation he began to sing and write worship songs to God. Those songs are recorded in the Bible; they are the Psalms. And Psalm 23 gives us the shepherd's eye view.

David must have wondered as a young lad what this was all about. To be anointed as King, receive the Holy Spirit and then go back into isolation! But God had things to do in his life – things to put into him and things to draw out of him. I believe that most of this was done using worship.

Most of us like singing to ourselves. Sing to God! Worship Him and maybe He will draw a new psalm out of you!

14

Then the apostles gathered to Jesus and told Him all things, both what they had done and what they had taught. And He said to them, "Come aside by yourselves to a deserted place and rest a while." For there were many coming and going, and they did not even have time to eat. So they departed to a deserted place in the boat by themselves.

Mark 6:30-32 (NKJV)

It's Friday and one of the things associated with this day is the modern expression, "Thank God it's Friday." I don't think this phrase has a very Christian origin, but there is a good sentiment there and it's this: I need a rest.

We all know that rest is a strong biblical concept, even being written into the Ten Commandments. One day in every seven we are to rest. It would have been strange if Jesus, being the Son of God, did not take notice of the divine imperative to rest. He did. We see Him in the Gospel accounts withdrawing into a lonely place to rest and pray. His times of solitude and rest were not long but were necessary.

Every day we talk about what we are going to do in lockdown but we overlook maybe the greatest advantage of all: rest. Now, I know that some people are working incredibly hard, even harder than usual, but most of us are freed from the endless round of things: work, shopping, travelling, eating out, sport, gyms, even going to church meetings! We are resting.

I have heard of people who say they haven't had a single headache since the lockdown began. Stress levels are falling. Our minds and bodies are getting a break. We are catching up with ourselves at last. If we do this right, when the time comes we will be so ready to meet the world, refreshed and renewed. "Come aside by yourselves to a deserted place and rest a while…" Don't feel guilty – rest!

15

But when God, who set me apart from my mother's womb and called me by His grace, was pleased to reveal His Son in me so that I might preach Him among the Gentiles, I did not rush to consult with flesh and blood, nor did I go up to Jerusalem to the apostles who came before me, but I went into Arabia and later returned to Damascus.

Galatians 1:15-17 (NIV)

Yesterday we looked at how Jesus took time out alone to rest. Today we are looking at someone else who purposefully put themselves into isolation, and that is the apostle Paul. Now, as most people know, Paul (or Saul, as he called himself when he was among his fellow Jews), had hated Jesus and His followers, and as a Pharisee he has obtained permission to hunt Christians down and imprison or kill them. Then, on a mission to do this in Damascus, he was met on the road by Jesus speaking to him from heaven. He was instantly converted and became perhaps the most significant follower of Christ there has ever been.

After getting healed, and baptised by the Christians in Damascus, Paul chose to go off by himself into the deserts of Arabia to self-isolate. This verse is the only reference to it in the Bible but it speaks volumes. He didn't immediately want to get together with the disciples in Jerusalem – who would have thought it a trick to catch them – but rather to get together with God alone. We don't know how long he spent in isolation – it could have been anything from a few months to a couple of years – but what we do know is this: God revealed to him His plan for the church, for missions and for the evangelisation of the world during that time.

Nobody ever had such a grasp of the importance of church as Paul did. He then laid down the blueprint he had received from God in his letters.

I believe that during our time of isolation we too will have a revelation from God about the importance of church and God's plan for it. We miss our physical contact with our brothers and sisters but we are beginning to realise, like never before, that *we are* the church and that it can function outside the walls of a building. Our community is thriving in isolation – it is unstoppable. It will never be the same again. Praise the Lord!

16

"...you have come into the Kingdom for such a time as this."

Esther 4:14 (NKJV)

Well, it's Holy Week now and it would be remiss of me not to talk this week about the passion of Christ. Why is it called the passion? Well the word 'passion' has changed its meaning; it used to mean 'to suffer, bear, endure'.

The passion starts on Palm Sunday with Jesus riding into Jerusalem on a young donkey – a colt.

Jesus told His disciples to go into the village of Bethpage and there they would find a colt tied up which they should untie and bring to Him. He borrowed a donkey. But it wasn't just any donkey – it had to be a donkey that no-one had ever ridden. To find a donkey like this meant that the animal had to be a very specific age: old enough to be ridden but not yet sold or used to bear weight. This is the most famous donkey in history and it was born at a certain time so that it would be this specific age, about four years old, when Jesus needed its services. It was born for that moment. This was its day. This was the reason it had been born.

We were born for now. This pandemic will probably be the greatest challenge of our lives. God has been preparing this generation of Christians for the task we now face. He has given us the tools to do the job. He has paved the way. We must rise to the task!

Last night in her address to the nation the Queen said, "I hope in the years to come everyone will be able to take pride in how they responded to this challenge." I'm not sure about the pride bit but we will be judged on how we responded, not least by God.

God is calling every one of us, even in self-isolation, to be His instruments at this time – to pray, to serve, to phone, to reach out, to witness, to encourage. "...you have come into the Kingdom for such a time as this."

17

He answered, "When you enter the city, a man carrying a jug of water will meet you. Follow him to the house he enters, and say to the owner of that house, 'The Teacher asks: Where is the guest room, where I may eat the Passover with My disciples?'"

Luke 22:10-11 (NIV)

Yesterday we saw that during the week of Jesus' passion, He borrowed a donkey – it was there ready and waiting for Him. Today we move on to the Passover. Jesus and His disciples needed a room in Jerusalem to celebrate the Passover meal in, but Jerusalem was packed with visitors that had come to celebrate the feast. Some scholars estimate over a million people!

How would they find an empty room? There was a need but there proved to be no difficulty. Jesus borrowed a room. The sign was a man carrying water – something you never saw, as that was a woman's job. There is no doubt that this was a miraculous provision. God set it up. God provided a room.

The lesson here is that God will always provide what we need to do His will. The Last Supper was something that had to happen. You cannot imagine Christianity without the Last Supper – without communion. And God provided what was needed to fulfil His will, and with it a way of finding that provision (the man carrying water).

If you have a job to do for Jesus, you will never be without what you need. God has supplied my needs on so many occasions in unexpected ways but the sign was always there. On one of my first missionary trips my friend and I arrived in Helsinki, Finland by train, hungry and disorientated. I walked the streets for an hour to try to find a sign. A car stopped and a man shouted, "Can I help you?" I told him I was looking for a church, or at least a Christian. He said, "Praise the Lord, brother, get in! God sent me to pick you up." In half an hour we were sitting down to a lovely meal with his family and later he called a church that had been praying for a preacher for their outreach weekend.

God will provide all that you need to do what He has told you to do. In this crisis situation, remember the Bible says, "And my God will supply all your needs according to his riches in glory by Christ Jesus." (KJV)

18

Christ Jesus came into the world to save sinners...

1 Timothy 1:15 (NIV)

In the last two talks we have seen how Jesus borrowed a donkey and borrowed a room; today we move on to Good Friday and there was something He needed to use on that day too: a cross. The Bible says, "When we were utterly helpless, Christ came at just the right time and died for us sinners." (Rom.5:6, NLT)

The ultimate purpose of Jesus coming into the world was to save sinners, to save us. The only way that this could be done was for Him to die. Only the blood of a perfect man could pay for the sins of the entire human race. But to die in the way that was prophesied, He needed a cross. Getting that cross was not easy. It needed the Jews and the Romans to agree – and they never agreed. Pilate tried to let Jesus off the death penalty – then there would have been no cross. Eventually there was such a wave of public opinion that Pilate caved and the death penalty was given.

But there were only three crosses. Barabbas, a notorious rebel and murderer was set free and Jesus took his place. He borrowed his cross.

It wasn't only Barabbas' cross that Jesus borrowed; it was ours. You see, the Bible says that because we have sinned we should die. Jesus did not only die in Barabbas' place but in ours too. I sometimes wonder if Barabbas realised the significance of this. If I had been him, I would have said, "You died for me – I will live for you!"

And I did say that – when I was fourteen – and I've been trying to live for Him ever since. How about you?

If you've never said that to Jesus, do it today. Say you're sorry for your sins and tell Him you will live for Him from now on.

19

He had done no wrong and had never deceived anyone. But he was buried like a criminal; he was put in a rich man's tomb.

Isaiah 53:9 (NLT)

We have seen that everything that Jesus needed to fulfil His passion was provided: a borrowed donkey, a borrowed room and a borrowed cross. To complete His work on earth, Jesus needed one more thing: a tomb.

As Isaiah had prophesied, he was put in a rich man's tomb. Amazingly, a secret follower of Jesus, Joseph of Arimathea, who was a prominent member of the council, happened to own a tomb in a nearby garden. He asked the Romans if he could take Jesus' body and bury it, thereby fulfilling the prophecy that He would be buried in a rich man's tomb.

But of course, burial wasn't the end. On Easter Sunday, the first day of the Jewish week, Jesus was raised from the dead. I love this story – especially the details. This is historical fact, not a fairy story.

The power of God's Holy Spirit zeroed in on that tomb and Jesus came back to life. They had mummified His body but He rose through the bandages and left them, like a butterfly's chrysalis, where He had lain. It was the sight of that that convinced the disciple John that Jesus was risen.

The release of God's power was so great in that garden of tombs that other dead people were brought back to life too and returned to their families, the Bible says!

It was Mary Magdalene who was the first person to see Him – thinking Him to be the gardener until He spoke to her.

Without the resurrection the whole Bible is meaningless. But with the resurrection we have the promise of new life. Romans 10:9 (NIV) says, "If you declare with your mouth, 'Jesus is Lord,' and believe in your heart that God raised him from the dead, you will be saved."

Over five hundred people saw Jesus after this. Many, even His own disciples, were sceptical until they saw Him for themselves. In the time between Easter Sunday and His ascension into heaven, Jesus gave the disciples a refresher course of His teaching, so it wasn't a fleeting glimpse that they had of the risen Christ.

Because Jesus is alive, we can know Him today. We can have a relationship with Him. If you have asked Him into your life this week, I would love to know.

God bless and Happy Easter!

20

We proclaim to you the one who existed from the beginning, whom we have heard and seen. We saw him with our own eyes and touched him with our own hands. He is the Word of life. This one who is life itself was revealed to us, and we have seen him. And now we testify and proclaim to you that he is the one who is eternal life. He was with the Father, and then he was revealed to us. We proclaim to you what we ourselves have actually seen and heard so that you may have fellowship with us. And our fellowship is with the Father and with his Son, Jesus Christ. We are writing these things so that you may fully share our joy.

1 John 1:1-4 (NLT)

The people who gathered around the cross to watch Jesus die were a diverse group indeed. In a strange way they are a microcosm of those who find themselves in church but continually miss the point – those for whom the penny has never dropped, so to speak.

First of all there were the soldiers – only one of them spotted what was going on in front of their very eyes and said, "Surely this is the Son of God."

Then there were the priests who, passing by, mocked Him. False religion is always a mockery of the truth of the gospel. Only concerned with the outward side of religion, not the inward reality, they were oblivious to what God was doing that day.

There were those who came just to watch the action. There are those today who like to spectate but never get involved; they keep their distance for fear that their lives might have to change if they encounter Christ for real.

There were the morbid. Today there are those who deal in death – the gravediggers, the funeral directors – and those who derive some kind of pleasure from suffering. Some of the people who spend most time in church sadly never discover who Jesus really is.

There were the relatives who were only there because of family ties. We know Mary was there but there were relatives of the other men on crosses. Some people only endure church because their wife goes, their husband goes. They never engage with the Christ of the cross.

But lastly there were the disciples; only John was close enough to speak with Jesus – maybe that's why he called himself the disciple Jesus loved. His account of what happened during Jesus' passion is the most detailed and extensive because he was not only there, he had a relationship with the man on the cross. Later in his life John was to write the words of today's reading.

21

For God so loved the world that he gave his only begotten son that whosoever believes in him shall not perish but have eternal life.

John 3:16 (NKJV)

These days we are used to sequels to popular films. In our talk today we have a return appearance of a character that first cropped up at the beginning of John's Gospel. I call it Nicodemus II. Nicodemus was an intellectual; he was known as the Teacher of Israel. He was a well-known and popular public speaker – the guy you would want for your keynote convention speaker but couldn't afford! He was an expert on Hebrew faith and law. But Nicodemus was intrigued by Jesus. Could he be the Messiah? He had to find out for himself but couldn't be seen to approach Him – his reputation was at stake. So he went at night to interview Jesus. As a result, we have one of the most well-known verses in the Bible (today's reading).

Nicodemus became a secret believer in Jesus. His position as a judge on the Sanhedrin (Israel's Supreme Court) would not allow him to go public.

At one point during Jesus' ministry, when soldiers were sent to arrest Jesus, Nicodemus spoke out, saying it was illegal to convict someone without hearing them speak.

Then, after the crucifixion, the moment comes for Nicodemus to shine. His friend Joseph of Arimathea, another secret believer, has asked for Jesus' body, to bury in his own tomb. He needs help with the burial and so Nicodemus brings seventy-five pounds of myrrh and fragrant aloes to put between the linen bindings. The two men carry this out together and so take their place in history.

There will come times in our lives when we are required by God to step up to the crease and do something for Him that nobody else can. The important thing is that we are in constant communication with God so that we can hear Him when it's our time. The job we have to do for Him might be a small one or a big one, it might be for one day or for many years, but one thing is certain: God has a job for all of us to do.

22

[Thomas said,] "Unless I see the nail marks in his hands and put my finger where the nails were, and put my hand into his side, I will not believe."

John 20:25 (NIV)

Someone that I always feel a bit sorry for at Easter is Thomas. We seldom reference him without saying 'doubting Thomas' and this is not fair. It's not fair because someone should not be forever labelled because of one remark they once made, but also because that remark was perfectly valid.

You see, Thomas was also known as Didymus, and *didymus* is the Greek word for 'twin'. Thomas had a twin brother. It is not such a stretch for us to think that Thomas had been the subject of mistaken identity all his life – as any identical twin will tell you. So when the other disciples said that they had seen the risen Lord Jesus, Thomas' first reaction was to think, "Ah! Mistaken identity again. They saw someone who looked just like Him."

Thomas wanted to see the evidence.

For a whole week Thomas maintained his position, but then, when all the disciples were together again, the Bible says that Jesus came and stood among them even though the doors were locked. "Peace be with you," He said (Jn.20:19,NIV), and then invited Thomas to do what he had said: "Put your finger here ... Don't be faithless any longer. Believe!" (Jn.20:27, NLT)

Thomas said, "My Lord and my God." We don't know whether he did (put his finger in Jesus' wounds) or not; most people think not and so do I. Meeting Jesus – hearing His voice, experiencing His presence – is enough to recognise Him; that is our evidence.

Christianity does not call for blind faith. That would be ridiculous! People think that though and compare our faith with believing in fairies!

We *do* have evidence. The evidence that God gives us is empirical: "...taste and see that the LORD is good..." (Ps.38:4, NKJV) Experience Jesus. If you haven't done it yet, why not try?

Thomas went farther in his missionary endeavours than any of the other disciples, founding a church in Kerela in India.

23

It was Mary Magdalene, Joanna, Mary the mother of James, and the other women with them, who told these things to the apostles.

Luke 24:10 (NKJV)

Joanna is someone easily forgotten from the Easter story, but not by us because our daughter is named after her. Joanna, Luke tells us in chapter 8, was the wife of Chuza, Herod's steward – a member of the Royal Court. The word that is used for "steward" suggests Chuza was in charge of the education of Herod's children.

King Herod lived in Tiberius, a town he had built on the Sea of Galilee; so when Joanna fell ill, she sent for Jesus who was nearby, and was healed. She became a disciple from that moment although it cannot have been easy for someone with her status.

She did not just *follow* Jesus, though. Luke tells us that she *provided* for Jesus and the disciples out of her own resources.

When Jesus went to Jerusalem, Joanna and the other women, Mary Magdalene, Mary the mother of James and others, went too. They were to witness all the events of His passion. They followed Nicodemus and Joseph of Arimathea to the tomb, saw how Jesus' body was laid and then went back to their lodgings to prepare more spices and oils. That's why some Christians call her St. Joanna the myrrh-bearer.

On Easter Sunday morning they returned to the tomb, found it empty and were spoken to by the angel.

Pastor Stan Hyde used to say that "God has His men in every strata of life" – well, it seems He has His women there also. Almost certainly, Joanna was the one who bought the spices and myrrh to use; the other women, who were fisher-folk, would not have been able to afford them.

In this time of great sadness and danger, Joanna was still giving to Jesus.

Joanna was one of just a few people that supported Jesus' ministry, and that makes her a very special person.

24

...Jesus himself came up and walked along with them.

Luke 24:15 (NIV)

Cleopas and his friend were walking back to Emmaus from Jerusalem on the day of Jesus' resurrection. As followers of Jesus, they had already heard the news that He had risen from the dead, but didn't know what to make of it. We don't know much about these two men and I have often wondered what made them so special that Jesus appeared to them personally. I have found out that some scholars believe Cleopas to be Jesus' uncle – Joseph's brother. That would give us a reason.

However, the story is a beautiful one. Luke tells us that as they walked they were joined by another who asked them what they were talking about. Jesus somehow hid His identity from them.

They stopped and replied rather petulantly, "Are you the only person who does not know what's been going on in Jerusalem?"

Jesus said, "What things?"

And so they told Him all that had happened and how confused they were about it.

"How foolish you are," Jesus said and explained the Old Testament prophesies concerning the Messiah.

As they got near Emmaus, Jesus made as though to go on but they persuaded Him to stay the night. When they sat down to supper and Jesus broke bread and prayed, they immediately knew it was Him and at that precise moment He disappeared.

I love the phrase in this story where it says, "...and Jesus came and walked with them." Two guys, confused, downcast, unsure about the future, a little afraid... Sound familiar? So many people are in that position right now. But what happened? Jesus came and walked with them.

I want to assure you today that in our isolation, confusion, fear for the future, Jesus comes and walks with us, His followers. He is there, involved and implicated in our lives. Have you recognised Him?

25

And you also were included in Christ when you heard the word of truth, the gospel of your salvation. Having believed, you were marked in him with a seal, the promised Holy Spirit...

Ephesians 1:13 (NIV)

If I told you that Pontius Pilate was born in Scotland, you would probably laugh. However, there is some suggestion that this could be the case. Also it is claimed that he was born in Taragona in Spain or Forchheim in Germany. Why anywhere would want to claim him seems strange. The fact is, we do not know where he was born. What is even stranger is that we don't know where he died – although there are legends aplenty. For history to lose track of a prominent Roman official is unusual and poses questions for us. Eusebius, a spiritual counsellor to the first Christian emperor, Constantine, claims that Pilate committed suicide out of remorse for sentencing Jesus to death.

Most people see Pontius Pilate as the bad guy of the Easter story and his name has gone down in infamy. You never heard of anyone calling their son Pilate, did you? But there is another side to the story. The famous Roman historian Tertullian claims in a letter that he wrote to the Emperor Tiberius that "Pilate was a Christian at heart". In fact, the churches of North Africa have always venerated Pilate, claiming that after the resurrection of Jesus he became a Christian. The Ethiopian Orthodox Church (probably the oldest church in the world) went as far as making him a saint. So we are left with several question marks. Where was he born? Where did he die? Was he a bad guy? Did he die a believer? Only heaven will tell. The point is this though: God knows. We can debate till the cows come home, but at the end of the day our opinions count for nothing. God's opinion is the only one that matters.

And it is the same with us. We are always trying to win people's approval and court their favour. What people think of us seems to matter so much to us, but what God thinks of us is the only thing that counts.

There are some whacky ideas about St. Peter standing at the Pearly Gates and the good and the bad we have done being weighed up. None of that is true. God doesn't look at us as other people do; He looks at the inner man. And what is God looking for? He is looking for the mark of Christ on us – the Holy Spirit. Jesus said, "I am the good shepherd; and I know My sheep." (Jn.10:14, NKJV)

26

When they came back from the tomb, they told all these things to the Eleven and to all the others. It was Mary Magdalene, Joanna, Mary the mother of James, and the others with them who told this to the apostles.

Luke 24:9-10 (NIV)

In the last of my talks on the Easter story I want to highlight one of the most important words in the Bible. Can you spot it in today's passage? It is mentioned twice in those two verses.

Well, the word I'm referring to is "others". This is such an important word. Without "others" this story would be much smaller and less believable. If Jesus only appeared after the resurrection to two or three people, we would immediately question it. There were the others at the last supper, the others on the mount of ascension and the others on the day of Pentecost.

We know the names of some of the others: Philip, Bartholomew, Jude. But there are a great many we don't know. Yet they were there. They were witnesses. They were followers, they were important. On the day of Pentecost there were over a hundred that we do not know the names of.

Of course, it would make the Bible very hard to read if it mentioned all their names all the time, but we do have a habit of making heroes. How often do we say, Hudson Taylor *and others* took the gospel to China, William Booth *and others* started the Salvation Army, Reinhard Bonnke *and others* took the gospel from Cape town to Cairo? They were all great men but without the others they could not have done it.

Let's face it: you and I are others too. Our names are not going to be recorded in history but that doesn't mean we are not valuable – actually, essential – to the work of God.

While history might overlook others, God never does! Jesus made this very clear in His teaching. He said, "…the last shall be first and the first last." (Matt.20:16, NKJV) He highlighted the widow's mite. He often went out of His way for others whose names are not recorded.

Never feel that because your name isn't mentioned or you are not in the limelight that you are not important to God. Others are the most important of all. As Jesus said, "…everyone who has given up houses or brothers or sisters or father or mother or children or property, for my sake, will receive a hundred times as much in return and will have eternal life. But many who seem to be important now will be the least important then, and those who are considered least here will be the greatest then." (Matt.19:29-30, NLT)

27

For this _cause_, I Paul, prisoner of Christ for you Gentiles...

Ephesians 3:1 (NKJV)

We are beginning to get used to using technology to communicate with each other during lockdown, and what a blessing it is! Even ten years ago we would not have been able to share our meetings with Facebook or Zoom. Thank God for this, because it is keeping us in touch and performing many functions of the church in this difficult time.

One thing that is missing though, and I almost hesitate to mention it, is *fellowship*. Facetime and Skype are better than just a telephone call but they don't replace actually being together. Several people say they are missing the hugs! Fellowship is so central to the concept of church, and it is more than just a coffee afterwards. The New Testament is full of references to fellowship, or *koinonia* as the original puts it, and there are many aspects of it.

Those familiar with *The Lord of the Rings* will know the first film in the series was called *The Fellowship of the Ring*. Around here we are familiar with King Arthur and the fellowship of the Round Table. The use of the word 'fellowship' in these settings is more akin to the Bible than the way we use it today. Let's face it – Frodo and his friends were not standing around drinking coffee and neither were Sir Lancelot and King Arthur's knights! There is a *cause*.

I love that word. We, as members of Christ's church, have a cause, the greatest cause of all. And we are united in the pursuance of it.

Koinonia is also translated 'partnership' and 'participation'. You, if you are a Christian, are a partner and a participator in the cause of Christ, and let me tell you this: no virus can stand in the way! In fact, I believe the opposite might be true. Has God pressed pause for the cause?! Friends, we have had a rest; now it's time to pursue the cause, taking advantage of this great opportunity that God has given us and with the tools that He has put at our fingertips... literally!

Ephesians 3:8-9 (NKJV) says, "To me, who am less than the least of all the saints, this grace was given, that I should preach among the Gentiles the unsearchable riches of Christ, and to make all see what is the fellowship of the mystery which from the beginning of the ages has been hidden in God..."

28

God is faithful, by whom you were called into the Fellowship of His Son, Jesus Christ our Lord.

1 Corinthians 1:9 (ESV)

Yesterday we started to look at the meaning of 'fellowship' and saw that it was more about people uniting in a cause than uniting around a cup of coffee. Covid-19 is not going to pause the cause either!

You have been *called!* You have been called into the fellowship of His son. *Invited!* We would get so excited if we were invited to a garden party at Buckingham Palace, but how much greater is this! To be invited into a band of believers with Jesus at the head! What a privilege!

The fellowship of His Son is a fellowship of love. It's not cold and clinical but warm and caring. It's a family; blood is thicker than water and we are related through the blood of the Lord Jesus Christ.

- We've got to look out for each other.
- We have lost our right to be islands.
- We are committed to connection.

Jesus told us that this fellowship has new rules. He said, "A new commandment I give unto you that you love one another; as I have loved you, you must love one another." (Jn.13:34, BSB) Of course, we know that love is an action not a sentiment and so *this love must be a doing kind of love.*

Again, the apostle John put it this way: "Dear children, let us not love with words or tongue but with actions and in truth." (1.Jn.3:18, NIV)

There has never been a better time than this for the church to get busy – *helping, phoning, collecting, shopping, comforting, reassuring,* and through these things taking the gospel and love of Jesus to a hurting world.

Do something today! No pause for the cause...

29

Therefore if there is any consolation in Christ, if any comfort of love, if any fellowship of the Spirit, if any affection and mercy, fulfil my joy by being like-minded, having the same love, being of one accord, of one mind. Let nothing be done through selfish ambition or conceit, but in humility let each esteem others better than himself. Let each of you look out not only for his own interests, but also for the interests of others.

Philippians 2:1-4 (NKJV)

This week we are looking at the real meaning of fellowship – *koinonia*. And today I want to look at a phrase that is found in Philippians: "fellowship of the Spirit".

The Holy Spirit brings power; He is the driving force, He brings the energy, the ability and the cohesion to the body.

Remember when the pregnant Mary met the pregnant Elizabeth and their unborn babies (Jesus and John the Baptist) both leapt in their wombs? That was because the Holy Spirit was in both babies.

Born again believers know each other too because the Holy Spirit lives in us. And that Holy Spirit brings us together.

Most people know about centrifugal force that makes things fly off when you spin. Well, the opposite of that is centripetal force that causes things to be kept together in the same circumstances. The devil exerts centrifugal force on the church – he wants us to fly off and do our own thing. The Holy Spirit exerts centripetal force which holds the church together.

We used to sing, "Bind us together, Lord, bind us together with cords that cannot be broken." That is the work of the Holy Spirit – the *fellowship* of the Spirit.

We all use the phrase from time to time, "I'm with you in spirit." I've never really known what that means! But at this time of forced physical separation we need to learn how to be together in spirit. We have to believe that the Holy Spirit will hold us together at this time and keep us in "one accord".

The apostle John, when isolated from his congregation on the prison island of Patmos, said, "I was in the Spirit on the Lord's day."(Rev.1:10, KJV) That is how he maintained fellowship with God and with His church – fellowship of the Spirit.

30

The cup of blessing that we bless is our fellowship in the blood of the Messiah, isn't it? The bread that we break is our fellowship in the body of the Messiah, isn't it?

1 Corinthians 10:16 (ISV)

This week we are looking at the true meaning of fellowship, which, as we have discovered, means a lot more than a social time after church. In 1 Corinthians Paul speaks about the breaking of bread, the communion, and 'communion' is the same word as 'fellowship'.

The broken bread represents the broken body of Jesus but it also represents the body of Christ, the church – one loaf split into many parts. In several of his letters Paul speaks about the way in which the body of Christ – like a human body – is made up of many members and each has a separate role to perform.

But there is unity as well as diversity in the body. A body is joined together. In Ephesians 4:16 (NLT) Paul says, "Under his direction, the whole body is fitted together perfectly. As each part does its own special work, it helps the other parts grow, so that the whole body is healthy and growing and full of love." The Greek word used here for "fitted together perfectly" is *synarmologeo* (pronounced soon-am-mol-og-eh-o) which is where the word 'LEGO'® came from!

So the members of a church are supposed to be fitted together perfectly. You can build great things with LEGO® because of the many different kind of bricks but also because they fit together so well.

Jesus wants to build great thing with His church – not buildings and structures but wonderfully organised and functioning teams that complement each other and get the job done so well that it is a thing of beauty.

You have a role to play in this! You are part of a team! Building something with LEGO® can be quite time consuming; the thing that takes the time is finding the right bricks! I think it's the same with the church. The trouble is, a lot of bricks don't know what kind of brick they are themselves!

This is our duty before God: to find out what our role is in His masterplan and then offer ourselves for His selection.

31

...that I may know Him and the power of His resurrection, and the fellowship of His sufferings...

Philippians 3:10 (NKJV)

Fellowship is the topic this week and we have looked at four different aspects of God's great invention. Today we look at one that is not quite so appealing: the fellowship of His sufferings.

At face value this seems like a big ask. Who would want to sign up to share in the suffering of Christ? But of course, we know that He went through that excruciating death so that we would not have to. He tasted death for everyone.

The rest of the verse is a clue. If we want to know Him and if we want the power of the resurrection in our lives then we have to go into partnership with Him (fellowship) in His suffering or death. In a partnership (let's say, in a football team) not all the players have to score goals or save goals – one does it for all the rest and they all benefit from what one did. So is the partnership of His sufferings.

The sad thing is that most people can't accept Jesus' sacrifice – they are saying, unless I score a goal it doesn't count. But if we are willing to humbly accept what He has done for us by going into partnership over the cross then we will be part of the winning team that can enjoy all the benefits of victory.

Now, I must say, we are not exempt from all suffering. Apart from that suffering that is common to all human beings, our partnership with Jesus will bring other suffering as well. I'm sure that one of the biggest heartaches for Jesus was being misunderstood, and that is something we as Christians have to face all the time. There is also the ridicule, rejection and even hatred that goes with the territory.

But Jesus said, "Blessed are you when men hate you, when they exclude you and insult you and reject your name as evil, because of the Son of Man. Rejoice in that day and leap for joy, because great is your reward in heaven." (Lk.6:22-23, BSB) In other words – it's all worth it!

32

...and to make all see what is the fellowship of the mystery, which from the beginning of the ages has been hidden in God who created all things through Jesus Christ...

Ephesians 3:9 (NKJV)

Today we are going to look at the biggest secret in history. It was such a secret that it was only known to God. Not even angels knew this secret. It was only revealed when Jesus came, and those who are told it and accept it become part of a privileged band. Paul calls this "the fellowship of the mystery".

The secret or mystery was God's rescue plan for the human race – that, at a given moment in time, He would send His Son Jesus into the world as one of us, and after He had lived a perfect life He would die as a perfect sacrifice redeeming the whole world.

We know this secret and have accepted Jesus as our saviour. By that very act, we are inducted into the fellowship of the mystery. The one aim of this fellowship is to let everyone know the secret.

Nothing is more important to God than this. The whole Bible revolves around this axis. Jesus' last words on earth were, "Go into all the world and tell this to everybody."

This week I have been reading about Henry Martyn, a man from Cornwall who, in 1805, sailed to India to share the secret. He was the first person to translate the New Testament into Urdu, Persian and Arabic – one of the greatest missionary linguists in history. He died at thirty-one years old. He is a member of this fellowship along with his friends John Newton, William Wilberforce and William Carey.

David Livingstone is a member, as are William and Katherine Booth, Billy Graham and Saint Piran. C.S. Lewis is, Francis Schaeffer is, Katherine Kulman is and Queen Elisabeth II is too!

You know the secret. It has changed your life. If you take up the challenge to tell others, you join the fellowship. How about it?

33

My peace I give to you; not as the world gives do I give to you.

John 14:27 (NKJV)

I've noticed that a word that I have been using a lot lately is 'peace', and I've felt the Lord leading me to talk about peace this week. It's a word so charged with meaning, a powerful word, but what does it actually mean? It is used in so many different contexts: from Tolstoy's *War and Peace,* to the hippy greeting, "Peace, man!"; from The Nobel Peace Prize and 'keeping the peace', to a bit of 'peace and quiet'. Peace can be the absence of war, a tranquil scene or a state of mind.

Jesus, who is called the Prince of Peace, said, "*My* peace I give to you," as though it were a different kind of peace. And perhaps it is. It is a peace that runs deep, a peace that lasts, abides in us and does not vary with our circumstances.

The word used in the NT for peace is *eirene* (i-ray-nay). It's where the name 'Eirene' comes from. But the literal meaning of this word is very strange; it means 'when all essential parts are joined together' – a kind of combination of having all your ducks in a row and having all bases covered; you have it sorted! Another translation of this word is 'wholeness'.

C.S. Lewis said that Christians have peace at the centre of their beings because all the great questions of life are answered for us.

Jesus gives us *His peace* (what better peace is there?) as a gift. This wholeness, this contentment, this tranquillity is a gift from Him to you. And He gives it to us when we are born again.

He follows His statement up by saying, "Not as the world gives do I give to you." The way the world gives its brand of peace is different; it comes in a bottle, or is inhaled or injected, it comes at a cost to us or to someone else. It is a compromise, a trade-off, and you have to keep coming back for more. I don't want that kind of peace.

I've never been drunk or stoned – but I have been high as a kite on Jesus' peace!

34

Then He arose and rebuked the wind, and said to the sea, "Peace, be still!"
And the wind ceased and there was a great calm.

Mark 4:39 (NKJV)

One of the most memorable times when Jesus used the word 'peace' was when He stilled the storm. I have preached on that miracle so many times and from so many angles but one thing that we often miss about that story is fact that Jesus *commands* peace!

I know in the storms of my life I have wished that Jesus would come and command peace. But when I think about it, some of the storms in my life are of my own making.

Jesus has already said, "Peace, be still," to *me,* but I didn't take any notice. The thing that I am learning through this enforced isolation is the blessing of peace. I can't be rushing around in endless busyness trying to juggle umpteen 'important' jobs, and the difference it has made to my life is phenomenal.

Jesus commands peace. I have often thought about that line in the 23rd Psalm, "He makes me to lie down in green pastures…" (v.2, NKJV) I used to think, why would He *make* you lie down? Now I know, because He has indeed *made* me lie down. I am learning that busyness and effectiveness are two different things. Here I am, so relaxed, so enjoying every day, and yet through these devotionals I am reaching more people each day than I would normally reach in a week!

This peace in our lives is so important to God that He legislated for it in the Ten Commandments: one day of enforced rest every seven. God knows that we are more effective, more productive, if we have a background of rest or peace in our lives – a day, not sitting around doing nothing, but of recharging our peace quotient from the Lord of Peace.

"Now may the Lord of peace Himself give you peace always in every way." (2.Thess.3:16, NIV) The Lord *be* with you.

35

When you enter a house, first say, 'Peace to this house' If a man of peace is there your peace will rest on him; if not it will return to you.

Luke 10:5-6 (NIV)

Yesterday I spoke about the importance of peace in the economy of God. Today I want to look something Jesus said that, at first glance, seems really strange…

From Jesus' words in today's passage, it looks like peace is thing – a tangible thing that you can give away! To be honest, I do sometimes say, "Peace to this house," when I visit someone – especially for the first time.

To put this verse into context, Jesus was sending out seventy disciples ahead of Himself to prepare the way, to take healing and good news about the kingdom of God. When they went to visit or stay with someone they took a gift – peace.

I think that somewhere here is a concept that we have lost. We know that Jews greet people with the word *"Shalom!"* and when I've been ministering in Italy and Romania the believers greet each other with *"Pace fratello!"* – "Peace, brother (or sister)!" This is a lovely thing and I wish we did it, but what Jesus was saying was more than this.

We have peace to give away. Amazing! Maybe we can give it to somebody by just saying it, I don't know, but what I do know is this:

1. If you have peace yourself you can change the atmosphere around you. You can be a peaceful influence, a calming catalyst – whether it's in your family, at your workplace or among your friends. People love to have you around because you still the storm. Jesus said, "Blessed are the peacemakers…" (Matt.5:9, NKJV) That is not just conflict resolution but bringing the peace of God into any environment.

2. We are, like those seventy sent out by Jesus – heralds of the gospel of peace. The best way of bringing peace into someone's life is introducing them to the Prince of Peace. I was thrilled to hear my friend and local MP say last week that the thing that the church should be doing more than anything in this crisis is sharing the gospel.

I pray that peace – and the gospel of peace – may rest on all those we speak to in the coming days.

36

Don't worry about anything; instead, pray about everything. Tell God what you need, and thank him for all he has done. If you do this, you will experience God's peace, which is far more wonderful than the human mind can understand. His peace will guard your hearts and minds as you live in Christ Jesus.

Philippians 4:6-7 (NLT)

One of the most well know phrases in the Bible concerning peace is "peace that passes all understanding". If ever there was a great advertisement for the Christian faith, this is it! If ever there was a time when it was right to make this known, this is it! My goodness, what a promise!

Have you ever thought about why or how the peace of God surpasses understanding? It's not because it is a kind of mystical thing that our finite minds are incapable of taking in. It's a lot simpler than that. It is the quality of the peace and when it shows up.

I know some people who have gone through extreme circumstances in their lives; one ninety-year-old lady I met in Estonia had just been released from a Soviet prison camp in Siberia where she had been for forty years because she owned two farms. Her demeanour was beautiful. I asked her, "How can you be like this? How are you so happy, so peaceful?" You see, the peace was past my understanding – I couldn't see how it was possible. She replied, "That's easy; I prayed and I forgave them every day."

I can't say I have ever been in such desperate circumstances but I have been at my wits' end and extremely frightened on occasions. When I prayed, a flood of peace poured into my heart and mind – it was almost a physical sensation. It made me exclaim, "Wow, what is that?" There was no rational explanation for it – it was beyond understanding.

In our present situation many people experience fear and anxiety – maybe waves of it come over you. The answer is right here in Philippians: pray about everything, tell God what you need and thank Him for all He has done. If you do this, you will experience God's peace.

Now is the time to pass the good news about God's peace on to your friends and family... Do it today!

37

But he was pierced for our transgressions, he was crushed for our iniquities; the punishment that brought us peace was on him, and by his wounds we are healed.

Isaiah 53:5 (NIV)

This week we are looking at the great gift of peace that God has given us through Jesus. This gift, that comes with salvation, is really one of the best and most valuable gifts God has given us. Part of the value is that it is because of the new peace in our hearts that we know we are saved, that something has really happened.

We always talk about salvation being the free gift of God, and it is. We cannot buy it and we cannot earn it; we can only receive it as a gift. But like all gifts, it is free to us but it had to be paid for somewhere. We know that Jesus paid the price for our salvation. He paid the debt that we owed.

We have to look in the Old Testament book of Isaiah, written seven hundred years before Jesus was born, to find the details of the transaction that Jesus made for us. You might call it an invoice for work done or to be done. Here, in today's verse, are four things that Jesus paid for with His sufferings. And we see that the punishment He took bought us peace. This helps us to understand what the basis of our peace is. The fact is, unless you have peace with God, you don't have peace at all.

Yes, there are all kinds of substitutes, counterfeits and placebos, but they are short-lived, and some do more harm than good. I used to have a sticker on my bible that said, "Real peace is Jesus," and that sums it up. The peace we have as Christians is based totally on our sins being forgiven. This brings us into a relationship with God – unlocking all the wonderful blessings of the kingdom of God for us, not least having the indwelling presence of Jesus 24/7.

This week an old warrior died in the depths of the Amazon jungle. His name, known to millions around the world, was Mincaye. In 1958, as a young man from the unreached murderous Waodani tribe, he speared missionary Nate Saint to death. When Saint's family then bravely came to live among the tribe, Mincaye gave his life to Jesus and received peace – peace with God, peace with himself and peace with the family. In fact, Nate Saint's son Steve and Mincaye became lifelong best friends.

His story, *The End of the Spear,* became known around the world as the greatest story of forgiveness and peace in a generation.

Real peace is Jesus!

38

You will keep him in perfect peace,
Whose mind is stayed on you,
Because he trusts in You.

Isaiah 26:3 (NKJV)

Today in the last of our talks on peace. I want to talk about *keeping* your peace. Once you have found the peace of God, it is important to hold on to it, because you can lose it. Usually this is a temporary loss but it can be longer.

We can think of different people in the Bible who lost their peace. One of them was Peter. When Peter denied knowing Jesus on the night before the crucifixion, the Bible says "he began to curse and swear" and then "he went out and wept bitterly" (Matt.26:74,75, NKJV). Peter was in a mess. Confusion, disappointment, anger and frustration were filling his mind because of what was going on around him. The result? He lost his peace.

He even told the other disciples he was going fishing – returning to his old life perhaps. I can imagine him thinking, "Well, at least there's one thing I know how to do!" He went fishing – all night – and caught nothing! His frustration grew; he could not find any peace by his own devices. He had taken his eyes off the ball – or more correctly, taken his mind off Jesus. He was trying to depend on himself and his own strengths to get him through.

Then Jesus came but they couldn't see it was Him. He stood there on the beach and shouted, asking them if they had caught anything. He told them to try the net on the other side of the boat, and to their surprise they caught a huge number of fish.

Peter's mind began to click into gear: "This doesn't happen; I know there weren't any fish there. There's only one person who could do this: Jesus!" He put his coat on and dived into the water swimming to Jesus. Finding his peace again.

In these uncertain days it is tempting to let our minds stray. If we do, we will lose our peace for sure.

You see, peace is a person. And to keep it we have to keep our mind focussed and dependent upon Him.

39

The Lord is my shepherd...

Psalm 23:1 (NKJV)

The Bible says, "The Lord is my shepherd." Who is yours? That's a good question. The thing about sheep is, they don't do well by themselves. They don't have much sense of danger; they wander off, get themselves in scrapes, and if they get on their back they die. What's more, sheep cannot defend themselves against predators.

Strange then, that Jesus should say that out of all animals, human beings are most like sheep. Sheep need a shepherd – someone to care for them, to lead them, to protect them – and so do we.

Deep down we are all looking for a shepherd – someone in whom we can put all our trust, someone to help us. Many of us put our trust in the wrong person and come out worse off.

Jesus, on the other hand, will never, ever let you down. He will stick by you like a limpet; He will guide you through your life with great wisdom. And He loves you regardless.

You don't have to do anything to win His love or to deserve His love. He loves you already, unconditionally – so much so that He died to pay the price for your sins.

As you know, He rose again and now invites you to be His sheep, to come under His care and protection.

The Lord is my shepherd – invite Him to become yours today.

40

In the beginning God created the heavens and the earth.

Genesis 1:1 (NIV)

"In the beginning God..." Most people know that these are the first words in the Bible. The wonderful story of creation unfolds from there. Actually, the Bible is full of beginnings – there is the beginning of marriage, the beginning of law, the beginning of sin, the beginning of worship, the beginning of nations – but the best beginning of all is the New Beginning that we are all offered in Jesus.

When this pandemic is over, a lot of people will be hoping for a new beginning for their business, their club or their social life, but today I'm giving you an opportunity to jump the gun. What about a new beginning for your *life?!*

Let's face it, most of us have not had the best track record; we have messed up in some of the most important areas of our lives. I often hear people say, "If only I could start again..." Well, you can! That is actually what the Bible is all about.

Our biggest problem is revealed to us every day when we look in the mirror: ourselves! Things are never going to be any different as long as we are the same. It's us that need to change and the only one who can do that is God. Let's face it, we have tried and failed. The root cause is sin – sins that have built up over the years, which we sometimes call 'baggage'.

People have tried everything imaginable to get rid of this but they can't. So God's own son, Jesus, came to the world to do it for us. By dying on the cross He took the punishment for us so that we could be forgiven. Not only forgiven but totally cleaned up. Not only cleaned up but born again into a new life.

I know what you're thinking: "Yes, but how long till I mess it up again?" Well, that's the second part of the equation. Now Jesus walks with you; in fact, He will be in you, giving you strength you never had before.

If that is not good news, I don't know what is – and believe me, it works!

So jump the gun and get a new beginning today.

Speak to God now and get instant access.

41

...seek and ye shall find...

Matthew 7:7 (KJV)

When I was a boy my dad often used to send me to fetch something for him. When I returned and said it wasn't there, he would say, "Seek and ye shall find." When I came back for a second time and told him I couldn't see it, he would go there with me, show me it was exactly where he had said it was and then sing, "He gave us eyes to see them..."[1]

It was always there, right under my nose, but I couldn't see it. I think the same is true in our quest for truth and meaning in life. We seek these things and look all over the place, even in obscure and sometimes crazy places – when all the time truth and meaning are right there under our noses.

It's true that familiarity breeds contempt. Could the answers you are looking for really be found in Jesus? I hear you say, "But that's church, that's the Bible, that's hymns and prayers – so uncool..." But don't mistake a living faith in Christ for a pastiche of second-hand impressions. It's like I often tell people: do you really think, if it was that tame and boring, I would want anything to do with it?

Jesus was the first one to say, "Seek and ye shall find," and it is a great invitation and a promise to find him and to know him.

Actor David Suchet, who plays Agatha Christie's Poirot, was brought up without any kind of faith. In the sixties he started seeking and got into gurus and meditation; then one evening, in a Seattle hotel room, he read Romans 8 and his seeking was rewarded. He says, "By the end of the letter [Romans], certainly by the end of the book, I was reading about a way of being and a way of life that I had been looking for all those years."[2]

You are invited to have a go and you are guaranteed success. Why not find a New Testament and start reading today?

---

[1] 'All Things Bright and Beautiful'; Cecil Frances Alexander (1848)
[2] *Daily Express;* 12 Dec 2012

42

Our Father...

Matthew 6:9 (NIV)

I think the words of Jesus in today's verse are two of the most remarkable words in the Bible – not in themselves of course, but for whom they are used.

The disciples had asked Jesus to teach them how to pray and He replied by saying, "...when you pray, say, Our Father..." (Luke 11:2, NKJV) *Our Father!* Not Almighty God, not Everlasting and Eternal God, not even Father of Jesus, but *our Father*. Nobody had ever called God Father before. The Jews were too afraid even to mention His name, yet here comes Jesus with "Our Father" – the most intimate and love-filled address possible.

Perhaps the most important message that Jesus brought with Him from heaven was how much God loves us and how much He wants to have a relationship with us. And this phrase says it all: "Our Father".

He told a story about a son who thought he knew best, left home with half his father's money and had a whale of a time until the money ran out. His newfound hangers-on abandoned him and he ended up living in a pigsty, literally.

He came to his senses and thought he might see if at least his father would give him a job – he'd burnt all his 'father-son' bridges and imagined the anger he'd have to face. So he began the long walk home. He was shocked, when he came in sight of the farm, that his dad ran out to meet him and threw a huge party to celebrate.

This is the picture that Jesus gives us of our own lives and our heavenly Father's love for us, when we have been going our own way: "Come home."

Love and forgiveness are waiting for you. Come home...

43

... if the Son sets you free, you will be free indeed.

John 8:36 (ESV)

I was watching the war film *A Bridge Too Far* this week and was once again touched by the scenes of liberation as the allies drove through those Dutch towns. The joy and the relief that men, women and children were expressing was palpable!

Liberation is a powerful thing; we remember the liberation of Terry Waite and other hostages when they were released from captivity.

Another of the best known phrases in the Bible is, "Whom the son sets free is free indeed." This is talking about that moment in our lives when we are set free, liberated, released. Like those Dutch people in the film, it is a moment of such joy and relief that we never forget it.

I can clearly remember the day of my liberation on January 21st, 1973. I can remember the feelings of freedom that swept over me and took my life in a wonderful new direction. What was I set free from? From self-destructive forces that were taking my life in a crazy direction. I have no doubt I wouldn't even be alive today if heaven's forces had not liberated me. So many of my old friends did not make it.

Jesus said that God had sent Him to proclaim liberty to the captives and, by dying on the cross, to pay the ransom demand on our lives. When we open our hearts to Him and He comes into our lives, we experience our liberation day!

The amazing thing is that we continue to live in freedom for the rest of our lives – we are no longer oppressed by the forces of evil or captive to our own habits.

"Whom the son sets free is free indeed!" Have your own Victory day today!

44

'You shall love the Lord your God with all your heart, with all your soul, with all your strength, and with all your mind,' and 'your neighbour as yourself.'

Luke 10:27 (NKJV)

Six times the Bible tells us to love the Lord our God with all our heart and with all our soul – three times in the Old Testament and three in the New.

When Jesus was asked which is the greatest commandment – a common question for debate at the time – this is what He replied: to love the Lord your God.

On another occasion an up-and-coming young man asked Jesus, "What do I have to do to get to heaven?"

Jesus replied, "What do you think? What does the Bible say?"

And he said, "'You shall love the Lord your God with all your heart, with all your soul, with all your strength, and with all your mind,' and 'your neighbour as yourself.'"

Jesus told him he was right – "Do this and you will live," He said.

This is obviously an incredibly important verse – but how do you do it? This week I am going to be trying to answer that question.

Love is a much misused word. We use it for everything from fish and chips to our latest grandchild! The truth is, you cannot love a thing, you can only love life. And only the kind of life that has personality. You cannot love an idea, or a concept or a force. We can only love God because He is real; He is Jehovah Shammah – the God who is there – as opposed to the god who is not there! His personality is so unique, so sublime, so perfect, that to know Him is to love Him.

The problem is that sin has drawn a veil between mankind and God so that He cannot be seen or known without His help. Jesus came into the world to reveal God to us and He will still reveal God to us today if we ask Him to.

Chares Spurgeon said, "The food of love is a sense of sin and a grateful sense of forgiveness."[3] When our sin is dealt with and we are forgiven, our first response is love for God.

---

[3] Metropolitan Tabernacle Pulpit Volume 14 (March 22, 1868); 'The Woman that was a Sinner'

45

'You shall love the Lord your God with all your heart...'

Luke 10:27 (NKJV)

How do I love God? How do I love Him with all my heart and soul? How do I keep the commandment that Jesus said was the greatest? Today we are looking at loving God with all your heart.

Just because the word 'God' is in this sentence, it doesn't mean that suddenly we don't know what love means. Of course we do. We are not talking about respect, admiration, acceptance, belief – all those are important – we are talking about *love!*

To love God with all your heart is to care about Him.

I never hear people talk about this! It seems to be always about His care for us, but surely love is a two-way thing. Reciprocal. It's a poor kind of love, a poor kind of relationship, if the care is only in one direction.

We need to care about how God feels. Did anybody ask Him how He feels about coronavirus? If the subject of what God thinks about something comes up, we seem to presume or guess what He thinks. Try that with your wife!

I once asked God how He felt about Camelford and I was shocked at His reply. The things that upset Him were not what I would have said at all.

As Christians we are so obsessed about getting the best. We are so quick to quote that all things work together for good for us – but what about Him? Do we desire the best for Him? When we pray in the Lord's prayer, "Thy will be done," what we are really saying is, "I pray that things go the way you want them to, that this works out best for you." That puts a whole new slant on things – on our choices.

To love God is to make Him the centre of your affections, His name to be the first on your lips in the morning and the last at night.

Just before I became a Christian, I remember getting annoyed at the older youth in our group. "It's 'the Lord' this and 'the Lord' that; can't you talk about anything else?!"

I didn't realise that they were just in love. I soon was too.

46

'You shall love the Lord your God with ... with all your soul...'
                                        Luke 10:27 (NKJV)

Y ou have heard of soul music and soulmates but what does it mean to love God with all your soul? Remember, Jesus said that the greatest commandment was to love the Lord your God with all your heart *and all your soul*.

Our soul consists of our intellect, our emotions and our will. In the same way as we say someone has put their heart and soul into something, meaning everything they have, so loving God with all your soul means with your whole being. That's easy to say, but how does it play out in everyday life?

Soul speaks of life; God made Adam *a living soul*. We are invited to love God not with our soul but with *all* our soul, with *all* our life, with every part of our life.

We are very good as human beings at compartmentalising. Some say this is how we deal with issues and keep sane, but compartmentalising can be a problem as a Christian if we put our spiritual life in a box and keep it separate from other things in our lives. Loving God with all our soul means to ask Him to be in every compartment, every area. This will bring us harmony within, as each part is singing off the same hymn-sheet and is not in conflict with other parts.

The Spirit of God wants to pervade our whole being – all our soul. He wants to bring His presence, His grace, His strength into every part. If you are struggling in a particular area – maybe relationships, maybe addiction or perhaps timidity – then it is very likely that God has not been invited into this part. That happens if we are ashamed of that area and try to hide it, or if our old nature is putting up a fight for squatters' rights!

Today, start to ensure God is in each compartment. You have to invite Him in, then stand back and watch Him work.

47

'You shall love the Lord your God with … with all your mind…'

Luke 10:27 (NKJV)

The human mind is something that has always fascinated me – but how do you love God with all your mind? First of all, we must not think that mind love is of any less value than heart love – it is just different. The word that is used in the original Greek suggests that we love God by using of our mind especially with deep thought.

There are four ways in which we can do this. The obvious one is by increasing our *knowledge*. Paul tells us to "Give attention to reading" (1.Tim.4:13, NKJV) and "study to show yourself approved" (2.Tim.2:15, KJ21). I find that reading or listening to something that makes me think will stimulate my mind to start thinking great thoughts of its own. To love God with your mind is to be a lifelong student of His Word.

Second is *imagination,* and the same Greek word for mind can be translated 'imagination'. Don't be afraid to use your imagination for Him. Where would we be without C.S. Lewis and his imaginative allegorical books? Where would children's work be without creative teachers? What about missionary innovator Steve Saint and his flying car and drones for jungle work and the inspirational painters, songwriters, composers and movie-makers?

Third is *wisdom* – using your mind to make wise choices yourself and for giving wise counsel to others who ask for help and advice. This is loving God with your mind.

And fourthly, *intellect* – whether we are clever in the conventional sense or not, we are all under the inspiration of the Holy Spirit, able to think great thoughts! Many of the Bible authors were people with no formal education yet able to convey the mind of God to us. Many uneducated preachers have stunned the world with their insight and deep thought.

You might never have thought of any of these as ways of loving God before, but I encourage you today to start employing your mind in His service with greater resolve.

48

'You shall love the Lord your God ... with all your strength...'
Luke 10:27 (NKJV)

Have you got what it takes to love God? A lot of people, for various reasons, would say no. But in today's verse the Bible says you have. The Greek word *ischus* used here for "strength" means 'potential or residual power' – possessing the strength to do something. So if Jesus tells us that we should love God with all our strength, we obviously have the power to do it.

As human beings we have a lot of potential. Some people think they know their strengths – but most of us have reservoirs of strength that we are unaware of. When we first heard about the pandemic and the lockdown, we wondered how we would ever cope with such a curtailment of normal life, but here we are fifty-three days in and we are OK. Actually, *better* than OK. We had strength we didn't know about.

When it comes to loving and serving God, we have potential that we don't know about either. It is hidden until we need it. It could surface at a time of extremity like persecution. We often think the Christians of the persecuted church are amazing in their courage and resilience, but they are no different to us. You would be just the same if the situation arose.

But think on this: why do we wait until bad things happen to find out how strong we are? Why not start using that incredible reservoir of power now by attempting something for God – maybe something that you have been holding back on because you thought you were not strong enough?

The father of missions, William Carey, wrote in the late 1700s, "Expect great things from God. Attempt great things for God."

Loving God with all your strength is using your potential for His glory.

49

'You shall love the Lord your God with all your heart, with all your soul, with all your strength, and with all your mind,' and 'your neighbour as yourself.'

Luke 10:27 (NKJV)

What is the most important law in the UK? Wow – what a question! Parliament and people could debate that until the cows come home but I don't think you would ever get agreement.

The people of Jesus' time used to debate this endlessly and one day they asked Him His opinion. He said, "You must love the Lord your God with all your heart, all your soul, and all your mind. This is the first and greatest commandment." Then He quickly followed it up by saying, "A second is equally important: love your neighbour as yourself." (Matt.22:39, NKJV)

Neither of these was part of the Ten Commandments but both were given to the people of God at other times. Yet Jesus – who devised all of the commandments in the first place – knew that these two were the spirit of the law. He said, "All the other commandments and all the demands of the prophets are based on these two commandments." (Matt.22:40, NLT)

And when you think about it, it is really true; if you really love God and really love others and that love is not all talk and feelings, but functioning and active, you will keep not only the other commandments but the will of God.

Neither of these commandments can stand alone. It is not good enough to just love God or just love people. You can imagine the outcome of that. The apostle John tells us that if we say we love God and don't love people, we are lying. There are many reasons for that, but for today let's consider this: we demonstrate our love for God by caring for others. Not just the loveable ones but the unloveable.

The most notable Christians that we know of and are inspired by are those that did this very thing: David Wilkerson loved God and gang members in New York; Mother Theresa loved God and the poor in India; General Booth loved God and the drunks of London; George Muller loved God and the orphans of Bristol.

Whom has God put on your heart to love?

50

For God so loved the world that he gave his one and only Son, that whoever believes in him shall not perish but have eternal life.

John 3:16 (NIV)

This week I want to celebrate what you could call 'the gospel of us'. We are always talking about the fact that Jesus *died* for us – but actually *everything* that Jesus did, He did for us. Jesus' mission to earth was totally humancentric.

It never ceases to amaze me that the God of the universe is so interested in our little planet. Larry Norman once sang that if there is life on other planets, Jesus has been there and died for them too. It's a nice thought but I don't think it's true. C.S. Lewis, in his science fiction books *The Cosmic Trilogy,* has other planets that were like earth but at different stages in their relationship with God – one that did not rebel against God, for instance. Again, an interesting idea and quite helpful for understanding our own experience, but just fiction.

When we read, "For God so loved the world…" it does not mean that it is His pet planet, His favourite. For the Bible to make sense, and indeed for cosmology to make sense, earth has to be His only populated planet. If earth were some kind of experiment, human zoo or hobby for God, He would not have taken the devastating step of sending His only Son to die such a cruel death for its inhabitants.

The Apostle Paul tells us, "He died for our sins, just as God our Father planned, in order to rescue us from this evil world in which we live," (Gal.1:4, MSG) and, "God sent him to buy freedom for us who were slaves to the law, so that he could adopt us as his very own children." (Gal.4:5, NLT)

There is no doubt that the one and only reason that Jesus came into the world was for us – not just to show Himself to us, as it were, but to die in order to rescue and redeem us. As the old hymn tells us, "There was no other good enough to pay the price of sin; He only could unlock the gate of heaven and let us in."[4]

So the first point in 'the gospel of us' is that Jesus came into the world and was born for us.

---

[4] 'There is a Green Hill Far Away'; Cecil Frances Alexander (1848)

51

The Word became flesh and lived among us...

John 1:14 (WEB)

Our theme this week is 'the gospel of us' – how everything that Jesus did was for us. Today we look at the fact that He *lived* for us.

"The Word" with a capital 'W' is another name for Jesus, but the Greek word used here is *logos,* which means 'meaning'. The Meaning became flesh and lived among us. Jesus came to live for us – to show us the meaning; to demonstrate it.

- He showed us how to love others but at the same time not to compromise truth.
- He showed us how to live with dignity and yet be the servant of all.
- He showed us how to be in the world but not of the world.

And so much more besides.

Later in his Gospel, John reports Jesus saying, "For I have given you an example, that you should do as I have done to you." (1.Jn.13:15, NKJV)

Have you seen that funny sketch were somebody says, "Please, walk this way," and the person follows them imitating the actual way they walk? In his first letter John says something similar, once again stressing the point that we should imitate Jesus: "He who says he abides in Him ought himself also to walk just as He walked." (1.Jn.2:6, NKJV)

All these things are vitally important to living the Christian life, but the primary reason Jesus lived for thirty-three years as a man was that He could live a sinless life. His death on the cross would not have paid for our sin unless He was sin-free. A sacrifice always had to be spotless. 2 Corinthians 5:21 (NKJV) explains, "For He made Him who knew no sin to be sin *for us,* that we might become the righteousness of God in Him."

Also, if He had arrived in this world as a grown man and a week later died for our sins, He could have *technically* been sin-free but not *experientially*. The fact that He was tempted in every way as we are and yet did not sin makes His sinlessness real.

And it makes it for us.

52

...who gave Himself for us, that He might redeem us from every lawless deed and purify for Himself His own special people, zealous for good works.

Titus 2:14 (NKJV)

Everything Jesus did, He did for us. In today's verse, Paul doesn't just say Jesus died for us or gave His life for us, but He *gave Himself* for us. That makes it so much more personal and so much more all-encompassing, summing up our theme: He gave Himself; He gave everything.

But notice that it says "Himself" twice in this verse. One is about giving, the other is about getting. He *gave* Himself to redeem us so that He could purify *for* Himself His own special people. He wanted people to be pure enough to be His – His special ones, His posse (as the kids would say).

There is something so charming and winsome about this. It has love written all over it. We can look in the mirror and say, "I am one of his special people."

These special people have a special role. They are distinguished from other people by their eagerness to do good and to do what is right. This is a simple but profound description of what a Christian is.

In various places we read that Jesus suffered for us, laid down His life for us, died for us... but I want to give attention to one more: "He was delivered over to death for our sins and was raised to life for our justification." (Rom.4:25, NKJV) He *rose* for us.

He rose for our justification – which means 'to make us right with God'. How does this work? Later in Romans Paul tells us that "if you confess with your mouth, 'Jesus is Lord,' and believe in your heart that God raised him from the dead, you will be saved" (Rom.10:9, NKJV).

Without the resurrection there is no salvation. If Jesus stayed dead there is no victory. If He did not rise we cannot rise either. He did it for us!

53

This hope we have as an anchor of the soul, both sure and steadfast, and which enters the Presence behind the veil, where the forerunner has entered for us, even Jesus, having become High Priest forever according to the order of Melchizedek.

Hebrews 6:19-20 (NKJV)

Today is Ascension Day and so of course we are talking about the fact that Jesus ascended for us. The ascension happened forty days after Easter. During that time Jesus had met with the disciples and given them a refresher course of His teaching, now that their eyes were open. Then, on Ascension Day, the disciples assembled on the Mount of Olives just outside Jerusalem, and Jesus was physically taken up into the sky until a cloud enveloped Him.

It is not easy to think offhand about how this could possibly be for us – but it was, as today's verse shows us. The key word here in this verse is "forerunner" – literally, 'scout'. Jesus ascends into heaven and enters the presence of God as our scout, as one who goes before to prepare the way. We could even say that the ascension is a trial run for the rapture when we will ascend to join Him in the air.

Hebrews 9:24 (BSB) goes on to say, "For Christ did not enter a man-made sanctuary that was only a copy of the true one; He entered heaven itself, now to appear for us in God's presence." So once in heaven, Jesus appears in the presence of God for us. *For us!* In what way is it for us? The phrase "appear for us" is the way we talk about a lawyer in court – appearing on our behalf – and we know from Romans 8:34 that Jesus "who is even at the right hand of God … makes intercession for us" (Rom.8:34, NKJV). He pleads our case.

Hebrews 10 finishes up this picture by telling us that we enter the presence of God by a new and living way which He consecrated, or inaugurated, for us through the veil – that is, His flesh. Our access to God the Father is made possible because Jesus has ascended back into heaven and presented His blood for our sins.

Lastly, a verse in Ephesians 4 shows us yet another 'for us'. "When He ascended on high, He led captivity captive, And gave gifts to men." (v.8, NKJV) Because of Christ's ascension and presence in heaven, He is able to send us gifts – the gift of the Holy Spirit and all the other gifts that come with it!

54

And if I go and prepare a place for you, I will come back and take you to be with me that you also may be where I am.

John 14:3 (NIV)

It is amazing that Jesus was born for us, lived for us, died for us, rose for us, ascended for us and today we see that He is coming again for us. There is a lot of talk at the moment about the second coming because of what is going on in the world right now. Bibles are flying off shelves and Christian websites are getting more hits than ever because people want answers. Why should a global pandemic spark such interest in the second coming? Because it is one of the signs of the end of the age.

Jesus said, "For nation will rise against nation, and kingdom against kingdom. And there will be famines, pestilences, and earthquakes in various places. All these are the beginning of sorrows." (Matt.24:7-8, NKJV) 'Pestilence' is an old-fashioned word for 'epidemic'. Jesus is saying that epidemics are the "beginning of sorrows" or birthing pains. Matthew 24 is not exactly bedtime reading! Let's put it this way: things are not going to get better.

I don't think we can brush off Covid-19 as a run-of-the-mill occurrence. It might not be the most dangerous disease ever but it is certainly the most widespread. This is a warning from heaven that Jesus is coming back. He is coming to take all those that belong to Him off this planet before God's final judgement falls on it. The last thing that happens before war is declared is that a nation removes its ambassadors, and we are the ambassadors of Christ!

Our job right now is to tell everybody that they can be saved too. I heard last week that a young man who is not living for Christ said to His mum, "Why are Christians not preaching the gospel? They need to preach the gospel right now. Don't they understand that?"

"For the Lord himself will come down from heaven, with a loud command, with the voice of the archangel and with the trumpet call of God, and the dead in Christ will rise first. After that, we who are still alive and are left will be caught up together with them in the clouds to meet the Lord in the air. And so we will be with the Lord for ever. Therefore encourage each other with these words."[5]

---

[5] 1 Thessalonians 4:16-18

I don't want to ruin your Friday, but we have to get busy! And we have to get busy *now!*

55

SATURDAY, 23RD MAY, 2020

*And I will ask the Father, and he will give you another advocate to help you
and be with you for ever – the Spirit of truth. The world cannot accept him,
because it neither sees him nor knows him. But you know him, for he lives
with you and will be in you. I will not leave you as orphans; I will come to
you.*

John 14:16-18 (NIV)

Our last talk on 'the gospel of us' is a good lead into Pentecost week next week because we are looking at Jesus coming to live in us.

Jesus told his disciples that it was to their advantage that He was going away. *What?!* What on earth could be better than having Jesus by your side day by day? How many of us would not want that right now? He could sort things out! He could heal us of coronavirus and all the rest of our aches and pains. He could bring life to our church and we could sit at His feet as He would teach us. Jesus with us – my goodness, that would be the best!

But Jesus said to them that night that this was *not* the best. What they had experienced for three years was not the best God had to offer. He told them that at the moment He was with them, but if He went away – to heaven – He could be *in* them! He said He would come to them and indwell them.

Galatians 4:6 (NIV) helps us understand this. "Because you are sons, God sent the Spirit of His Son into our hearts, the Spirit who calls out, 'Abba, Father.'" The Holy Spirit is the Spirit of Jesus. That's why we can say that Jesus lives in our hearts and that we are filled with the Holy Spirit.

Now, if you put two and two together, we are in the same boat as the disciples. Jesus has gone to heaven but His Spirit is sent back by God to indwell us and that is better!

All the things that Jesus did, He can still do but now through us. It really is to our advantage. And instead of having one physical body, He now has thousands, millions!

Next week we are going to be looking at the things that the Holy Spirit does to us and through us.

56

When the Counsellor comes, whom I will send to you from the Father, the Spirit of truth who goes out from the Father, he will testify about me. And you also must testify, for you have been with me from the beginning.

John 15:26-27 (NIV)

This week, as we look forward to Pentecost next Sunday, we are going to be looking at the work of the Holy Spirit. Before Jesus ascended into heaven He promised the Holy Spirit to His followers. The Holy Spirit will live in us and help us in all manner of ways. But something that is often overlooked is that the Holy Spirit has His own work to do as well. "He will testify about me," Jesus said. Some versions say "bear witness". What does "testify" or "bear witness" mean? It means 'provide evidence'. The Holy Spirit will provide evidence about Jesus.

As the disciples were about to step out into the greatest challenge ever given ("Go into all the world and preach the gospel to every creature" – Mk.16:15, NKJV) – a challenge which two thousand years later is still being worked at – the prospect for them must have seemed incredibly daunting. Men who had never been more than a hundred miles from home were told to become international travellers.

They must have thought about the obstacles that they faced: the languages, the lack of money, the pagan religions, the hostile authorities... How on earth?! Literally!

But Jesus told them they would have a helper and this helper would testify about Him, just as the disciples would testify about Him – He would provide evidence.

And this is just what He does. He prepares the way for the gospel by providing evidence to people – before we get there! Most people that I speak to about Jesus have already had some kind of experience that made them think that there was a spiritual side of life, that God did exist. The Holy Spirit had already been there, providing evidence.

A friend of mine, whom I actually baptised many years ago in Malta, today has a large church in Iraq made up entirely of Muslims that met Jesus in a dream and woke up Christians! The Holy Spirit was there – providing evidence.

We are not asked to do this thing alone. We have a very capable co-worker: God the Holy Spirit!

57

Believe me when I say that I am in the Father and the Father is in me; or at least believe on the evidence of the miracles themselves.

John 14:11 (NIV)

Yesterday we saw how the Holy Spirit works by providing evidence about Jesus to people who don't yet know Him. He does this by arranging encounters with Christians, through dreams, using circumstances to make them think, putting a bible in their hands and so on.

Another kind of evidence that the Holy Spirit provides is the miraculous. I love the story in Acts 14 of when Paul and Barnabas visited Iconium in Turkey. They had great success there initially, with many people believing what they said and accepting Jesus as their Saviour. (Remember, they had never even heard of Jesus before this.) But then some people started try to undermine their work by poisoning the minds of the community against them. It must have been heartbreaking.

Instead of retreating, the Bible tells us the pair "stayed there a long time, speaking boldly in the Lord, who was bearing witness to the word of His grace, granting signs and wonders to be done by their hands" (Acts.14:3, NKJV).

There it is again: "the Lord ... bearing witness" – the Holy Spirit providing evidence. This time the evidence was "signs and wonders" – in other words, miracles. People saw that when these men preached, things would happen – amazing things, impossible things; people were healed and set free.

I remember that back in the eighties when I was doing lots of open air meetings in Malta, we were not at all well received. I was threatened, abused and ignored. One day someone even drove a truck at our loudspeakers. One afternoon, in the town of Vittoirosa, I prayed for a man with a disabled hand. God healed him immediately. The man in his fifties began jumping up and down and shouting, "I'm healed!" The people around – who had been very 'anti' up to then – suddenly turned and became friendly. From that moment we never had opposition again.

The Holy Spirit provided evidence.

58

On one occasion, while he was eating with them, he gave them this command: "Do not leave Jerusalem, but wait for the gift my Father promised, which you have heard me speak about. For John baptised with water, but in a few days you will be baptised with the Holy Spirit."

Acts 1:4-5 (NIV)

Let me ask you a question: have you been baptised? I mean, did you go to the sea or a river or a church baptistery and get dunked? Let me ask you another question: how do you know you did? Are you sure that's what happened? You are probably saying right now, "What a stupid question! How could you forget a thing like that or not realise what was happening to you?" Well, that is my point.

Jesus told His followers that they would be *baptised* in the Holy Spirit. Same word – baptised (immersed, submerged, dipped, overwhelmed).

If you can be sure you were baptised in water, I think you would know if you had been baptised in the Holy Spirit, especially as this is (according to Matthew 3:11) a baptism of fire.

We are talking about the Spirit of God; about being immersed, submerged, overwhelmed by the Spirit of God – the same Holy Spirit that raised Christ from the dead, that filled the hundred and twenty on the day of Pentecost. *The same.*

Think about it. You cannot be submerged in an inch of water. Neither can you be baptised with a little bit of the Holy Spirit. Whoever is filled with the Holy Spirit gets the lot, the same amount. If you have been baptised in the Holy Spirit, you have had the same experience as they did on the day of Pentecost.

Have you been baptised in the Holy Spirit? You can be, you must be. But just like when you are baptised in water, you must surrender to the water and let it overwhelm you, let it fully take you – so you must let the Holy Spirit have you completely. You have to give in.

God is speaking to you today.

59

When the Day of Pentecost had fully come, they were all with one accord in one place. And suddenly there came a sound from heaven, as of a rushing mighty wind, and it filled the whole house where they were sitting. Then there appeared to them divided tongues, as of fire, and one sat upon each of them. And they were all filled with the Holy Spirit and began to speak with other tongues, as the Spirit gave them utterance.

Acts 2:1-4 (NKJV)

Jesus had promised the baptism of the Holy Spirit to His followers. They were to wait in Jerusalem until this happened to them – they stayed in the upper room for ten days after His ascension and then it happened.

We can only imagine what the sound of the heavenly wind was like as it filled the house where the hundred and twenty were gathered. We can imagine, too, the forked flames sitting on every one of them. But we don't have to imagine the Holy Spirit filling them because that is our experience too!

They were filled, it says – not touched, not blessed, not moved, but *filled* with the Holy Spirit. This was a new experience that no-one had ever had before. In the Old Testament the Holy Spirit had come upon people when they were in need of great faith or strength but this is new – filled. In the Old Testament it was a transitory experience but now the infilling was here to stay.

The word used here for "filled" is *pletho* – that's where our word 'plethora' comes from and it means 'a large amount'! The Holy Spirit is a person. You can't have a bit of a person; you either have all of Him or none of Him. He came to live in them – the Spirit of Christ.

And they began to speak in other tongues. Why? Surely being filled with the Holy Spirit would enable them to heal the sick, do miracles, love the unloveable. Why new tongues? All those other things would come later; for now they needed evidence. A wind, a fire – the rational mind could have reasoned them away. But the ability to speak in the language of heaven whenever you felt like it? That's evidence!

60

THURSDAY, 28TH MAY, 2020

Now there were staying in Jerusalem God-fearing Jews from every nation under heaven. When they heard this sound, a crowd came together in bewilderment, because each one heard them speaking in his own language.

Acts 2:5-8 (NIV)

Something that absolutely fascinates me is the next part of the Pentecost story, seen in today's passage. Utterly amazed, the people hearing the disciples speak their own languages asked, "Are not all these men who are speaking Galileans? Then how is it that each of us hears them in his own native language?" (Acts.2:7-8, BSB)

To begin with, these hundred and twenty people gathered in a room upstairs must have been making a lot of noise, because it attracted a large crowd – it certainly wasn't a sedate meeting!

Secondly, the crowd agreed that they could all hear them speaking in their own language. To emphasise this, Luke lists at least fifteen different language groups there. If each one of the disciples was speaking a different language and the people heard that person, this would not have made them bewildered; they would simply assume that each disciple knew how to speak that language.

The one hundred and twenty were all speaking in tongues and none of it was a language that was discernible. It doesn't say that they were all speaking in different languages. They weren't. What it does say is that the listeners all *heard* it in their own language. The miracle was in the hearing.

I know from personal experience that God can give you the ability to instantly be able to speak another language but this is not what the hundred and twenty were doing.

Miracles always have purpose. The purpose of this one was to amaze and so to draw an enormous crowd. They were sufficiently fascinated to stick around and hear what Peter had to say, and we know that when he preached Jesus to them, three thousand of them were converted.

It has always been part of the mission of the followers of Jesus to amaze people. How are we doing that today?

61

"...(both Jews and converts to Judaism); Cretans and Arabs – we hear them declaring the wonders of God in our own tongues!" Amazed and perplexed, they asked one another, "What does this mean?" Some, however, made fun of them and said, "They have had too much wine."

Acts 2:11-13 (NIV)

We heard yesterday how the international crowd on the day of Pentecost were baffled by the disciples speaking in tongues. After this, some of the onlookers laughed and said that they must be drunk. This is not the only place in the New Testament where being filled with the Holy Spirit is compared to being drunk. Ephesians 5:18 (NKJV) says, "And do not be drunk with wine, in which is dissipation; but be filled with the Spirit..."

I was talking to a young man the other day and told him that I had never taken drugs and I had never been drunk but that didn't mean I had never been high! There is no doubt that when the Holy Spirit moves within us there is a euphoria and excitement that is perhaps similar to being drunk. So Paul says, "Don't get drunk; get filled with the Spirit instead."

But there is a more serious reason that the two experiences are similar. I have asked people why they get drunk and one of the main reasons is to lose their inhibitions. This is a great reason to be filled with the Spirit; to be honest, I can't think of anything that we need more as Christians than to lose our inhibitions!

Along with that goes boldness. Did you know that this is one of the most common requests that we get when we are praying for people? I always say, if you need boldness, you need the Holy Spirit – there is no other source.

When we look at the disciples before and after Pentecost, the most striking difference is their boldness – they became incorrigible and unstoppable in their pursuit of the gospel.

In these days of extremity and opportunity we need the boldness the Holy Spirit gives us. I've got a good idea: let's get drunk this weekend! It's Pentecost after all!

62

"...(both Jews and converts to Judaism); Cretans and Arabs – we hear them declaring the wonders of God in our own tongues!" Amazed and perplexed, they asked one another, "What does this mean?" Some, however, made fun of them and said, "They have had too much wine."

Acts 2:11-13 (NIV)

When Peter stood up to preach on the day of day of Pentecost, any notion that he was drunk vanished. He gave a superb sermon and three thousand people were saved.

But hold on a minute. This was, as far as we know, the first time Peter had ever preached. He was a fisherman. Yet his words held the attention of a vast crowd and the impact of his sermon was enormous. People in Jerusalem were to comment on the fact that he was not educated and wonder at where he got this ability.

And we could wonder too. Here is a man becoming instantly gifted – and gifted to a high level. How did this happen? How is this possible?

The clue is in the word – 'gifted'. Peter had been given a gift and that gift was the Holy Spirit – a gift from heaven. At the end of his sermon he says, "Repent, and let every one of you be baptised in the name of Jesus Christ for the remission of sins and you shall receive the gift of the Holy Spirit." (Acts.2:38, NKJV) He has only just received it and he is advertising it!

Nobody was more amazed at his new ability than he was himself! The gift of the Holy Spirit, the promise of the Father. And as we can see, this gift made him gifted. He was instantly a gifted speaker.

Jesus had told the disciples not to leave Jerusalem – not to do anything; not to spread the good news about His resurrection; nothing – until they received the baptism in the Holy Spirit. It was so vital to ministry and so vital to the normal Christian life that to attempt anything without His presence within them would have been useless.

As we look at our lives today, are we being effective? Are we changing things? Do you feel you have what it takes to be a powerful influence for Christ on the people around you?

In the next verse Peter says, "For the promise is to you and to your children and to all who are afar off – as many as the Lord will call." I think he is talking about you!

We all need to receive the gift and become gifted!

63

For the promise is to you and to your children and to all who are afar off as many as the Lord will call.

Acts 2:39 (NKJV)

In 1920 an American radio station promoted its new radios with the catchphrase, "The gift that keeps on giving." Nothing could describe the gift of the Holy Spirit better than that!

Yesterday we heard that the gift of the Holy Spirit is a promise to everyone that becomes a Christian. And when Peter received it, he also received the gift of preaching.

The same thing happened to me when I was fourteen years old. I was not a person who liked standing in front of others. One Sunday evening a few weeks after I had received the baptism in the Holy Spirit, our youth group were on our way to take a service at another church. I was just along for the ride, but in the car the leader asked me to give my testimony at the service. I said no – but he would not take no for an answer.

The time came and I reluctantly stood before the congregation. I spoke for so long they had to close the service; there was no time for our leader to preach. I thought, "I'm for the high jump now!" But as we drove away he was all smiles. He turned to me and said, "David! You are a preacher! You didn't testify, you preached!" He was so happy.

Like Peter on that first day of Pentecost, no-one was more surprised than me. That was forty-six years ago and I have been preaching ever since. I still rely totally on the Holy Spirit to inspire every single sermon. I relied upon Him this morning to give me something to say. It's the gift that keeps on giving.

Jesus said, "...if you sinful people know how to give good gifts to your children, how much more will your heavenly Father give the Holy Spirit to those who ask him." (Lk.11:13, NLT) Who knows what other gift your heavenly Father will give you when He gives you the Holy Spirit? Why not ask Him for it today?

64

Those who believed what Peter said were baptized and added to the church that day – about 3,000 in all. All the believers devoted themselves to the apostles' teaching, and to fellowship, and to sharing in meals (including the Lord's Supper), and to prayer. A deep sense of awe came over them all, and the apostles performed many miraculous signs and wonders.

Acts 2:41-43 (NLT)

A baptism of three thousand people was what Jerusalem witnessed after Peter preached. That must have been some spectacle. Sadly, the Bible doesn't record where it took place, but I'm sure there hasn't been another such event in Jerusalem since.

I don't know about you but just by reading these few words I feel the buzz of excitement that was abroad in the new church. How must the disciples have felt when they saw this huge move of God? Let's face it, they had no idea what was coming and whether anything would actually work now that Jesus had left.

But work it did! Jesus had told them that they would do greater works than He did, and here in one day they saw three thousand saved. But not only that, the disciples, it says, performed many miraculous signs and wonders.

Remember, the Holy Spirit is the gift that keeps on giving and here we see that because of the Holy Spirit's power within them, they were able to perform miracles. This is what happens when the Holy Spirit is in a believer. This is not extraordinary; this is normal.

When we say that we are believers, we usually mean that we believe in God and that we believe in Jesus. We would also say that we believe that God loves us and that Jesus died for us, that He rose from dead and is coming again. The Apostles' Creed also states, "I believe in the Holy Spirit," and we would all agree with that. The question is, what do you believe about the third person of the Trinity?

Just as believing in Jesus means believing in what He does, believing in the Holy Spirit must mean believing in what *He* does. Here in Acts 2 we have a graphic account of what He does. We must believe it and have faith that He will do today through us what He did then through them.

65

And the Lord added to the church daily those who were being saved.

Acts 2:47 (NKJV)

This is a verse that we love as evangelicals – people being saved every day. Wow! We try to imagine what that would be like and hope and pray that we see something like that in our churches.

I can't help thinking, though, that the preceding verses have a bearing on this harvest of souls. "And they continued steadfastly in the apostles' doctrine and fellowship, in the breaking of bread, and in prayers. ... So continuing daily with one accord in the temple, and breaking bread from house to house..." (Acts.2:43,46, NKJV)

It wasn't just that people were being saved daily – the teaching and fellowship, the breaking bread and prayer were daily too. Do you think that might be a contributory factor in this revival? This is the church at work – working as it should. This is normal New Testament church.

I have seen people getting saved every day. I've seen it in many countries and I have seen it, back in the eighties, right here in north Cornwall. What was the secret? What was the formula?

Actually, it was very simple. We were trying to get people saved every day. We were having meetings every day. We called them various names: crusades, campaigns, missions – it was all the same thing. Because we were doing this, there would be prayer, fellowship and often teaching every day too.

There are no such things as campaigns now. We don't do them any more. People are too busy to come out every night.

Mark 16:20 (NKJV) also talks about this time in the early church. It says, "And they went out and preached everywhere, the Lord working with them and confirming the word through the accompanying signs. Amen." The Lord was working with them. There is one thing you need to do if you want the Lord to be working with you: *work.*

66

Then they knew that it was he who sat begging alms at the Beautiful Gate of the temple; and they were filled with wonder and amazement at what had happened to him.

Acts 3:10 (NKJV)

This time last year I was in Israel. It was the trip of a lifetime seeing all the places that I had only imagined all my life. But there was one unexpected outcome of the trip. We attended a service at Mount Carmel Church. To be honest, it was one of the best meetings I have ever been in. Partway through the service the leader said, almost in passing, "If you need healing today put your hand on the part of your body where the problem is." Then he prayed a simple prayer of healing. I was healed.

For many years I had had IBS and took pills every day for this painful condition. From that moment on I have not had any pain and have not taken one more pill.

Following the day of Pentecost, Peter and John were going into the temple in Jerusalem when a man asked them for money. He was there every day begging; it was his only means of support because he had had no use of his legs from birth. Just imagine what his legs looked like. There were no muscles at all; they were just skin and bones. Peter replied to the man, "We haven't got any money but what we have got you can have – in Jesus' name stand up and walk." And Peter took his hand and pulled him to his feet.

To everyone's surprise he could stand. To everyone's shock he could walk. To everyone's astonishment he could leap around. And he did – praising God! It was an outstanding miracle (pardon the pun); a full set of toned and strong muscles was created instantly – no physio needed.

Healing is one of the gifts from the gift that keeps on giving. I have experienced it on the receiving end and on the giving side many, many times. The fact that the Holy Spirit lives in us makes healing possible. Jesus heals through us by the power of the Holy Spirit.

There are many questions about this – "Why does it not always happen?" being one. I don't know. I will never know. But this I do know: sometimes it does and that's good enough for me!

67

"So if you sinful people know how to give good gifts to your children, how much more will your heavenly Father give the Holy Spirit to those who ask him."

Luke 11:13 (NLT)

In the village of Albaston near Callington in Cornwall there lies a cottage where on 22nd July, 1862 a great hero of the faith was born. He was to change Europe as profoundly as any political leader. Thomas Ball Barratt was the son of a Cornish mining engineer and Wesleyan Methodist who went to church in the village.

When Thomas was four, his family moved to Norway for his father's work but Thomas was sent back to school in Taunton. As Thomas grew up, he accepted Christ as his saviour and went on to train for the Methodist ministry. He also studied music in Oslo under the famous Norwegian composer Greig.

Barratt was the minister of several churches in Norway before starting the mission in Central Oslo which today is known as Filadelfia Church.

In the early days of this mission in 1906, he journeyed to America to raise funds. It wasn't very successful, but while in New York he heard about an outpouring of the Holy Spirit in California. He didn't have the money to get to Azusa Street in L.A. so instead started seeking God for it in his hotel room in New York. He received it – alone in the room. He had had no teaching, beside what he had read in the New Testament, but he got the Pentecostal experience, was filled with the Holy Spirit and began to speak in new tongues.

He returned to Norway, not much richer financially, but immeasurably richer spiritually. A whole new world opened up to match his new zeal.

68

"Behold, the virgin shall be with child, and bear a Son, and they shall call His name Immanuel," which is translated, "God with us."

Matthew 1:23 (NKJV)

There are many examples of rich and famous people who limit their interaction with common people. They become recluses or only venture out heavily guarded or with gloves and mask to protect them from contamination. The U.S. President takes an entourage of hundreds of people to cover every eventuality!

But see today's verse. God came into the world as a man: Immanuel, God with us, Jesus. What an amazing thing – God leaving the purity and perfection of heaven and walking among us, with no PPE, no entourage, no bubble!

Jesus arrived in a cattle shed as a baby. What does this tell you about Him? It tells us He humbled Himself. He loved us so much that He left all His heavenly attendants and became one of us. He took a job. He got His hands dirty. He hugged lepers. He befriended outcasts. He slept rough. He only had the clothes that He stood up in. He got into trouble. He went to prison. He was tortured. He was executed. He bled. He died. He was one of us. He was one *of* us so that He could be one *with* us – and us one with Him.

All this. How can we ignore Him, reject Him, keep Him at a distance, forget Him, marginalise Him? How can we not let Him do what He wants – be with us, be in us, be involved now, today, with us?

Why not pray with me right now?

Oh Lord Jesus, thank you for your wonderful sacrifice, for your expedition to earth. Thank you that you love me so much that you never give up trying to be my Immanuel – God with me. I welcome you today – walk every step with me. Amen.

69

"I am the Alpha and the Omega, the Beginning and the End," says the Lord,
"who is and who was and who is to come, the Almighty."

Revelation 1:8 (NKJV)

We have all heard of an alpha male. This term means 'the highest ranking individual' in any group. There is no doubt that Jesus is the alpha male of the human race. He called Himself "the Alpha". What He was referring to, though, was not His rank or position but the fact that He was and is "the Beginning".

He was there at the very beginning of everything and kicked it off. If there was a big bang, He was the one who made it. The Bible says, "He was in the beginning with God. He created everything there is. Nothing exists that he didn't make." (Jn.1:2-3, TLB)

Jesus is in the creation business. As you look around you, you will see that He is very good at it. There is one thing that He loves to create and He is still doing it now, every day, and that is new hearts.

Ezekiel 36:26 (NIV) says, "I will give you a new heart and put a new spirit in you; I will remove from you your heart of stone and give you a heart of flesh."

We sometimes say that someone is stony-hearted. The fact is, we all are. Sin makes our heart calloused and hard. We get set in our ways and change becomes virtually impossible. In our most reflective moments we don't like who we have become.

Jesus offers us re-creation, a fundamental makeover, new lives for old. He wants to forgive our sins, create a new heart and give us a new beginning. He is the Alpha – the God of new beginnings.

Many who are reading this can say, "Yes, that happened to me," but if it hasn't happened to you, why not pray today and ask Him to give you a new heart today?

70

"I am the Alpha and the Omega, the Beginning and the End," says the Lord, "who is and who was and who is to come, the Almighty."

Revelation 1:8 (NKJV)

Yesterday we looked at Jesus being the Alpha – the beginner not only of all things but also of our new lives. You will be expecting Omega today, I'm sure! He is not only the initiator of our Christian walk but the finisher also. That well-known verse in Hebrews 12:2 (NKJV) says, "...looking unto Jesus, the author and finisher of our faith..."

One of my great uncles used to say of someone, "He's a good starter but a poor finisher." I am often reminded of this as I see lots of incomplete projects around the place, especially paintings that I have left unfinished. I don't want my life to be like that, do you?

In Hosea 7 we read about the tribe of Ephraim being like a cake half-baked! I'm afraid there are a lot of half-baked Christians around. That is not God's will for our lives.

Jesus started us off when we were born again, and the Bible says He will complete us if we let Him. If we are left to our own devices we would all be poor finishers, but in Jesus' hands you can be a good finisher. He wants to make you complete. Philippians 1:6 (NKJV) says, "He who has begun a good work in you will complete it until the day of Jesus Christ..."

I'm sure that each one of us wants to complete our life's purpose rather than leave both ourselves and our mission incomplete when we die. The best way to ensure that we become complete is to co-operate with the Lord and say yes to all He asks of us.

Pray: *Lord Jesus, I am sorry I have been uncooperative and stubborn. I want to say yes to your plans for my life. I say yes today to the next step in my development as a person. I say yes today to the ministry you have given me. Help everyone find their place in our church, Lord, so it too can be complete. Amen.*

71

And the scripture was fulfilled that says, 'Abraham believed God, and it was credited to him as righteousness,' and he was called God's friend.

James 2:23 (NIV)

How many friends do you have on Facebook? The word 'friend' has never been used so much as it is today but we all know there are friends and *friends!* A few months ago I met up with my old friend Desmond. He lives near Aberdeen now and we only get to see each other about once a decade, and yet when we meet it's like we have never been apart.

We sometimes sing, "What a friend we have in Jesus." *What a friend!* It's utterly amazing that Jesus would want to be my friend. You can choose your friends and He has chosen me. When you choose a friend, you usually look for someone who is like you and shares the same interests. When we first met, I was nothing like Him. I hope I'm a little more like Him now. Being friends with someone means you will gradually pick up their ways.

It says something about Jesus that He can be our friend. World religions and philosophies venerate their founders but they are all dead. Dead people make pretty boring friends. Jesus makes a great friend – He is alive!

James 2:23 tells us that Abraham was called the friend of God. *The friend of God!* As amazing as that sounds, do you know that that is the very reason behind the creation of the human race – to become friends of God?

We can grade our friends as to how good a friend they are. Proverbs 18:24 (NIV) tells us that Jesus wants to be the "friend that sticks closer than a brother". We all need a friend like that – one who is loyal, faithful and true, who will fight for us, and encourage and comfort us too – a friend who will always be there for us and never let us down.

Maybe there is someone who is reading this today that has been separated from their friend Jesus for some time, and He wants me to tell you that it's OK – you can be friends again and take up where you left off just like me and Desmond. Do it!

72

And He said to them, "Cast the net on the right side of the boat, and you will find some." So they cast, and now they were not able to draw it in because of the multitude of fish.

John 21:6 (NKJV)

Was Jesus a fisherman? He could certainly catch fish better than those who were! He was better at winemaking than a vintner, better at healing than a doctor, better at teaching than a teacher, even better on water than a boat! He is the jack of all trades and the master of all. Hallelujah! Whatever you do for a living, Jesus is better at it than you. He will help you, advise you and inspire you.

My dear friend Professor Roy Peacock, who is now with the Lord, told me this story. As an authority on gas turbines, he was once called in by the Indian Government. They had built a state-of-the-art power station that had been sitting idle for more than a year because they couldn't get it to fire up. They had exhausted all their expertise. He asked the government committee for the blueprints and went back to his hotel room.

In his own words, he didn't have a clue! He knelt by the blueprints and asked God to help him. Immediately the Holy Spirit said, "You need to look at the fluidic switches." He had no idea what these were but the next day he went back to the power station and said, "You need to look at the fluidic switches!" They immediately replaced these components and pressed start. The power station sprung into life. They were all amazed.

The government minister asked Roy to stay behind when the others left. "Tell me," he said, "how did you know? You have only been here a day." Roy told him about his prayer and God's answer. "Can I know your God too?" the minister said and Roy led him to Jesus there and then.

Exodus 31:3-5 (NKJV) says, "And I have filled him with the Spirit of God, in wisdom, in understanding, in knowledge, and in all manner of workmanship, to design artistic works, to work in gold, in silver, in bronze, in cutting jewels for setting, in carving wood, and to work in all manner of workmanship."

Consult the expert, the omniscient Christ, with problems in your day job or anything else you need help with. He knows, you know!

73

Jesus turned around and when he saw her he said, "Daughter, be encouraged! Your faith has made you well." And the woman was healed at that moment.

Matthew 9:22 (NLT)

One of the easiest things to do as a Christian is also one of the most neglected. It doesn't cost anything, it doesn't take any time, it doesn't require any special gifting. I'm talking about encouraging each other.

Encouragement is huge in the New Testament. Any new movement needs it more than almost anything else, especially when it is subject to persecution and hard times. That's why we need to encourage each other at the moment.

For us, encouragement usually means an uplifting word or two from a friend. For Jesus, encouragement meant action! We might have said to this woman, "Look on the bright side." Jesus took her to the bright side.

He is the light of the world! As you look into the future from the lockdown, there might be things you are dreading apart from coronavirus, like getting older, financial issues, exams – but be encouraged. Jesus is not just there to pat you on the back and say it will be OK – He is with you to *make* it OK!

He goes before us to level the path, remove obstacles and dismantle booby-traps! Then He walks with us as our "ever-present help" (Ps.46:1, NIV). Yes, trouble may come, but let's look at it in the way an icebreaker ship looks at the freezing sea: not plain sailing, maybe, but we've got the equipment to deal with it. Jesus' encouragement is practical.

The Holy Spirit is known as the comforter but that same word is better translated 'encourager'. In the Bayeux tapestry depicting King Harold's war with France he is shown with his sword poking one of his soldiers in the back; underneath it reads, "Harold comforteth his troops." He was encouraging him to fight.

We need God's encouragement but we also need to pass it on. Make up your mind that you are going to be an encourager from now on.

74

"O LORD, God of Abraham, Isaac, and Jacob, prove today that you are God in Israel and that I am your servant. Prove that I have done all this at your command. O LORD, answer me! Answer me so these people will know that you, O LORD, are God and that you have brought them back to yourself."

1 Kings 18:36-37 (NLT)

A year ago today I was standing on the top of Mount Carmel in Israel. Some of you will know that is where Elijah had a showdown with the prophets of Baal – the false god that the king and queen had adopted.

Elijah challenged the pagans to a contest: whichever god answered prayer, let him be the God of Israel. The prayer that was to be prayed was for fire – fire that would consume a sacrifice on an altar.

The false prophets performed an elaborate ritual that got more and more frenzied until they gave up. Elijah prayed a simple prayer, seen in today's passage. And God immediately answered with fire.

This week we are going to look at how to have your prayers answered. Elijah is going to be our example.

The first thing we can learn from Elijah is *Elijah*. His name. Elijah means 'Yahweh is God'. It's like you being called 'Jesus Saves'. It is a statement, a declaration. Now, in a country where everyone, at the King's command, is worshipping another god, having that name is radical. If anyone ever nailed his colours to the mast, it was Elijah.

The first step to having our prayers answered is to claim Christ – to give your life to Him and declare it. Don't make a secret of it – make it your identity, just like Elijah.

God only promises to answer prayer for those that belong to Him, and to do that we must ask Him to forgive our sins and make our lives His home.

Making a public stand for Jesus glorifies God, and He said, "Everyone who acknowledges me publicly here on earth, I will also acknowledge before my Father in heaven." (Matt.10:32, NLT)

75

Elijah was a man just like us. He prayed earnestly that it would not rain, and it did not rain on the land for three and a half years. Again he prayed, and the heavens gave rain, and the earth produced its crops.

James 5:17-18 (BSB)

How do you get your prayers answered? That's this week's subject. Yesterday we saw that in a very hostile society Elijah very publicly declared that he belonged to God. This is step one in having your prayers answered.

The Bible introduces Elijah as a "Tishbite, from Tishbe in Gilead" (1.Kgs.17:1, NIV). That's it. Unusually for the Bible, it does not say who his father was or give any family information. In other words, he was a nobody – at least, nobody special.

The point in today's passage is that Elijah was just an ordinary person like you or me. He didn't try to big himself up in any way or claim any special revelation or anointing by God. He was just a man from the mountains. He was humble.

Step two in getting your prayers answered is to be humble. God loves humility.

A sure way of getting God to ignore your prayers is to be proud. I'm not just talking about being proud in the way you pray but being a person that is full of pride. James 4:6 (NKJV) says, "God resists the proud, but gives grace to the humble."

Do you know why traditionally people kneel down to pray? To remind themselves to be humble. Psalm 10:17 (HCSB) says, "LORD, you have heard the desire of the humble; you will strengthen their hearts. You will listen carefully..."

76

"But be careful. Don't let your heart be deceived so that you turn away from the LORD and serve and worship other gods. If you do, the LORD's anger will burn against you. He will shut up the sky and hold back the rain, and the ground will fail to produce its harvests."

Deuteronomy 11:16-17 (NLT)

Elijah was a man who knew how to get answered prayer. The New Testament holds him up above everyone else in this department. We have seen that he prayed as someone who belonged to God and publicly declared it, and that he was humble. Today we look at the content of his prayers.

You see, it's no good asking God for things that He doesn't want to do. When we pray, it's good to pray in line with God's promises. If He has said He will do something, then we can pray that with confidence.

Elijah prayed that it would not rain, not because they had had too much, but because Israel needed to be taught a lesson. Led by the wicked royal family, Israel had started worshipping idols rather than God. Elijah knew God had said something about this.

When Elijah prayed, today's verse was the promise he was standing on. This was the ground for his confidence and this was one of the reasons why it brought an immediate response from heaven.

The Bible is full of promises, and if we know them we can claim them in prayer. Just this morning I found myself in a situation where someone needed peace very quickly. The ambulance crew were there but were unable to help. I prayed using Philippians 4:7 (NKJV): "...and the peace of God, which surpasses all understanding, will guard your hearts and minds through Christ Jesus." Within a few minutes that peace came.

When we pray, our prayers should line up with scripture; sometimes we know a verse that we can use like I did today, but all the time our prayers need to be in line with the spirit of the Bible. It's no good praying, "Lord help me to win the lottery," or, "God make so-and-so fall in love with me."

When we pray, the Holy Spirit will help us to know how to pray by reminding us of what the Bible says and nudging us to pray that way.

77

What is faith? It is the confident assurance that what we hope for is going to happen. It is being certain of things we cannot yet see.

Hebrews 11:1 (TLB)

What is faith? Elijah seems to have had it in bucketloads! Is this why his prayers were answered? Well, it's one of the reasons. Did you ever hold back in a prayer meeting from praying what you really wanted to pray because you were worried that if it wasn't answered you would look silly? It's one thing to pray something and quite another to pray it publicly.

Elijah's faith was courageous – he prayed his prayers publicly, even in front of the king and queen. He put everything on the line.

Most people think that faith is some special quality like a superpower – that some people have got it and some people haven't. It isn't that at all. The verse in Hebrews says faith is the confident assurance that what we hope for is going to happen. Let me ask you a question: who is going to make it happen? You? No, God. Our faith is not in our own superpower but in God – God's ability to do anything.

There's an old saying, "Prayer changes things." No it doesn't – God changes things.

We also hear, "There's power in prayer." No there isn't – there is power in God. It's no wonder we don't pray out loud if we think the answers depend on our level of faith.

What the answers do depend on is our confidence in God – that what we pray for is easy for Him to do. It is our confidence that He is listening when we pray. It is our confidence that He would take any notice of our prayers.

Elijah's prayers show us his confident assurance that what he hoped for would happen because he knew God was able, God was willing and God was listening! This is the secret to answered prayer.

So when you pray, ask yourself these questions first, and when you realise that the answer is yes to all three, you can pray in confident faith.

78

And Elijah the Tishbite, of the inhabitants of Gilead, said to Ahab, "As the LORD God of Israel lives, before whom I stand, there shall not be dew nor rain these years, except at my word."

1 Kings 17:1 (NKJV)

This week we have been getting prayer tips from one of the greatest prayers in the Bible. Elijah, though an ordinary guy, was such a spiritual person that when Jesus came on the scene, many thought that Elijah had come back! Also, Elijah is one of just two people in the Old Testament that did not die but was airlifted to heaven like Jesus!

What was it about Elijah that made him, a man just like us, so special to God and so used by Him? I think the answer to that is that Elijah was in tune with heaven – he knew God's heart; he cared about God. I'm not sure that there are ever many people around like that.

If we go back to the verse introducing Elijah, we read this: "As the LORD God of Israel lives before whom I stand..." This tells us a lot. The word in Hebrew translated "stand" here is the word *amad*. It means 'to dwell with' and 'to be ordained by'. Interesting. A picture is emerging here of a man who had such a close relationship with God that he could say he lived with Him and that he was personally commissioned by Him.

Because of that, Elijah knew what God was thinking; he had God's best interests at heart. The driving force of his life is seen in his prayer. "O LORD, answer me! Answer me so these people will know that you, O LORD, are God and that you have brought them back to yourself." (1.Kgs.18:37, NLT)

"You ... are God and ... you have brought them back to yourself."

Does that ring a bell? You see, God's heart has not changed since the Garden of Eden. His desire is to bring people back to Himself. Everything else is subsidiary; everything else we do as Christians has to serve this cause!

How many people today are passionate about bringing people back to God and satisfying the desire of *His* heart?

79

And he answered, "I have not troubled Israel, but you and your father's house have, in that you have forsaken the commandments of the LORD and have followed the Baals. Now therefore, send and gather all Israel to me on Mount Carmel, the four hundred and fifty prophets of Baal, and the four hundred prophets of Asherah, who eat at Jezebel's table."

1 Kings 18:18-19 (NKJV)

This week we have been learning from Elijah – the Bible's prayer expert. Today we close this study by looking at what Elijah did once he had prayed. Read this story today and you will be amazed at Elijah's bravery – considering he was a nobody and his challenge to the king could have resulted in instant execution.

But Elijah wasn't content just to pray, as many people are; he worked with God to bring the answers to his prayers about. He was part of the answer.

Someone once said that the difference between prayer and intercession is involvement. Are we willing to be involved in God's answer to our own prayers?

In 1864 a boy was born in my hometown of Camelford who was to follow Elijah's example. By the age of twenty-two he was a civil servant in Clapham, London. One evening at a rally, he heard the great China missionary Hudson Taylor speak about the millions of Chinese who had never heard about Jesus.

Sam and his friends started to earnestly pray for China in their prayer meetings, asking God to send workers to the mission field of Yunnan in South West China. Before long, Sam himself realised that God was calling him to be the answer to his own prayers. In 1887 he left for China with his boyhood friend who had also been called by God.

Incredible adventures awaited him: he was shipwrecked on the way up the Yangzee river; he was often threatened with his life by the Chinese who called them foreign devils. For the first number of years Sam saw no fruit for his labours. He busied himself with not only learning the local language, Miao, but inventing a written form of it and then translating the New Testament into it. He saved hundreds of people from suicide by opium poisoning and preached tirelessly throughout the region.

Then a mighty revival broke out – thousands were born again and little whitewashed chapels sprung up on every hillside. Sam Pollard was God's answer to his own prayers.

Today his memory is honoured in China; even a skyscraper is named after him. I have over a dozen books written about him – he is my hero.

Be ready to be the answer to your own prayers – like Elijah and Sam Pollard.

80

...suppose a woman has ten silver coins and loses one. Doesn't she light a lamp, sweep the house and search carefully until she finds it?

Luke 15:8 (NIV)

In New Testament times a married woman would wear a headband of ten coins. She had saved up for them and wore them proudly – it was equivalent to a wedding ring. They were so precious to a woman that they could not be taken from her, not even by a court of law in payment of a debt. It was one of these coins that Jesus told a parable about. He said, a woman had ten silver coins and then she lost one.

She frantically searches for it, lights a lamp and looks in every corner, sweeping the floor and looking under the furniture – this might have gone on for days – and then she finds it. (It's a familiar story with things in our house!) She is so overjoyed at finding it, she throws a party for her neighbours, telling them, "Come and help me celebrate finding my coin!"

Jesus followed this little story with this: "In the same way, I tell you, there is rejoicing in the presence of the angels of God over one sinner who repents." (Lk.15:10, NIV)

The coin represents a person who doesn't know Jesus and is lost – lost to Him, lost their way, lost hope and is going to a lost eternity.

The thing about the coin is this: whatever happened to it, whether it was under the bed, in a dark corner or fallen down the drain, it never lost its value. It wasn't just the intrinsic value of the coin (about a day's wages); it was what it meant to the woman. It was something to do with love, something to do with belonging.

God wants you to know that wherever or whatever you are, lost or not, your value to Him is never in question. You cannot lose your value any more than the coin could. It's not just your face value that is important; you are loved, your life means something to Him.

He searches for you, and when He finds you and you find Him, there's going to be a party in heaven. Why don't you let Him find you today?

81

Suppose one of you has a hundred sheep and loses one of them. Doesn't he leave the ninety-nine in the open country and go after the lost sheep until he finds it?

Luke 15:4 (NIV)

My grandchildren Isabelle and Levi raised an orphan lamb by hand. It became so tame. But imagine if they came out one morning and the fourteen-week-old lamb wasn't there – he had run off and got lost on the moors nearby. What a fuss there would be; all the family would be out searching.

Sheep are prone to wandering off, which is a bit silly because they are so ill-equipped to take care of themselves. The Bible says, "All we like sheep have gone astray; each one of us has turned to his own way." (Is.53:6, BSB)

It's easily done. The sheep, head down eating grass, sees some juicier grass over there and wanders over to eat it, then some more a bit farther on and so on. When they eventually look up they don't know where they are. Here in North Cornwall sheep simply wander onto the cliffs like that and need rescuing.

Many people get lost in life, not because they did anything terrible, but because the grass was a little greener a bit farther on. We get tempted to go after just a little more... just a little more... until we are lost. We can't go back; we are stuck in a trap of our own making.

Jesus told a story about a shepherd who lost a sheep. He left the rest of the flock to go and find it. "And when he has found it, he lays it on his shoulders, rejoicing." (Lk.15:5-7, NIV) He really cared about that sheep – at that moment, more than all the others that hadn't run off.

Jesus said, "I am the good shepherd. The good shepherd gives His life for the sheep." (Jn.10:11-12, NKJV) He is the shepherd; we are the sheep. He cares so much for the individual that He goes looking when they get lost. In fact, He loves us so much that He died on the cross to get us back in the fold. He paid the price for our wandering.

His disciple Peter wrote to God's sheep and said, "Once you were wandering like lost sheep. But now you have turned to your Shepherd, the Guardian of your souls." (1.Pet.2:25, NLT)

We all need a shepherd.

82

Jesus continued: 'There was a man who had two sons. The younger one said to his father, "Father, give me my share of the estate." So he divided his property between them. Not long after that, the younger son got together all he had, set off for a distant country and there squandered his wealth in wild living.'

Luke 15:11-13 (NIV)

His son had been missing so long he thought he was probably dead. He hadn't heard a word since he had taken off with his inheritance to the city. But still the father did not give up. There was still a glimmer of hope and so every day he climbed the hill to see if he could see his son returning.

His son had gone to find himself, or at least to find a new life, but things had not gone to plan. The money had not lasted as long as he thought it would because he had spent it recklessly, leaving himself penniless.

His dream had turned into a nightmare. Now he was sleeping rough and taking handouts. He had found himself, alright, and he didn't like what he had found: a selfish idiot. He beat himself up every day for his stupidity. He found a job of sorts eventually – feeding pigs. What a comedown for a Jewish boy!

One day, hungry and desperate, he came to his senses. "My dad looks after his hired help better than this!" he thought. "I'll go home and ask him to take me on as a servant – I've lost the right to be a son."

But when he was still half a mile from home, his dad spotted him. "I'd know that walk anywhere." He ran to greet him, hugged him and kissed him. That night there was the biggest party ever. "My son was dead but now he's alive – he was lost but now he's found!"

Jesus told this story for one reason and one reason alone: to illustrate out heavenly Father's love for us. Yes, the prodigal had spent all the money; yes, he'd wallowed in sin; yes, he'd disrespected his father; but now he was home.

God loves us so much, He never gives up hope of us coming home. He is waiting, longing. All will be forgiven if we will just come back to Him. The disciple John wrote, "See what great love the Father has lavished upon us, that we should be called children of God! And that is what we are." (1.Jn.3:1, NIV) Come home!

83

Jacob's well was there, and Jesus, tired as he was from the journey, sat down by the well. It was about noon. When a Samaritan woman came to draw water, Jesus said to her, 'Will you give me a drink?'

John 4:6-7 (NIV)

We're having a mini heatwave here at the moment but it's nothing compared to being in Israel last year. In hot countries people stay indoors during the hottest time of the day. Why then was a woman fetching water at midday when Jesus met her?

The reason was that she was lost – well, she had lost her reputation. She had had five failed marriages and was living with somebody else now. She had made a name for herself and the other women didn't speak to her any more. So she came to the well at that time to avoid them.

But Jesus spoke to her; in fact, His conversation with her is one of His longest on record. He broke several social rules of that time by speaking to her. He knew everything about her but He still spoke to her. He said, "For the son of man came to seek and to save those who are lost." (Lk.9:10, NLT)

Jesus doesn't avoid the lost; He homes in on them. He told her to forget the well water – He would give her *living* water and she would never thirst again.

Her encounter with Jesus changed her life and earned her a new reputation because she went and told everyone in the town what had happened and they came to meet Jesus too. They said, "We no longer believe just because of what you said; now we have heard for ourselves, and we know that this man really is the Saviour of the world." (Jn.4:42, NLT)

Christians are not people that *believe in* Jesus; they are people who have *met* Jesus – encountered Him and their lives changed forever. He is still seeking and saving the lost. Nobody is too bad, nobody is too far gone – these are the ones He is looking for. I invite you today to meet Him.

Stop right where you are and ask Him to come into your life. You will never thirst again.

84

You sympathized with those in prison and joyfully accepted the confiscation of your property, knowing that you yourselves had a better and permanent possession.

Hebrews 10:34 (BSB)

Some years ago when I was in Sicily, I was taken to a Roman amphitheatre. Instead of an arena it had a large swimming pool with two pillars in it. The guide told us that a Christian would be put on each pillar and they were given poles to try to knock each other off into the water. The trouble was, the water was filled with crocodiles. As I walked out of the tunnel that led into the area, I could feel the spiritual stain on that place.

Towards the end of the New Testament we start to see the state turn against those who believed in Jesus. From the emperor down, the Roman Empire threw all its weight against the church and tried to snuff it out.

The believers written to in today's passage had all their worldly goods confiscated and were thrown out of their properties, but *joyfully accepted it*. Hold on a moment… Did I read that right? Yes, joyfully accepted it. And the reason? Because they knew they had something better and something no one could take away. This kind of thing still happens today.

Contrast that to the verse in Luke 9 where Jesus says, "What good is it for someone to gain the whole world, and yet lose or forfeit their very self?" (Lk.9:25, NIV)

The society in which we live is all about possessions, money, property. And people, it seems, are willing to lose their soul to get it. How many celebrities are willing to trade everything to make it big? How many business-people are willing to trample on humanity to succeed? How many politicians become corrupt to further their cause?

At this time of a global pandemic, are we any closer to realising what is really important? We are only here for a short time – eternity is forever!

85

If you cling to your life you will lose it and if you let your life go you will save it.

Luke 17:33 (NLT)

Today I want to talk about losing your life, but don't worry, it's not really about death. There are several reasons why we would want to cling on to our life – or maybe we should say *lifestyle*.

Firstly, we don't like change; we are creatures of habit. We might moan about life being predictable but that's the way we like it to be. This current crisis is testament to that. But Jesus calls us to change; He wants to change almost everything about us. He wants to change our identity, to change our citizenship, to change our allegiance, to change our desires, to change our outlook and to change our destiny! There is no greater change known to man than becoming a Christian.

In today's verse, Jesus was saying that if we stubbornly want to cling to our life as it is, then that will be our undoing because the sinful life cannot survive – it is condemned. If, however, we are willing to lose that old life – to let go and let Him change us from the inside out – then our future is secure: eternal life awaits us!

You would think it was a 'no-brainer' really, wouldn't you? Would you like to live in heaven forever and have a great adventure with God on the way? Uh… yes! But as we know from the story of the rich young ruler, he loved his life too much to change. Jesus asked him to lose his life, to let go of it, but Mark tells us, "At this the man's face fell. He went away sad because he had great wealth." (Mk.10:22, NIV) He couldn't do it. Even if his life depended on it (and it did) he couldn't do it. Many people love their life too much; they want to cling on to their identity of 'the rebel' or 'the sex-bomb' or 'the drunken joker' or whatever it is. It can even seem like a respectable persona – 'the intellectual atheist' or 'the aloof businessperson'. But whatever it is, if you hang on to it, it will kill you.

Let it go and let Jesus change your life and your destiny.

86

And the Angel of the LORD appeared to him, and said to him, "The LORD is with you, you mighty man of valour!"

Judges 6:12 (NKJV)

Do you ever feel completely useless? You are not alone. We all feel like that sometimes. And I'm pleased to say that some of the great men and women in the Bible felt it too.

Gideon considered himself the most insignificant person in the world. He was the poorest member of his family, his family was the poorest in the tribe, the tribe was the poorest in Israel, and Israel (which had been ransacked by the Midianites) was the poorest country in the world. This was his outlook on life.

But it is amazing whom God chooses to be His ambassadors and generals. It is often someone like Gideon – someone who thinks they are useless.

The Midianite raiding parties frequently came across the border grabbing whatever they could, and the Israelites were living in terror. Gideon hit on the great idea of threshing his corn in the winepress – which was basically a hole in the ground – so that if the Midianites came it would already be hidden from them. The only problem was that you needed wind to thresh corn. But desperate times etc.

While he was doing this, a stranger appeared at the top of the pit. Gideon did not know it was an angel – they don't often come with wings. I can see Gideon looking around to see whom the angel was talking to. But there was no one else in the pit. "Mighty man of valour" was not something Gideon would have considered himself to be in a million years! But that was what God said – and God is never wrong.

God saw something in Gideon that transcended his view of himself. That is always the way God sees us. He sees things in us that we have never seen. He sees potential that we have not realised. He sees what He has put there.

There comes a time when those latent qualities must be brought out. For some of you that time is now. So let me say to you today, "The Lord is with you – mighty man or woman of valour." It's time…

87

Gideon said to Him, "O my lord, if the LORD is with us, why then has all this happened to us? And where are all His miracles which our fathers told us about, saying, 'Did not the LORD bring us up from Egypt?' But now the LORD has forsaken us and delivered us into the hands of the Midianites."

Judges 6:13 (NKJV)

When Gideon looked in the mirror he saw someone who was useless looking back at him, but when God looked at Gideon he saw a mighty man of valour.

God loves to take people who think they can't and show them they can. Today people would say, "Well, he just has to believe in himself." That is utter rubbish. No amount of self-belief could have rallied an army or produced a victory. There is no evidence in the account of Gideon that he had a seminal moment of self-confidence. In fact, the opposite is true. Throughout this story Gideon has to rely totally on God.

It is his confidence in God that changes. See the first question he asks the angel in today's verse. He starts off with these doubts about God's faithfulness and care for Israel, but soon is shouting, "For the sword of the Lord and for Gideon!" as he leads an army into battle.

What made the difference? He came to know God personally by speaking with Him and he came to trust God implicitly as he obeyed Him.

When Gideon obeyed he received strength; when he obeyed he saw God move.

The apostle Paul said, "I can do all things through Christ who strengthens me." (Phil.4:13, NKJV) That isn't self-confidence; that is God-confidence. Paul could only say this because, like Gideon, he had proved it. He obeyed God, and God met him with strength.

I have found this to be so true in my life. I have no more confidence in myself than I had when I set out on this ministry journey thirty-nine years ago this month. But I rely daily on God to meet me with strength as I obey Him. It's my confidence in God that has grown.

88

His Divine power has given us everything we need for life and godliness through the knowledge of Him who called us by His own glory and excellence.

2 Peter 1:3 (BSB)

Have you ever been looking for something, only to realise that it is in your hand or pocket? My favourite is looking for my glasses when they are on my head!

As Christians we are often looking for things we already have and asking God for things that He has already given us. When Moses was tasked with being God's representative to Pharaoh, he made all kinds of excuses, but God said to him, "What is that in your hand?" It was his staff. God said, "Throw it on the floor." He did and it turned into a snake. God said, "Pick it up." He did and it turned back into a stick.

God wanted to show Moses that what he needed he already had. God had already invested in him, already equipped him. Until he tried, he would never know what he could do.

What is that in *your* hand?

None of us know how well equipped we are in God until we attempt something for Him. If we have been filled with the Holy Spirit, nothing really is impossible.

During the Indonesian Revival in the 1960s, every miracle in the New Testament was replicated. I once sat next to Cliff Dudley who wrote the book *Like A Mighty Wind* about that revival. He assured me that everything in Mel Tari's account was true and verifiable.

The gifts of the Holy Spirit are like a toolbox. When you are faced with a certain task, you can take out the appropriate tool. We so often shy away from God's will and His prompting to do something for Him because we think we are incapable. But our ability comes from Him. "Not that we are competent in ourselves to claim that anything comes from us but our competence comes from God." (2.Cor.3:5, BSB) We don't have to wait around and pray to be given this competence either... It has already been put in us.

So stop putting off what God has called you to do. He's given you the tools; get on with the job!

89

But God chose the foolish things of the world to shame the wise, God chose the weak things of this world to shame the mighty.

1 Corinthians 1:27 (NIV)

If you are looking for a good excuse, can I recommend looking in the Bible? It is full of excuses. Here are a few: "I've just bought some oxen and I haven't tried them out yet." "I've just bought some land and I haven't seen it yet." "I just got married." Gideon's excuse was, "I'm too poor." Moses' excuse was, "I have a speech impediment." Isaiah's was, "I have a dirty mouth." Jeremiah's was, "I'm too young." And so on.

But what do you notice about Gideon, Moses, Isaiah and Jeremiah? God still used them. God is bigger than our excuses, bigger than our disqualifications, bigger than our limitations. My dear Norwegian friend Finn Arne Lauvaas wrote a brilliant song entitled 'He Broke All My Limitations'. And that is exactly what God does!

Someone who had more reason to excuse himself than most was the Apostle Paul. He had hated Jesus and everything to do with Him; he had waged a personal war against the new church; he had rounded up Christians and had them thrown into jail, flogged and even executed. He was very aware of his own sinful nature, even calling himself the chief of sinners. He was often afraid and lacking in courage.

He had had some very bad experiences once he became a Christian: being beaten, stoned, shipwrecked, imprisoned, left for dead. Even some Christians disliked him and made up things to try to discredit him. You would have thought he would have learnt his lesson, wouldn't you?

Did he make an excuse and bow out of what God asked him to do? Did he ever! His reaction to his own disqualification was this: "For when I am weak, then I am strong!" (2.Cor.12:10, NKJV) He writes that God had said to him, "My grace is sufficient for you, for my strength is made perfect in weakness." (v.9, NKJV)

Our weakness, whatever it might be, is not an excuse but a qualification. Today's passage tells us that this is even God's strategy.

Just remember today, don't make excuses; when you are weak then you are strong.

90

But we have this treasure in jars of clay to show that this surpassingly great power is from God not from us.

2 Corinthians 4:7 (NIV)

This week we have been looking at how God takes people who think they are useless and makes them useful to Him. The expression '*used* of God' is one of the highest accolades that we give a person. There are several reasons why God works this way. If He uses people who think they cannot do what He asks, they will be reliant on Him for help – they will do it in His strength, not their own, and do it His way rather than their way. When the task is complete, all the glory will go to Him and not to them as they humbly acknowledge that it was only through the Lord's enabling that they could do it at all.

Today's verse tells us that God put the treasure of His indwelling presence and power in the most basic kind of containers – you and me. If we will stay humble and pure, He will use us to surprise the proud and the self-important.

All through history we see this happening. In the Old Testament God chose shepherds, ploughmen, even criminals; in the New Testament Jesus chose fishermen and a tax collector. In church history we see the same pattern.

The leader of the Welsh revival, Evan Roberts, was a miner, as was Billy Bray here in Cornwall. Author of *Pilgrim's Progress*, the first novel in the English language, John Bunyan was a tinker (a mender of pots and pans). Martin Luther was a poor parish priest whose church was a 20x30 wooden shack in Wittenberg, Germany, the walls propped up on all sides. All around were imposing churches and lavish cathedrals but God chose the man from the shed rather than those from the basilicas to change the world.

Revivals, too, don't start in the notable churches of the world; the Welsh revival started in a simple chapel in the Welsh Valleys, the Hebridean revival on a far-flung Scottish island and the Pentecostal revival began with a half-blind black preacher in a disused warehouse in Los Angeles. The Son of God chose to be born in a cattle shed in an obscure Jewish village and set the pattern long ago.

You and I need to develop a stable mentality too!

91

But God chose what the world considers nonsense to put wise people to shame, God chose what the world considers weak to put what is strong to shame.

1 Corinthians 1:27 (GW)

Yesterday we were considering how the treasure of God's presence and power is contained in jars of clay – how God prefers to use weak and foolish people and obscure places to do and to birth His work.

Crackington Haven in North Cornwall is my wife's homeplace. This village is the place farthest from a hospital in the whole of England. Three hundred years ago it had a population of eighty families. The parish church, St. Genny's, is stuck on top of a cliff on a dead-end road. Yet there a most remarkable thing happened. In 1732 Revd. George Thompson, a thrill seeker and adventurer, was appointed vicar. Not long after this he had a recurring dream of his own death. Terrified, he asked the congregation for their prayers. Two weeks later he came to know Jesus as his personal saviour.

George had attended Cambridge University with some notable people, and he ask one of them to fill in for him for six weeks in 1738. It was the none other than the renowned evangelist George Whitfield. In 1744 another friend, Charles Wesley, came and preached, and some gave their lives to Christ. The next year John Wesley came and preached morning and evening to a packed church, and both he and Charles returned year after year to preach, winning souls and encouraging George Thompson, who had started branch works in several places including Port Isaac. Revival was happening and Methodism was being born, to the annoyance of the Bishop of Exeter.

In the spring of 1750 a meeting took place in the church when present were John Wesley, George Whitfield, George Thompson and four more of Wesley's notable preachers – it went on for hours! This obscure little church on the very fringe of England became a hotbed of revival. It was one of only three churches in Cornwall that would receive John Wesley, although revival was winning thousands in the county.

As Francis Schaeffer once wrote, with God "there are no little places and no little people".

92

*By night I went out … examining the walls of Jerusalem, which had been
broken down, and its gates, which had been destroyed by fire.*

Nehemiah 2:13 (NIV)

Do you ever feel defeated and overwhelmed? Have you lost battles
in your life and your relationship with God suffered because of
it? This week I'm going to address this by talking about God's
secret code of restoration.

It was night-time when God took Nehemiah on a tour of Jerusalem
and showed him the walls broken down and the gates destroyed. The
Jews had returned from captivity in Babylon, and Ezra had rebuilt the
temple, but it was so vulnerable without the city walls and gates. There
was something new and beautiful; it needed to be protected.

This, to me, is a picture of the new Christian. God has given them a
new heart, a place where He dwells at the centre of everything, but it is
vulnerable. It needs protecting. Walls need to be built and gates need to
be shut – some permanently.

We live in a land of castles. When a castle comes under attack, the
first thing you do is pull up the drawbridge and lower the portcullis!

Sometimes a follower of Jesus can be robbed of the things God has
given them by the devil and his schemes because people haven't been told
to shut the gates!

Here in Nehemiah we see a kind of code embedded in the text which
helps us to build these protections into our lives. There are ten gates
which represent ten principles, and we are going to look at them this
week.

Before we begin we need to realise that the devil hates God and wants
to hurt Him and frustrate His plans. God Himself, of course, is
unassailable and so the devil picks a softer target, something that is
precious to God, something He loves: you and me.

Jesus, speaking about the devil, said, "The thief's purpose is to steal
and kill and destroy. My purpose is to give them a rich and satisfying
life." (Jn.10:10, NLT) The devil wants to steal our peace, kill our faith
and destroy our relationship with God. This is an ongoing battle and the
only ones who will emerge victorious at the end are those that have learnt
to build the walls and shut the gates.

93

...I went out through the Valley Gate...

Nehemiah 2:13 (NIV)

The ten gates of the ancient city of Jerusalem have a hidden meaning. If we see our life as a city, we can protect the citadel of our heart by building a wall of protection and gates that can be closed to the attacks and influences of the devil.

The first gate we are going to consider is the Valley Gate. This is the gate that Nehemiah went out through when God took him on a night-time tour of the broken-down walls.

The Valley Gate led to the Hinnom valley, the most inauspicious side of Jerusalem. It had been in this valley that an altar to Baal, a false god, had been erected and human sacrifice had taken place. (I have visited Macchu Picchu in Peru and although the spectacle is breathtaking, I found the spiritual atmosphere the worst I have ever encountered because it was a place of human sacrifice.) This worship of Baal was one of the reasons God sent the Jews into exile.

Another name for this valley was Gehenna – the valley of the flame. It was the city's rubbish dump and the fire of burning rubbish was said to never go out. This is why the Jews called hell 'Gehenna'.

In the middle of all this was a well called the Serpent Well or Dragon Well. Jackals used to drink from it as they were rifling through the rubbish. Not a pretty picture.

The image that this gives us is of a place to stay away from. I don't know about you but I wouldn't want to drink from that well. What God is saying to us is that if we want to be restored and protected from the devil's attacks, we need to shut the Valley Gate – the gate that leads to and from hell.

We need to stop drinking from the devil's well, whatever kicks / fixes / pleasures you were getting from that source you need to shut the door on permanently. There are some TV programmes you need to stop watching, some music you need to stop listening to, some company that you need to say goodbye to. Close the gate!

Paul says, "Yes, everything else is worthless when compared with the infinite value of knowing Christ Jesus my Lord. For his sake I have discarded everything else, counting it all as garbage, so that I could gain Christ and become one with Him." (Phil.3:8, NLT)

94

*I went out through the Valley Gate, past the Serpent's Well, and over to the
Dung Gate to inspect the broken walls and burned gates.*

Nehemiah 2:13-14 (CSB)

The ten ancient gates of Jerusalem have a hidden meaning. I call it
'God's restoration code'. The gates need to be operational to
prevent attack from the enemy and restore the city – our lives – to
spiritual health.

God had tasked Nehemiah with rebuilding the walls and gates. The
second gate that Nehemiah came to on his tour of the city was the Dung
Gate. This, too, led into the Valley of Hinnom where Jerusalem dumped
its waste. The Jews, because of the commandments that God had given
Moses, were the first nation on earth to understand sanitation and the
importance of getting rid of human and animal waste – hence the Dung
Gate.

Did you know that this is as important spiritually as it is physically?
Just as the city would have a daily cleansing and take the dirt out through
the Dung Gate, so God is telling us here that we must have a daily
cleansing spiritually and get the things that are dangerous to our
wellbeing out of our lives.

I am a great believer in saying the Lord's prayer. Jesus gave this to us
for a reason – so that we don't forget any important things we should
pray for daily. One line says, "…forgive us our sins as we forgive those
who sin against us." (Lk.11:4, NLT) Here we have the waste removal
system of prayer. We need to ask forgiveness daily for our sins. Allowing
them to accumulate in our lives is like letting waste pile up in the street –
it is a spiritual health risk.

But the second phrase is as important: "…as we forgive those who
trespass against us." Unforgiveness is a spiritual pollutant, a dangerous
pathogen that needs to be removed from our lives as quickly as possible.
Did you know that every cell in our body has a waste removal system
built into it? That is God's design – one of His building blocks for life
and health. Spiritual health needs the same mechanism.

Ephesians 4:31-32 (MSG) says, "Make a clean break with all cutting,
backbiting, profane talk. Be gentle with one another, sensitive. Forgive
one another quickly as God in Christ forgave you."

95

Then I went on to the Fountain Gate and to the King's Pool, but there was no room for the animal under me to pass.

Nehemiah 2:14 (NKJV)

Just like Nehemiah rebuilt the walls and the gates of the Jerusalem, making the temple (its heart) secure, so God wants us to rebuild the walls and gates of our lives, making our new life in Him secure. The Bible says, "Above all else guard your heart." (Prov.4:23, NIV)

Each gate of the old city of Jerusalem gives us a part of God's restoration code. Today we look at the Fountain Gate.

The Fountain Gate was the gate that people in Jerusalem used to use every day to go and draw water from the stream Gihon, which was the main water source for Jerusalem. It was called 'the fountain' because it was running water, a spring that had made life possible in Jerusalem – *living water.*

The stream ran into the Pool of Siloam which acted as a small reservoir for the city's water supply. This pool was also known as the King's Pool because, like the underground aqueducts, it was built by King Hezekiah.

Do you see the parallels here to the Christian life, to God's restoration plan? Just as the citizens of Jerusalem had to come every day through the Fountain Gate to draw fresh living water from the King's Pool, so, if we are to be restored and kept in good spiritual health, we need every day to get living water from the King of kings' pool.

Once, when Jesus saw the priests carrying pitchers of water from this pool through the Fountain Gate to the temple, He shouted out at the top of his voice, "If anyone is thirsty, let him come to Me and drink." (Jn.7:37, NIV)

So every day we are to go to Jesus and get living water from Him to sustain us. We drink it in by simply being in His presence in prayer and by reading His Word. Our spiritual lives are restored and maintained by the activity of going to fetch water.

96

Then Eliashib the high priest rose up with his brethren the priests and built the Sheep Gate; they consecrated it and hung its doors.

Nehemiah 3:1 (NKJV)

We are discovering that the ten gates of the old city of Jerusalem represent things in our lives that need to be taken care of to complete and maintain our restoration and our walk with God.

The first gate to be rebuilt under Nehemiah's direction was the Sheep Gate and it was rebuilt by a very unlikely group of people. Who would expect the high priest to be involved in building work?! But I'm sure there were reasons for that – priests or pastors should always set an example and be ready to get their hands dirty.

The name of this gate, the Sheep Gate, says a lot. The Bible says, "All we like sheep have gone astray; We have turned, every one, to his own way; And the Lord has laid on Him the iniquity of us all." (Is.53:6, NKJV) We, like sheep, have a propensity to go our own way, to do our own thing. In Judges we read, "In those days Israel had no king; all the people did whatever seemed right in their own eyes." (Jdg.21:25, NLT)

Today, more than ever, people are doing what is right in their own eyes. Selfishness and pride make people say, "You can't tell me what to do; you can't tell me how to live." Everybody is going their own way. "There is a way that seems right to a person," the Bible says, "but eventually it ends in death." (Prov.14:12, GW)

To rebuild the Sheep Gate, we have to get rid of this attitude and deal with our selfishness and pride. Oswald Chambers described sin as "my claim to my right to myself"[6] – never a truer word has been spoken! We need to surrender our rights to Jesus. He is our high priest and we need to let Him rebuild this part of our lives so that we live in dependence on Him – going His way, not our way, in everything.

If you have never done it before, do it today. Pray, "Lord, I surrender myself completely to you. I give you the throne of my life and make you my Lord, my Boss, my King. Help me to live in obedience to you."

---

[6] Oswald Chambers; *My Utmost for His Highest*

97

After him Malchijah (God is King), one of the goldsmiths, made repairs as far as the house of the Nethinim and of the merchants, in front of the Miphkad Gate, and as far as the upper room at the corner.

Nehemiah 3:31 (BSB)

The gate we are looking at today is mentioned in today's verse. In some Bible versions it is referred to by its Hebrew name – the Miphkad Gate – and in some it is translated "Inspection Gate". *Miphkad* can mean 'inspection', 'appointment' or 'muster'. I prefer 'muster'. It was by this gate that the army was assembled or mustered and inspected. We would call it a parade ground.

God musters His army once a week. It is called church! Interestingly, we see an "upper room" mentioned in this verse – the birthplace of the church! Assembling of ourselves together on Sundays is an important part of the restructuring of our lives. Hebrews 10:25 (NLT) says, "And let us not neglect our meeting together, as some people do, but encourage one another, especially now that the day of his return is drawing near."

In this Holy-Spirit-charged atmosphere we are 'inspected' and supplied. As we participate in the breaking of bread, we are told to examine ourselves. Also, as we gather we get our marching orders!

The work on Jerusalem's walls and gates is one of the most amazing corporate ventures you will find. The rebuilding was completed in fifty-two days! Everybody joined in with the work, from priests to goldsmiths, and worked on the section nearest their home! This is a lovely picture of church, where people from all families and professions work shoulder to shoulder for God. We must not underestimate the power and significance of building one another up.

There is of course another 'muster': our appointment in heaven, when God assembles all His people together for the heavenly census. To complete our wall and gates, in the building of the city which is our life, our eyes should be on the goal: the heavenly city!

98

Next to him were Pedaiah son of Parosh, with the Temple servants living on the hill of Ophel, who repaired the wall as far as a point across from the Water Gate to the east and the projecting tower.

Nehemiah 3:25-27 (NLT)

The last of our gates is the Water Gate – so named because it was part of a fortified tower that overlooked and protected the Spring of Gishon – Jerusalem's water supply. It was also the gate nearest the temple.

Something really wonderful happened here and it is a fitting conclusion to our talks. When the rebuilding was complete, Ezra the priest and Nehemiah the governor called the people together at the Water Gate. Ezra brought out the book of the Law of Moses and began to read.

During seventy years of captivity the people had forgotten a lot of their traditions and even their feasts. Ezra stood on a stage constructed for the occasion and read all morning long. As he read, they realised that it was the date for the Feast of Tabernacles.

Nehemiah 8:6 (NLT) says, "Then Ezra praised the Lord, the great God, and all the people chanted, 'Amen! Amen!' as they lifted their hands toward heaven. Then they bowed down and worshiped the Lord with their faces to the ground."

Ezra told the people to go and celebrate and be joyful – the feast had been revived ! And so a time of revival began.

It is so fitting that this happened at the Water Gate because water is a symbol of the Holy Spirit. The Holy Spirit is our source of supply, and when we receive the Holy Spirit into our lives, revival and joy are the result.

So our last gate is a reminder that we need to keep our heart alive to God through the Holy Spirit so that the walls and gates are protecting a living heart at the centre of our being.

Pray today and ask God to fill you with the Holy Spirit – we all need revival!

99

She said to her husband, "I am sure this man who stops in from time to time is a holy man of God. Let's make a little room for him on the roof and furnish it with a bed, a table, a chair, and a lamp. Then he will have a place to stay whenever he comes by."

2 Kings 4:9-10 (NLT)

Have you thought about putting on an extension to your home? Did you know that the Bible speaks about this? There's a lovely story in 2 Kings. Elisha the prophet was passing through the town of Shunem when a wealthy woman invited him in for a meal. This became a regular occurrence when he was in the area, so she and her husband decided to set up a permanent room for him.

That's exactly what happened in a little Hamlet called Trewint on the old coach road (now the A30) just south of Launceston. It wasn't Elisha this time but John Wesley – the eighteenth century preacher who famously said, "The world is my parish." The nearby parish church of Altarnun was one of just three churches that welcomed his ministry and so he was often passing through – this road being the main road through Cornwall in those days.

Digory Isbell and his wife Elizabeth welcomed Wesley to stay in their cottage in the summer of 1744 and felt much blessed by his presence. Sometime later Digory was reading 2 Kings and the story of Elisha and the Shunammite woman. He suddenly said to his wife, "I know what we have to do – build a prophet's chamber!" So they built a little two-storey extension to their home for Mr. Wesley.

He often stayed there and today there it is a museum with artifacts that he himself used – including a tea cup! The little downstairs room is said to be the smallest Methodist meeting place in the world.

Elisha repaid the Shunammite woman with a miracle baby as she was barren. I don't know how God repaid Digory and Elizabeth but I think it was with their neighbours and friends being born again as revival swept the area!

100

And whatever you do, do it heartily, as to the Lord and not to men, knowing that from the Lord you will receive the reward of the inheritance; for you serve the Lord Christ

Colossians 3:23-24 (NKJV)

One of my favourites in the New Testament is Stephen. Most people know him as the first Christian martyr but it's a shame if that is all we take from this remarkable man. His story begins in the book of Acts (chapter 6) when a problem arose for the young church. A group of women were protesting because they were not getting a fair share of the daily distribution of bread to the widows. The apostles felt that this was not something that they should give a lot of time to so they decided to appoint seven deacons to distribute the bread. Stephen was one of these men.

Imagine being a young man called before the apostles because they had a job for you. The excitement and anticipation must have been palpable! But then when you found out the job was giving out bread to crotchety ladies... how would you feel then?

Stephen's character shone through. Acts defines him as "a man full of faith and the Holy Spirit", so how does such a man respond to such a task? You can do big things in a little way or little things in a big way. Stephen did the latter. He put all his effort into serving the widows and so made the insignificant significant by the spirit he put into it. How do we know this? Because as we will see, Stephen did the job so efficiently that he had time to go out preaching afterwards.

There is a huge lesson for us here: when we have a job to do for Jesus, no matter how small, insignificant, even how demeaning it might be, we should always give a hundred percent, pray about it, do it as unto the Lord.

As we will see, this is God's way of testing us. We will never be allowed to do big things unless we will do little things in a big way.

101

Therefore, brethren, seek out from among you seven men of good reputation, full of the Holy Spirit and wisdom, whom we may appoint over this business...

Acts 6:3 (NKJV)

Yesterday we saw how Stephen was given a little job and did it in a big way and made the insignificant significant by the spirit he put into it. Another reason that God used Stephen was that he was of good report. When the apostles wanted to appoint the deacons, see what they said in today's verse.

When God wants to use someone, the first question that is asked is, "Is he or she of good report?" – or, do they have good reputation? The word that is used in Greek for this is rather surprising: *martyroumenous*. It's the word that we get 'martyr' from. A martyr is literally someone with a good reputation or witness. Timothy and Ananias of Damascus (who ministered to Paul after his conversion) are both described using this word – men that people spoke well of.

Is it strange that character is what God looks for first? Actually, it's quite understandable because character is the one thing God cannot give us; it is something of our own making. God will supply all the tools that we need to do the job but character is our responsibility. So if you want God to use you, start working on that.

The task of feeding the widows (or "waiting on tables", as the apostles put it) was not the most spiritual job you can think of, but the two other qualifications that the deacons needed were to be full of the Holy Spirit and wisdom. How different is that from our modern-day job descriptions? Which is right? Well, the Bible, of course.

What we fail to realise is that every job in church, every job for Jesus, is a ministry – it is all spiritual and therefore requires spiritual people to do it.

These three criteria guarantee success: reputation, Holy Spirit and wisdom. This worker ticks all the boxes and Stephen was a shining example of it.

102

Now Stephen, a man full of God's grace and power, did great wonders and miraculous signs among the people.

Acts 6:8 (NIV)

E. Stanley Jones called Stephen "the most Christian man in the Bible" – quite an accolade! What made him say that? We saw yesterday that Stephen was of good report, full of the Holy Spirit and wisdom. Today we see in Acts 6:8 that Stephen was a man full of God's grace and power. He is the only person in the Bible described in this way! In fact, the only other person in the Bible of whom it is said they were full of grace is Jesus Himself. Remember, "And the Word became flesh and dwelt among us, and we beheld His glory. The glory as of the only begotten of the Father, full of grace and truth." (Jn.1:14, NKJV)

Grace (*charis* in Greek) is a word that means a lot of things, but here it implies graciousness, being kind, tender-hearted, compassionate and also charming and endearing. There is no doubt that this is one of the main things we mean when we talk about becoming more like Jesus.

Here was a young man, plucked from the ranks, so to speak, who had only been a Christian for twelve months, described in a way that makes us marvel. It just shows you what can be achieved if we let God have His way in our lives and are serious about developing our own character and walk.

I always say, the fast-track in the Christian life is achieved by saying yes. Whatever God asks of you, say yes and do it immediately.

Back in the 1990s I was privileged to be involved in the Estonian revival. Large numbers of people were turning to Christ, eighty churches were planted in a year and people were becoming pastors who had not been even saved for a year – and it worked.

I asked them, "How did you grow so quickly in the Lord?"

"That's easy," they said, "we just kept saying yes."

I can't help thinking that in the current pandemic environment we need a bit more of this personal rapid growth in Christ. Remember, it's easy; all you have to do is say yes.

103

Yes, all of you be submissive to one another, and be clothed with humility, for "God resists the proud, but gives grace to the humble." Therefore humble yourselves under the mighty hand of God, that He may exalt you in due time...

1 Peter 5:5-6 (NKJV)

This week we are considering the ministry of Stephen, a man who was appointed to be a deacon – that is, to do a practical job distributing food to widows. We have seen how the Bible describes him as a man full of God's grace and power, who did great wonders and miraculous signs among the people. Wow! That's really something – especially for someone who was supposed to be doing a practical job. Stephen and his six co-workers did the job so efficiently that he had time to preach and see God do great wonders and miraculous signs.

I am always wary of people that want power. Power is not something that we should crave. Power comes with responsibilities and can be dangerous. Those who seek power never get it – but those who seek God get power as a bonus. Many people are powerful and don't even know it. Some of the most powerful people I have met are the most unassuming. I think Stephen was one of those.

To protect the church, ourselves and the world, God has made sure that the power of Christ can only be contained in the character of Christ; that is why there are fruits of the Spirit alongside the gifts of the Spirit. Can you imagine what someone would be like if they had the power of the Holy Spirit but an unscrupulous character?

Remember, it was Simon the Sorcerer who said, "Give me this power," and offered money for it. The Apostle Peter was only too aware of this danger, as we see in today's passage.

So the advice is this: seek God, develop your character, serve others and be gracious – seek first the kingdom of God and His righteousness and all these things will be added unto you. You will receive power but you might not even know it.

104

Therefore, brethren, seek out from among you seven men of good reputation, full of the Holy Spirit and wisdom, whom we may appoint over this business ... And they chose Stephen, a man full of faith and the Holy Spirit...

Acts 6:3-5 (NKJV)

As we look at the description of Stephen, we notice that it says he was full of the Holy Spirit, full of faith, full of God's grace, full of wisdom and full of power! My goodness – there wasn't much room for anything else! And perhaps that's it; he was so full of the things of God that there wasn't room for the things of the world.

Today I want to consider the fact that he was full of the Holy Spirit and wisdom. Only he and Barnabas are so described in the New Testament.

Some of you might have heard me say before that I pray every day that the Lord will fill me with the Holy Spirit and wisdom – I believe it is so important. First of all, we need a daily filling of the Holy Spirit; when the Bible says, "Be filled with the Holy Spirit," the tense means, "Be *being* filled," a continual filling, not a one-off.

But I couple that, as with Stephen, with wisdom. These two things need to go together. Spirituality directed by wisdom is awesome; spirituality directed by ignorance is awful! To have the Holy Spirit and no wisdom is dangerous, and to have wisdom and no Holy Spirit is suffocating and extremely boring!

We see these two gifts at work in Stephen in one of the following verses: "...but they could not stand up against the his wisdom or the Spirit by whom he spoke." (Acts.6:0, BSB) Wonderful! The combination of the Spirit and wisdom is unbeatable – it's what we need today – and they are two things which the Lord loves to give and promised to give if we ask for them.

James 1:5 (NIV) says, "If any of you lacks wisdom, you should ask God, who gives generously to all without finding fault, and it will be given to you." Start asking today!

105

But as the believers rapidly multiplied, there were rumblings of discontent. The Greek-speaking believers complained about the Hebrew-speaking believers, saying that their widows were being discriminated against in the daily distribution of food. So the Twelve called a meeting of all the believers.

Acts 6:1-2 (NLT)

Stephen made a great impact in his short ministry; for instance, his sermon is one of the longest sermons recorded in the Bible! The job that Stephen and the six other deacons were asked to do was not as simple as it sounds. The problem was a serious one: it necessitated a meeting of all the believers; it was of a racial nature; and it involved a dispute between women. Good luck with that!

The surprising answer that they came up with was that they appointed seven men to deal with it who were all from the Greek speakers' (or Hellenist) side. It was very awkward.

I don't know about you but I would have been extremely apprehensive about getting involved. I would have prayed much before doing anything and I am sure that's what Stephen did. Stephen was made by a job that was too difficult for him.

That is the kind of job that God loves to give us. You see, if we are only ever given jobs that are simple or only accept jobs that are within our comfort zone, then we will never develop. God calls us to jobs that are too difficult for us so that we cannot do them in our own strength and have to throw ourselves upon Him and ask for His help.

My life has been full of jobs that were too difficult for me – from the year I started in 1981 when God called me to Malta as a twenty-three-year-old evangelist when Joy and I experienced the worst week of our lives, to teaching in Bible colleges when I had not been to one myself, to buying a building for our church with no money in the bank!

God often puts an impossible task before us to test us and to see if we will draw upon His resources or our own – actually, to force us to draw upon His.

This was the making of Stephen and it will be the making of you. Don't shy away from things that you think you cannot do – those are exactly the things you should be doing.

106

"It is not desirable that we should leave the word of God and serve tables."

Acts 6:2 (NKJV)

We are going to continue looking at Stephen for a couple more days. When the disciples appointed deacons to distribute the bread to the widows, they said it was because, "We apostles should spend our time preaching and teaching the word of God, not running a food program." (Acts.6:2, NLT) Yet that was exactly what Stephen managed to do – and do to great effect.

Now, I can see that there are times when ministers or pastors become very busy with preaching, teaching, leading, counselling, personal prayer and so on, but I think that it is a mistake to cut yourself entirely from practical work.

Too many have divorced themselves from the everyday world and common tasks and in doing so lost touch with their people and their lives. There is a phrase that is used for this: 'to be in an ivory tower' – detached, unreal.

When this happens you start to lose the ability to communicate with people in a meaningful way. Jesus didn't, and Paul maintained his tent-making, as we know.

Stephen comes across as a people's champion. He bridged the gap between secular and sacred.

Paul emphasised this in his first letter to the Thessalonians: "Make it your ambition to lead a quiet life, to mind your own business and to work with your hands , just as we told you, so that your daily life may win the respect of outsiders and so that you will not be dependent on anybody." (1.Thess.4:11-12, NIV)

Notice that there is a connection between working with your hands and winning people's respect. We must never get the idea that we are above certain jobs – that's a dangerous train of thought.

107

But he, being full of the Holy Spirit, gazed into heaven and saw the glory of God, and Jesus standing at the right hand of God...

Acts 7:55 (NKJV)

In the last of our talks on Stephen, I want to highlight the fact that he excelled in everything he did. We saw yesterday that he not only did the practical tasks well but he preached well and ministered wonderfully, God blessing his work with the miraculous.

Stephen wasn't swamped by the day job; he had plenty of time to serve God and fulfil what was the main calling of his life (even though it was short-lived). There are so many people who let their job completely take over their lives and do not leave any time for the Lord's work. My grandfather used to bemoan his job. He had a petrol station and garage business. He rarely took time off and holidays were almost non-existent. Sundays, of course, were always a day of rest. He used to say, "Never have your own business; don't be self-employed." But there you are, he *was* self-employed; he was his own boss, it was his own doing.

You have probably heard the saying that we should work to live, not live to work. When I was at school we were told that in the future we would all retire at fifty as there would be so many labour-saving devices that there would not be much work to do. What happened? The opposite! People are busier now than then; you never hear the expression "labour-saving device". We have to *make* time to serve God and fulfil what He has given us to do.

Lastly, Stephen died well. His is probably the most wonderful departure in the Bible, as seen in today's verse. When I attended my pastor Arthur Neil's funeral a couple of years ago, the Lord profoundly touched me. I came home saying to Joy, "Wow! He touched me in death as he touched me in life." The final service Steven did, the Lord was in his death. There was one looking on, maybe even organising the stoning, and that was Saul. Acts 8:1 (BSB) notes, "And Saul was there, giving approval to Stephen's death." I believe that his death, or more precisely the way he died, had a tremendous effect on Saul and was one of the "goads" that Jesus mentioned to him at his conversion.

Stephen's ministry, according to Bible scholars, lasted only about a year, but here we are talking about it two thousand years later – that is impact!

108

He restores my soul.

Psalm 23:3 (NKJV)

One of the phrases in the Bible that has always intrigued me is "He restores my soul", found in Psalm 23. When you start to delve into these words, you begin to see a world of meaning that is so inspiring and helpful. It sounds good in English but when you see the meaning in Hebrew – in which it was written – it is truly wonderful.

As you know, David wrote most of the Psalms. This was David the shepherd boy who fought Goliath, David who was to become king of Israel, David of whom God said, "[He is] a man after my own heart." (Acts.13:22, NIV) His psalms certainly show us how much he loved God and was dependant on Him.

So David wrote, "He restores my soul" – but what is our soul? Our soul is our mind, our will and our emotions – the very heart of who we are. Do you think that our mind, our will and our emotions need restoring? You bet they do, and they need restoring on a regular basis. God knows this better than anybody. Jesus Himself needed restoring in His presence through prayer and waiting on Him.

Our minds are bombarded daily with all the detritus of the world – bad news, fake news, sad news – the filth and garbage that the media constantly throw at us; the fears, worries and doubts that the devil fires at us; the burden and anguish of our friends' and family's problems; and our own thoughts, which are sometimes far from righteous and faith-filled. Such is the trouble of our soul.

Last year this time, the heart consultant told me to avoid stress. How is that possible? It's been interesting trying to navigate around and away from it. But He restores my soul. The constant round of decisions, judgement calls and motivation that make up my will need God's restoring touch, so I stay in His will and decide for Him and not myself.

Our emotions are strange things and difficult to control. They make great servants but poor masters. Sadly, the whole world seems to be led by their emotions rather than reason. We need God's restoring power in our emotions to keep them under control and in check. God uses our emotions – what is love if it is not an emotion? – but we must try to keep them in line with His heart, like David. It's going to be great exploring this wonderful phrase and promise together.

109

He prays to God and finds favour with him, he sees God's face and shouts for joy; he is restored by God to his righteous state.

Job 33:26 (BSB)

Psalm 23 says, "He restores my soul." Being of a certain vintage, I always want to say, "He restoreth my soul!" The word that is translated "restore" in our bibles is the Hebrew word *shuwb* (pronounced 'shoove'). *Shuwb* has an incredibly rich meaning. It is the original 're' word; it can mean 'recover', 'refresh', 'relieve', 'rescue', 'retrieve', 'return', 'reverse' and 'reward'. Also it can mean 'to bring back home' or 'put back to the beginning'.

Now, when you say, "He restores my soul," you can substitute any of those words for 'restore' and the impact and scope is multiplied wonderfully.

If you are a bit computer-literate you will know that computers have what is called a restore point. If something goes wrong with the software, it is often because you have downloaded something the computer doesn't like, something that has interfered with its smooth working. So then you go into the control panel of the computer and choose a restore point – a time and date before things started going wrong. You click on that and it takes your computer back to that moment and erases what has happened since that point. Pretty clever.

But God thought of it first. "He restores my soul" means exactly this – that God is able to take you back, take your soul back, to a time before your problem occurred and so restore it to how it worked at that time, also erasing the hurt and damage that has been caused since.

People often say, "What's done is done. You can't go back and change it," but you can. You can change the damage that it has done to your soul. This is an amazing provision from the Lord.

Of course, the main restore point is the day you were born again. When we give our lives to Jesus, He clicks the restore point and we are born again. Everything is erased and put back the way it should be. Has this happened to you? If not, why not do it right now?

110

*Repent therefore and be converted, that your sins may be blotted out, so
that times of refreshing may come from the presence of the Lord...*
Acts 3:19 (NKJV)

As we heard yesterday, the word for 'restore' in Hebrew – *shuwb* – can be translated in a number of ways. Today I want to look at 'refresh'. He *refreshes* my soul.

'Refresh' is a powerful word in the English language; it is a buzz word in advertising, as people are drawn to it. It harmonises with a desire within us for refreshing which all of us need in some area – it could be anything from our sleep to our marriage!

But here we are offered a refreshing of our soul. A common expression that we use is "refresh my memory" when we have forgotten something. This is something that God loves to do. The children of Israel had this written into their worship – they recited all the things God did for them like bringing them out of Israel and opening up the Red Sea for them to cross on dry land.

I noticed when I first visited Norway that when people prayed, they would invariably start with, "Thank you God for saving me" – refreshing their memory. It is a very important thing to remember and be thankful for all that the Lord has done for you.

Our mind is an aspect of the soul that needs to be refreshed – we could spend a week on this! But suffice to say, we need the junk, the dirt, the dust and the negative washed out of our mind daily. We need that crystal clear living water from heaven to course through our mind and return it to the healthy, vibrant and righteous thing that it is meant to be. Morning devotions are the way to do this: "He refreshes my soul."

Acts 3:19 is one of my favourite verses. We, as Christians, are meant to live in those times of refreshing. As we walk with the Lord, it is not only our mind that is refreshed, but our faith, hope and love. Let's face it, life has a habit of dulling and draining us – we can sometimes be living in a kind of stupor. If Christ offers to refresh our soul, let Him! Ask Him for it – ask Him now!

In that lovely little letter Paul says to Philemon, "For we have great joy and consolation in your love, because the hearts of the saints have been refreshed by you, brother." (Phm:7, NKJV) When we have been refreshed, let's make it our aim to refresh others!

111

Eye has not seen , nor ear heard,
Nor have entered into the heart of man
The things which God has prepared for those who love Him.

1 Corinthians 2:9 (NKJV)

The Hebrew word *shuwb* in Psalm 23:3 can also be translated 'reward' – so the verse would read, "He rewards my soul" – and isn't that the truth!

This week my dear father-in-law went to be with the Lord. Christians sometimes say someone 'went to his reward'. Gordon certainly did. His life was one of quiet but continual service of Jesus as a steward in his local chapel. As he got older, he seemed to do more and more. He did it because he loved the Lord – but listen, God is no-one's debtor; there was a fabulous reward waiting for him in heaven.

Those of us who walk with Jesus are aware, though, that we do not have to wait to get to heaven to be rewarded – our soul is continually rewarded by God. As I sit preparing these talks each morning, a thrill passes through my soul – I can't really describe it but it's like a sudden wave of ecstasy. A reward.

The Lord knows each of us so well and tailor-makes the rewards that He gives us. I knew that my grandson Levi would love some little offcuts of wood when I gave them to him – he would use them for bales in his toy farm – none of my other grandsons would have been too impressed.

God knows how to reward me too. I was in Norway on my birthday a few years ago – staying with dear friends on the Island of Bomlo. They threw a little party for me, and as we went out onto the balcony overlooking the fjord, what a sight met us. A huge eagle – only a few metres away – put on a display of aerobatics right there! My hosts said they had never seen an eagle near the house before. I knew it was for me. It was a reward. He does that for me with birds. He rewards my soul.

How does He reward you? Do you recognise where it comes from when He does?

112

Then the Lord said to [Saul], "Arise and go into the city, and you will be told what you must do."

Acts 9:6 (NKJV)

When Jesus intercepted Saul on the road to Damascus, the first thing that Saul cried out was, "Who are you, Lord?" The second thing he said was, "Lord, what do you want me to do?" Interesting.

There is something in salvation that provokes this response in us – there is a calling. Every Christian is called into the Lord's service. We need to discover, like Saul, what He wants us to do.

The Lord did tell Saul. But first He told Ananias, and so Ananias must have told Saul when he came to him in the lodging in Straight Street. Saul, or Paul (as he would call himself by his Greek name from now on), was healed, baptised by Ananias, filled with the Holy Spirit, and after spending some days with the believers in Damascus, immediately he preached in the synagogues that Jesus is the Son of God (see verse 20).

This week we are going to be looking at the subject of guidance – how do we know what the Lord wants us to do? Here we have our first lesson: we have to ask Him and when we ask we have to mean it – we have to be willing to do whatever He says, not just have a curious interest of what He would want us to do if we chose to accept it! This is not Mission Impossible – it is mission possible.

God knows what we are capable of when filled with His Holy Spirit and our mission will be tailored to our personality. I believe that God has been shaping us all our lives, unbeknown to us, to prepare us for the task He has for us. Everything you have gone through has made you the person you are today and made you uniquely suited to the job.

I have heard people say, "I love the ocean but God sent me to the desert!" I think that is nonsense – the Bible says He gives us the desires of our heart, and there will be something in the mission that He has for you that will thrill you.

113

Now may the God of peace who brought up our Lord Jesus from the dead, that great Shepherd of the sheep, through the blood of the everlasting covenant, make you complete in every good work to do His will, working in you what is well pleasing in His sight, through Jesus Christ, to whom be glory forever and ever. Amen.

Hebrews 13:20-21 (NKJV)

Guidance is always a popular subject – people seem to get so hung up on it. One thing is for sure: as we saw yesterday, God has no problem in making Himself clear. Although He usually has a still small voice, He is quite capable of shouting and knocking us to the ground if necessary. In my case He had to throw me through the windscreen of a car to get my attention!

A friend of mine, Albert, is a clay pigeon shooting expert (that's skeet, for our American friends). He says the problem most people have is that they try too hard. It's instinctive reaction you need, to be a good shot.

And that's the problem with guidance; people try too hard. There are certain things to remember. Let's go back to the story of Paul.

Paul knew what the Lord wanted him to do with his life within days of his conversion but it was eleven years before he started. Wow! Suddenly your mind is filled with questions and comments. Surely he could have done a whole lot more if he had started sooner – he could have reached many more people, many more nations. He could have written many more letters and trained many more pastors.

And you know this how? If he had started before God deemed him ready then his ministry might have been a total disaster and we would never have heard of him. Our first lesson is that God is not in any hurry. Jesus never ran. God's timing is perfect and we have to relax and work to His timetable.

Like Paul we have to be prepared. God must work *in* us before He can work *through* us. He has to make us complete in every good work to do His will and then what He works in us will be well pleasing in His sight. This doesn't mean that we can sit around doing nothing until we are ready. We'll talk about that tomorrow.

114

The steps of a good man are ordered by the Lord,
And He delights in his way.

Psalm 37:23 (NKJV)

This week we are looking at guidance. Yesterday we saw that there is often a period of preparation and waiting on God before we are released into the task that He has for us.

So, what do we do – sit around waiting? Some people rather foolishly do. We must understand that God has two sorts of will for your life. One is His general will and the other is His specific will. While we wait for His specific will – when He speaks to us personally and tells us what to do – we get on with doing His general will.

There are things that all Christians are supposed to do, the most important of which Jesus impressed on His disciples before He left for heaven: "Go into all the world and preach the gospel to every creature." (Mk.16:15, NKJV) We all have to find a way of spreading the good news.

We are all called to serve God in whatever way we can to make ourselves useful to the church at the direction of the church leaders.

There is a very good reason why we should be "about the Master's business" and not sitting around waiting. Have you ever noticed how difficult it is to turn the steering wheel of a stationary car? When it is moving it becomes much easier to steer in the right direction. Human beings are the same – we are much easier to guide when we are already in motion, already doing something.

Often we find that the very thing that we found to busy ourselves with is the very thing that God wants us to do, our calling. He has a way of steering us without us realising we are being steered!

The word used here in Hebrew for "ordered" in today's verse means 'set up'. It's very interesting how God has a way of setting us up!

115

For it seemed good to the Holy Spirit and to us to lay no greater burden on you than these requirements:...

Acts 15:28 (NKJV)

There is a phrase relating to guidance that is repeated several times in the New Testament: "it seemed good to us". When we first read it, maybe we are surprised at how casual it sounds, but that is not the intention or the reality. As we work with God, a kind of sixth sense emerges; it is more accurately captured in today's verse: "...it seemed good to *the Holy Spirit* and us..."

We must never forget we are co-workers with Christ; we are not slaves or programmed robots. He cares what we think and feel about certain situations and we are free to make suggestions. He always has the casting vote, of course, but He has given us a mind and a heart to use.

I remember being in Malta on one occasion and agonising over what to preach that evening. I wanted the Lord to tell me which of two things that were on my heart I should use. He clearly spoke to me as I prayed. "You choose," He said, "and whichever you choose, I will bless it." So I went with the one that seemed good to my spirit.

There are lots of things that we should not expect God to guide us in; again, He has given us a brain and sanctified it too by His Spirit. He has given us His Word as a reference to guide us. There are decisions we make every day that must be made within this framework. I even believe that God has nothing to do with whom we choose to marry – the Bible clearly says the decision is ours; we have free will, after all.

But back to our scripture, "For it seemed good to the Holy Spirit and to us..." The way this works is that we have peace about the decisions we make. We pray about them either generally or specifically, and then decide. I often find myself looking to my heavenly Father for a divine nod. That's good enough for me.

116

Trust in the LORD with all your heart, and lean not on your own understanding; in all your ways acknowledge Him, and He shall direct your paths.

Proverbs 3:5-6 (NKJV)

I have found that guidance is something that you have to be experimental with. My case was a bit unusual. When I started serving God in full time ministry, He clearly told me that He wanted me to be available. That is something that very few people are, because of commitments and organisations. He wanted me to be able to go anywhere at any time. This meant that I had to rely totally on His guidance on a daily basis. I would pray every morning and get my orders for the day.

Many times the directives were not earth-shattering; it would be something like, "Go and visit old Mrs. Jones." I would arrive there to be greeted at the door with, "Praise the Lord! I was praying God would send somebody to help me." I would ask how I could pray for her, to which she replied, "Oh, it's nothing like that, dear; I need a wardrobe moved."

Another day the Lord might say to me, "Go to Liechtenstein."

The point is that God's will is extremely varied and if He is to use us to answer people's prayers, we could be asked to do anything. Today's verse says, in *all* your ways acknowledge Him. We have got to be willing to do anything; we cannot be choosy. Often God will test us in small things, humble things, even boring things, to see if we are really willing to obey.

God's guiding voice can come to us in many ways. I had to develop an acute sense of hearing to get guidance on a daily basis. I often tell people that God's voice is like an invasive thought. Suddenly it pops into your head when you weren't thinking about anything like it.

Sometimes it is through the Bible, sometimes a strong urge or feeling, sometimes – oftentimes actually – it can come through a request from your pastor or another believer.

With really big things, like, "Go to Liechtenstein," I would always ask God for three confirmations, one of which was to be the money for the ticket. He never failed. Hudson Taylor famously said, "God's work done in God's way will never lack God's supplies."

117

And everyone who has this hope in Him purifies himself, just as He is pure.

1 John 3:3 (NKJV)

Something seems to have happened in our society – not only here in the UK but also in America. Since the lockdown lifted some people seem to be behaving differently. There is a craziness and it's not a good kind of crazy. There is a violence, a rebelliousness, a disregard for authority, and what we used to call a devil-may-care attitude.

To start with I thought this was the phenomenon that country folk are used to seeing when cattle are let out for the first time after winter indoors. They kick and buck and run around enjoying the freedom. But the effect is lasting too long for that. As I prayed, the Lord reminded me of today's verse from 1 John.

Hope has a purifying effect on our lives and on society. If we have a future, we want to be there to see it and enjoy it. Eternal hope has an even stronger sanctifying influence.

But if that is true, the converse must also be true: everyone who does not have hope does not purify themself. If you take hope away from someone or if they lose their notion of a future, then they will not purify themself; they will let go – or, more correctly, let *themself* go. They will have no thought of tomorrow; it will be, "Eat drink and be merry for tomorrow we die."

The pandemic has damaged people's vision of the future – maybe even destroying it completely. This is extremely dangerous for a society because, as the Bible says, "Where there is no vision, the people cast off restraint." (Prov.29:18, ASV) This is what we are seeing, and with governments predicting a once-in-a-century recession, the future is damaged even more. The unrest will get worse.

There is absolutely only one answer for this dilemma. Where can you find hope when there is none to be found? What kind of hope is impervious to hopelessness? "…hope in Him…"

As England slid toward revolution in the eighteenth century and everything said it would follow France down that road, all hope was lost. Hope came. It came from above in the form of the Wesleyan Revival, and England was saved.

The gospel of the Lord Jesus Christ needs to be preached fearlessly and preached widely – it is hope.

118

I was in the Spirit on the Lord's day.

Revelation 1:10 (NKJV)

We can talk about getting into the spirit of everything from a political rally to a Christmas party. The dictionary tells us that this means 'to enter into something enthusiastically'. But the expression has its origin in the Bible (see today's verse). What John was describing was more than enthusiasm – although that very word means 'to be possessed by God'! John was describing a spiritual state. He was alone, not in church, not with other believers, but by himself in a penal colony – the prison island of Patmos. And on the Lord's day, Sunday, he did what he usually did: got into the Spirit.

I'm sure some Christians don't ever do this, but without it Christian experience is very lacklustre and hard work. It is very noticeable to me whether I am "in the Spirit" or not when I stand before a congregation. It is the difference between flowing and halting speech, between inspiration and perspiration, between being a God thing or my thing!

Over the next few days we are going to look at how to be "in the Spirit" and why we need to be.

Of course, the Spirit that John is talking about is the Holy Spirit.

John saying he was in the Spirit on the Lord's day means that he could be *in* the Spirit or *not in* the Spirit. This is true; whilst the Holy Spirit is always in us (if we are a Spirit-filled believer) we are not always *in the Spirit*, nor should we be. We cannot live "in the Spirit"; it is a state of deeper communion with God – a time when we hear more clearly, are led more instantly and are used more powerfully.

We choose when to be in the Spirit. I believe it is what the psalmist was referring to when he wrote, "Enter his gates with thanksgiving and his courts with praise…" (Ps.100:4, NIV)

The first thing we have to do is ask ourselves, "Do I want to be in the Spirit? Do I want to enter into His courts, into the presence of God?" And if the answer is yes then we choose to do it.

119

Therefore, I urge you, brothers, in view of God's mercy, to offer your bodies as living sacrifices, holy and pleasing to God – this is your spiritual act of worship.

Romans 12:1 (NIV)

The Apostle John tells us that "for the word of God and for the testimony of Jesus Christ" (Rev.1:9, NKJV) he had been sent in exile to the island of Patmos. It was here during his Sunday devotions that he received the revelation which is the last book in the Bible. He says he was "in the Spirit" on the Lord's Day, which, as we saw yesterday, means 'being in a state of heightened communion with God'.

Anyone who has been filled with the Holy Spirit can and should practise this, and for ministry situations like leading worship and preaching it is absolutely essential. It's something that you have to decide to do.

How do you do it? Firstly your will needs to be engaged – or, to put it more simply, you need to say to yourself, "Right now I'm going to get into the Spirit." Then you start worshipping God either by singing or praying, either of which may be in tongues (our spiritual language). You turn your spiritual eyes upwards (often your physical eyes will follow and your arms will often reach out). You allow God to have 100% of your attention and abandon yourself to Him completely so that He is able to work in you and through you. It only takes a minute or so to get into the Spirit.

In a meeting it is natural to do this. Many of us do it automatically. But when you are alone, as John was, you have to be more disciplined. We must realise that this is not just something for Sunday mornings; it is a part of our lives.

Paul describes it exactly in today's verse. The Greek word used here for 'body' is *soma* which means 'your entire person'. So as we are entering into the Spirit we are offering God our entire being to fill and to use. And this is what He does. When I am in the Spirit, I feel that I'm not calling the shots any more but I am being directed and used by God. It's wonderful.

120

"But you, when you pray, go into your room, and when you have shut your door, pray to your Father who is in the secret place; and your Father who sees in secret will reward you openly."

Matthew 6:6 (NKJV)

This week we are considering being "in the Spirit" as the apostle John mentions in Revelation 1. Yesterday we saw that we achieve this spiritual state through prayer and praise and abandoning ourselves to God.

Jesus, too, spoke of the process of deeper communion with God and being in the Spirit, as we see in today's verse. There is more to this verse than meets the eye. Firstly, Jesus says we should go into our room – in other words, get alone somewhere. Then we should shut the door. This is interesting – why the emphasis on shutting the door? When we shut the door it makes the space private – no one can hear us.

Then it says, "...pray to your Father who is in the secret place..." This is not talking about your room any more; it is talking about a place where God is – a spiritual place which we can enter into. When we close the physical door, God closes the spiritual door. The place becomes secret.

"So what?" you might say. Well, actually this is very important. Our prayers need to be kept secret from the evil one. Imagine the havoc that he could wreak if he knew your innermost thoughts and feelings, your fears and struggles! No, your prayers are locked in. It's the difference between putting your conversation on Facebook and private messaging. God has always been in the business of private messaging.

This is the secret place, the spiritual realm, being in the Spirit.

And as if this wasn't good enough, Jesus says that the Father, who is in the secret place (we could add *with you*), will reward you. You actually get a reward for praying and being in the Spirit. The word "openly" is incidentally not in the original text.

So, my friends, it is well worth taking the time to get into the Spirit and spending time alone with God. I wonder how He will reward you today!

121

In the same way, the Spirit helps us in our weakness. We do not know what we ought to pray for, but the Spirit himself intercedes for us with groans that words cannot express.

Romans 8:26 (NIV)

The Apostle John says in Revelation 1:10, "I was in the Spirit on the Lord's day." What was the reason that he got into the Spirit on the Lord's day? There can only be one answer to that, and that is to pray. He would not have known that the Lord would give him the amazing revelation.

Yesterday we saw how being in the Spirit protects our prayer life from the enemy. Today we are going to look at how the Spirit enhances our prayer life. Paul writes about "praying always with all prayer and supplication in the Spirit, being watchful to this end with all perseverance and supplication for all the saints" (Eph.6:18, NKJV).

So we should always pray in the Spirit. That is, we should make sure that we enter His gates with thanksgiving, praise and speaking in tongues, abandoning ourselves to God. Charles Wesley wrote in his transcendent hymn 'Love Divine, All Loves Excelling' the line, "Lost in wonder, love and praise," which beautifully describes being in the Spirit.

How many of us struggle with prayer? It's hard to know what to pray for and how to pray for what we know! When we are in the Spirit, the Holy Spirit helps us. The Holy Spirit will lead us in our prayers, giving us direction, giving us words showing us how to approach a subject, giving us avenues of intercession. But where words absolutely fail, the Spirit interprets even our groans to God. One writer once said there is often more in the "Oh" at the beginning of a prayer than in all the rest of the prayer put together!

Being in the Spirit allows me to pray in tongues and so be eloquent before God at times when I don't know what to pray or don't even feel like praying. It also allows me to pray for situations that I have no knowledge of at all. "But you, beloved, building yourselves up on your most holy faith, praying in the Holy Spirit..." (Jud:20, BSB)

122

But the manifestation of the Spirit is given to each one for the profit of all.
1 Corinthians 12:7 (NKJV)

This week we have found that being in the Spirit is a spiritual state of heightened communion with God, something we choose to do before we pray or minister. We enter into this state by thanking and praising God and abandoning ourself to Him.

Speaking in tongues helps us clear the mind of interference and paves the way for the Holy Spirit to speak to us and direct our devotions.

The Apostle John found on that first day of revelation that God had something incredible to say to him and through him which is now the triumphant closing book of the Bible. I'm so glad that John was in the Spirit on that day.

In the book of Revelation we see not only prophecy, but wisdom and knowledge and maybe the discerning of spirits. Perhaps John's experience also involved speaking in tongues and interpretation too. In other words, the gifts of the Spirit were in operation in him as he was alone and in the Spirit.

The nine spiritual gifts listed in 1 Corinthians 12 are called manifestations of the Spirit. When are these manifestations likely to happen? When we are in the Spirit of course. It is then that the Holy Spirit who lives in us will manifest Himself, showing His presence by one or more of the spiritual gifts starting to function.

When this first happens one can be a little taken aback. What is this? Where did that thought come from? For me it was, "FOOT, FOOT, FOOT!" What in the world is 'foot'? I asked the pastor I was with at the front to that meeting. He stopped everything and said, "David has a word from the Lord that there is someone here with a bad foot. Would they come forward, please?" A lady hobbled from the back. "Now pray for her foot to be healed," he told me. I had never done anything like it before. After the meeting the lady came and told me that her foot was healed.

What adventures are waiting for you in the Spirit? "As each one has received a gift, minister it to one another, as good stewards of the manifold grace of God." (1.Pet.4:10, NKJV)

123

Do not despise these small beginnings , for the Lord rejoices to see the work begin.

Zechariah 4:10 (NLT)

This week we are going to be considering the *nano principles* of the kingdom of God – or the principle of the very small, if you like. I read in the newspaper today that an apple tree died in Washington State, USA. Why did that make headline news? Because it was the original one. One hundred and ninety-four years ago Lieutenant Aemilius Simpson of the Royal Navy found five apple seeds in his pudding. He went ashore and planted them. They grew. And from those five little seeds a huge industry came about – Washington State is famous for its apples! This is a nano principle. And we even know who planted the first seed.

God rejoices because this is the basis on which the kingdom of God works. We see this every day in the natural world. Even Jesus was once a single cell – a human egg.

The Bible encourages us by constantly reminding us that we are not insignificant and our efforts, though small, are not inconsequential either. From a mustard seed, the least of all seeds, the biggest of all the herbs grows. From an apple seed a regional industry is formed. From one person the world can be changed.

The Ethiopian eunuch returned to his nation a born-again believer after meeting Philip, and somehow Ethiopia became a Christian nation. Paul was able to say that from Jerusalem around to Illyricum (Albania) "I have fully preached the gospel of Christ" (Rom.15:19, NKJV). Job done.

The small beginnings that we are most likely to despise are our own. Don't! God knows what mighty trees are going to grow from your little seed today.

124

We do not want you to become lazy, but to imitate those who through faith and patience inherit what has been promised.

Hebrews 6:11 (NIV)

The kingdom of God grows from small beginnings. Every revival started in a small way, and importantly almost every revival started with *one person* or at the most two or three. It was Evan Roberts in Wales, Henry Guinness in Northern Ireland, Hans Nielsen Hauge in Norway, Billy Bray here in Cornwall. It is a fascinating study tracing the paths of these revivals to their small beginnings – to the prime mover.

These individuals, though often obscure and seemingly insignificant in society, have one thing in common: mustard seed they may be, but they are good seed! They are dedicated, sold-out men and women, humble and unassuming yet on fire for God.

From these little seeds mighty trees grow. Who can quantify the influence of John Wesley or Charles Finney – in fact, they are still influencers today.

So what does this have to do with us? We can't just celebrate these people and certainly not idolise them – they would 'turn in their graves', as we say, if they thought we were doing that! We have to apply the things their lives teach us to our own. The apostle Paul said, "...I urge you to imitate me." (1.Cor.4:16, NIV) We have to imitate their devotion to God, their prayerfulness, their zeal.

Think about the people that influenced you personally. What grabbed you about them? What did they sow in your life? Imitate them – pass it on. The amazing thing about a seed is that it doesn't just reproduce itself once but it produces much fruit, many seeds and so it goes on down the generations. Small beginnings – the nano principles of the kingdom of God.

125

Again he asked, "What shall I compare the kingdom of God to? It is like yeast that a woman took and mixed into a large amount of flour until it worked all through the dough."

Luke 13:20-21 (NIV)

We are looking at God's nano principles. The kingdom of God uses small things to make a big difference. Yeast is a single-celled organism which is only visible under a microscope. It takes twenty billion yeast cells to weigh one gram and yet its effect is dynamic!

It's a fallacy that Jewish people only eat unleavened bread; Jesus would have been used to seeing His mother make bread every day, taking some of the yeast she kept in the house and adding it to the bread mixture to make it rise. Jesus knew that just a tiny bit of yeast would work its way through the whole batch and change it.

Yeast is not only a powerful agent, but it works unseen, invisibly, and that is very often how the kingdom of God works. Its influence is spreading invisibly all the time, night and day, unobserved, unexpected, unwittingly. Even we as Christians don't appreciate it. God is doing much more than we can see. It's funny how we only thank God for what He is doing when we can see it – why not thank God for what He is doing that we don't know about, working in the hearts and minds of those that He is preparing for salvation?

Just like yeast we influence all those people around us. Put a person who lives for Jesus in any group of people – a factory, a school, an army platoon – and wait a while. There will always be results. This is how the kingdom of God works.

So don't be discouraged when you aren't seeing anything. Have faith in the invisible.

126

The righteous keep moving forward, and those with clean hands become stronger and stronger.

Job 17:9 (NLT)

I read somewhere that a nanometre is the amount that your fingernails grow in one second – one billionth of a metre. That's small! But fingernails do grow and have to be cut once a week.

Most growth is imperceptible and we get surprised by things like beans and sunflowers that grow quickly. This is the way the kingdom of God works, in small increments but 24/7 – it just keeps on going like the yeast, hidden but relentless.

Ships seem like a slow form of transport; most containerships travel at around twenty-five miles per hour, while super-tankers travel at half that. But they are a good form of transport because they do not stop. Night and day they just keep steaming on.

So what does this tell us about our own growth in the Lord? It tells us that it seems slow but it is happening. Little by little, precept by precept, we are growing. Just like Samson's hair. Compared to our fast-paced lives this seems too slow and many people are tempted to give up because they don't see their own progress.

Have you noticed that when a relative comes to visit, the first thing they say to our children is, "My, haven't you grown!" We don't notice it because we are there all the time.

Put yeast in a bowl with water and a little sugar, keep it warm and it will grow. Nothing can stop it if it is in the right environment and has the things it needs. The same is true of a Christian – if we have the food of the Word, the water of the Holy Spirit and the warmth of fellowship, we will grow. Nothing can stop us (except ourselves choosing not to). We must make sure we keep ourselves in the right environment for growth.

Today's verse is another nano principle of the kingdom of God

127

"What shall I compare the kingdom of God to? It is like yeast that a woman took and mixed into a large amount of flour until it worked all through the dough."

Luke 13:20-21 (NIV)

We are talking about God's nano principles and specifically about yeast, or 'leaven' as the Bible calls it. We have seen how yeast, though a tiny organism, has a powerful effect but it has to be placed into the mix to have any effect at all. As Christians, we have to be in the mix, in society, to have the effect that God has calculated. We have to be, as Jesus said, in the world but not of the world.

Some years ago I read a book which analysed the dramatic growth of the Pentecostal church in Brazil. The author Peter Wagner came to the conclusion that the church started seeing success when it stopped being an inviting church and became an invading church. This makes a lot of sense. We are very good at inviting people to come to church but not so good at taking church to people.

I believe that this is one of the main reasons that God has allowed the Covid-19 pandemic. Never in history has the church been so mobilised in getting the message out as during the last five months. The internet is full of church – and may it continue to be so. We cannot go back to our cloistered existence.

But that is the church – what about individual believers? Remember Jesus' words in today's passage. The yeast has to be mixed with the dough; it has to invade the lump! Food science calls yeast a raising agent. We could adopt the same label. In the book I mentioned earlier a transformation was seen in society when the Christians started to invade; it was called "salvation and lift". People were lifted out of poverty and crime when they became Christians. The believers were a raising agent.

I am totally convinced that God is speaking to the church through the pandemic and saying it's time the yeast got out of the packet and into the lump.

128

"...if you have faith as a mustard seed, you will say to this mountain, 'Move from here to there,' and it will move; and nothing will be impossible for you."

Matthew 17:20 (NKJV)

One hundred and fifty years ago Delabole Slate Quarry was the largest man-made hole in the world. Even today it is impressive and still a working quarry. They know all about explosives, and today it's 'explosive' that I want to talk to you about.

Jesus famously spoke the words in today's verse. Obviously this means that you only need a tiny bit of faith for incredible things to happen. This always bothered me a bit; I ended up thinking, "Well, my faith must be microscopic then!"

But then I found another verse: "I know your works. See, I have set before you an open door, and no one can shut it; for you have a little strength, have kept My word, and have not denied My name." (Rev.3:10, NKJV) Jesus said this to the church at Philadelphia and it was meant to be a compliment! Would you count it a compliment if someone told you that you only had a little strength? But if you look at the words in the original Greek, something else pops out. The words in Greek are *micro dunamis* – a little bit of dynamite! Now that is a compliment!

Anyone who knows about explosives knows that you don't need a lot. The important thing about explosives is what they are in rather than how much you have. The stronger the container, the more powerful the effect.

God's nano principle is this: you only need a little faith or a little strength; it is you yourself that are important, it is your relationship with God that counts. *Dunamis* in a weak container will just make a loud noise; *dunamis* in a strong container will effect everything in the vicinity!

God is in the business of causing small things to have a big effect. I want to be one of those small things – how about you?

129

Do not remove the ancient landmark.

Proverbs 22:28 (NKJV)

There is a little obelisk on Bodmin Moor, at the foot of Rough Tor. It is a memorial. On 18th April, 1844, Charlotte Dymond, a pretty eighteen-year-old, was walking across the moor when she was attacked and killed by Matthew Weeks right there. The people of Camelford were so affected by this that they clubbed together and paid for the stone. The landmark isn't very important in the great scheme of things but it is a reminder, a signpost to the past – a warning perhaps.

When the Bible speaks of landmarks it is speaking of the altars and the memorial stones that were erected in Israel to mark the places where God had done something wonderful. Something important. Jacob built an altar at El Bethel "because it was there that the Lord revealed himself to him" (Gen.35:7, NIV), for instance.

A little way down the road from the obelisk is a building which is a landmark of mine. It is a holiday home now, but in 1973 it was a chapel and it is where I preached my first sermon. God started something there – something in me.

Landmarks are important, not just to the people concerned but to successive generations. People have built them from time immemorial because they wanted others to know. They wanted to point the way to plant a marker.

The Bible says landmarks are important too – so important that it is unwise to remove them. This week we are going to look at some landmarks and the way that they are being removed. The building I mentioned is physically still there but is it a landmark any more? Does it still point the way? Who would know that this was once Highertown Chapel? But it's not just buildings, altars or standing stones that I'm talking about; it is landmarks that are being removed from our lives and from the very fabric of society.

130

Do not remove the ancient landmark.

Proverbs 22:28 (NKJV)

It's a dangerous thing to remove signposts. This week our subject is landmarks. Landmarks in the context of today's verse means things that act as a reminder to us and point the way to God.

All over Cornwall one can see granite Celtic Crosses. There are nearly a thousand of these dotted around the county. They were put at crossroads and busy places to remind people of Jesus as they went about their daily business. I can imagine someone in times past seeing this cross and thinking, "Oh I didn't have my devotions this morning. I'd better do it now."

Not so long ago all life was framed by faith: farming, business, politics, family life – both believers and non-believers had God in their reckoning. The landmarks were there.

Not only physical landmarks like this, of course, but those in conversation. 'Goodbye' is a shortened version of 'God be with ye'. And 'bless you' when someone sneezes was once 'God bless you'.

Now even Christians sign off their emails with the meaningless 'Every blessing'. See what happened there? The landmark was removed. God was taken out of the phrase. 'God bless you' is one of the most wonderful greetings. When the word 'God' is there it becomes a prayer.

Some Christians have taken to shouting "Woo!" in meetings rather than "Hallelujah!" – they removed the landmark.

When the river Jordan opened up so that the Israelites could get across on dry land, Joshua told his men to take twelve large stones from the riverbed and set them up on the bank "to serve as a sign" so that in the future when people passed there the children would ask their parents, "What do these stones mean?" (Josh.4:6, NIV) Then their parents would be able to tell their children about the great thing God had done there. That is the purpose of a landmark.

Landmarks pointing to Jesus are disappearing from our culture at an alarming rate. I don't want any part of it; I will fight to keep the landmarks...

131

Fight the good fight of faith.

1 Timothy 6:12 (NKJV)

Yesterday I mentioned how Christianity used to be part of daily life. You couldn't avoid it even if you wanted to, from church bells to wayside crosses, from school assemblies to Easter parades and nativity plays. One by one these landmarks are disappearing and many of them on our watch.

What is happening is the marginalisation of the Christian faith. The enemy, Satan, wants Christianity to be regarded as an irrelevance – a quaint hobby, or something for an interest group like trainspotters. Political correctness is the latest tool in his arsenal, which has been extremely effective in removing more landmarks for nonsensical reasons.

Christmas festivals have become winter festivals, the Gideons have been banned from many schools, local radio has dropped the 'God slot'. We could go on...

Something that is under attack at the moment is prayer in parliament. Did you know this: where you sit in the House of Commons is very important? You have to be able to catch the Speaker's eye if you want to speak. So each morning MPs go in early and put their name cards where they want to sit, so reserving a place for later in the day. Each morning there is a prayer meeting before proceedings begin. If you don't attend that prayer meeting then your card is removed and you lose your place. Not a lot of people know that.

This prayer meeting is at the moment subject to an attempt to remove it. Will this landmark be removed too? Sadly, there is not much fight in today's church; we are accepting the removal of landmarks without any struggle as if it is a *fait accompli*. With every landmark that disappears, Christianity becomes more marginalised and society more secularised.

But there is another verse in Jeremiah that says this: "Set up signposts, make landmarks..." (Jer.31:21, NKJV) Now that gives me an idea!

132

You shall teach them to your children, speaking of them when you sit in your house, when you walk by the way, when you lie down, and when you rise up. And you shall write them on the doorposts of your house and on your gates.

Deuteronomy 11:19-20 (NKJV)

I've been on a bit of a hobby-horse of mine this week and I realise it's quite negative to bemoan the secularisation of society, and it's not a good exercise to lament the past and do nothing to change the future.

We ended yesterday with the verse from Jeremiah which encourages us to, "Set up signposts and make landmarks." (Jer.32:21, NKJV) For all the talk in the media about the church dying, there are an awful lot of churches being born – new landmarks. During the pandemic hundreds of churches have taken to the internet on Facebook and YouTube – new landmarks. Some, like us, have started drive-in services – new landmarks. As I keep saying, I believe that one of the reasons that God is allowing coronavirus is to get the church into the public square once more.

But where do you fit in? How can you erect a landmark?

When we were in Israel last year, we noticed that there were little plaques on the doorposts of many homes. These, we found out, were *Mezuzahs* – a representation of the Word of God. There are several reasons behind this but the obvious outcome is that people know that a practising Jew lives there. It is a landmark.

In the 1970s believers went through a phase of wearing 'Jesus Loves You' stickers on their lapels, on their car bumpers and actually sticking them all over the place. You don't see them any more. We have become silent, hidden – we have marginalised ourselves. But what if every Christian started advertising, started declaring publicly, that they believed in Jesus? What effect would those landmarks have?

Years ago I longed for a window on the main road where I could display a text. Now our church has several large windows on a public car park. Do I display a text? No. What happened? What's wrong with me?

It's time to stand up and be counted before we go completely into hiding.

133

FRIDAY, 4TH SEPTEMBER, 2020

And you are living stones that God is building into his spiritual temple.

1 Peter 2:5 (NLT)

In considering landmarks this week, we haven't yet looked at the most important landmark of all: *you*. Landmarks were traditionally made of stone but the Bible says that "you are living stones" (1.Pet.2:5, NLT)!

One of our roles as a Christian is to be a signpost. There are many things that we can do to point people to Jesus – we can witness to them, tell them our testimony, invite them to church – but by far the most effective way we are signposts is by the way we live. We are fulfilling our role as signposts best when we don't even realise it.

As we live for Christ, people will see Him in us – in our actions and our reactions, in our attitude and outlook, in our kindness, gentleness and love.

Years ago there was a shop in Camelford that I used to visit a lot. I got to know the owner Les quite well. Then one morning when I walked in, he said, "Hey David, you come in here nearly every day and you are always the same, always smiling; how do you do that?" I had been a signpost without even knowing it. Of course, then I had a great opportunity to tell him about Jesus.

John the Baptist was the best signpost for Jesus. He actually pointed to Jesus and said, "Behold the Lamb of God that takes away the sins of the world." (Jn.1:29, NKJV) That was the fulfilment of his mission, his reason for existing, but it didn't start there. John had attracted people to his desert hangout by his unusual behaviour. He wasn't like other people; he dressed differently, spoke differently and behaved differently, and people were fascinated.

Now, I'm not saying, wear a camel-hair shirt and eat locusts. What I am saying is that we are called to be different. The word 'holy' actually means 'different'. Surprise people with your kind words, your unusual take on the world, your generous spirit. When we are different we are signposts and people will stop to ask us the way.

134

Behold, I lay in Zion a chief cornerstone, elect, precious, and he who believes on Him will by no means be put to shame.

1 Peter 2:6 (NKJV)

Remember, the Bible says, "Do not remove the ancient landmark," in Proverbs 22:28 (NKJV). A few hundred yards from my home in Camelford, Cornwall is a little granite cross by a road junction. This cross was not there when I was a boy; someone found it buried nearby and decided to erect it again. I was looking at this cross the other day and Frank, who lives nearby, came out and told me how he keeps the grass around it cut short so that everyone can see it. As I spoke to him, a lovely man, he began to see another landmark in me.

That's one way that the enemy gets rid of landmarks: if he can't remove them he buries them! Let me explain what I mean…

Christianity in the UK is the state religion – it is enshrined in law and cannot be easily be removed – so the enemy has buried it under pageantry and ritual so that it looks like an historical re-enactment and loses its relevance.

- The teaching of Christianity in schools in the UK is mandatory but it has been buried under comparative religions.
- The historical facts of Christianity cannot be removed but they can be buried under bias, cynicism and dust.
- Christian TV is an amazing landmark and perfect vehicle for the gospel but truth gets buried under weirdness, extremes and false teaching.
- The existence of the church and its ministers cannot be removed but society buries it under comedy, ridicule and smears.

Can we dig out the true cross and set it up again? We have to. There is no choice. God is depending on us to present the cross to the world.

This is the landmark: the Lord Jesus Christ (see today's verse)! This is the mission: "And I, if I am lifted up from the earth, will draw all peoples to Myself." (Jn.12:32, NKJV) Let's do it!

135

Therefore encourage one another and build each other up.

1 Thessalonians 5:11 (NIV)

It's funny the things that stick in your mind, isn't it? Some little moments in time leave an indelible impression; you can remember them vividly even though they took place years ago.

One such moment in my life was when I was fourteen and my dad came home from work and gave me a *Thompson Chain Reference Bible*. I remember it was in a gold-coloured box, and the edges of the pages were embellished with gold too. I had just started preaching and in those days every preacher needed one of these.

I don't know what I would have done without it – a one-volume reference bible, encyclopaedia, concordance and much more. That one gift, that one moment, would have a great impact on me. I still use this bible regularly today.

I hadn't pestered Dad to buy it for me. I had just mentioned I needed one. He was a generous man but this went beyond generosity; this was inspired, some people might even say a prophetic act. He had seen something in me and wanted in some way to encourage it, to stimulate my growth in the right direction, to give me a tool.

What a moment! I will never forget it and will always be grateful for it. But now it's my turn. I have to have my eyes and ears open for an opportunity to encourage someone else. I have to be ready for God when I get the divine nod and create a moment for a young believer. And maybe, as it did for me, that moment will turn into a lifetime of service to God.

You can do that too. There are so many critics around, so much cold water is thrown over emerging ministries, but you could, through kindness, generosity and perception, propel someone in the right direction.

136

For our light affliction, which is but for a moment, is working for us a far more exceeding and eternal weight of glory...

2 Corinthians 4:17 (NKJV)

Yesterday we saw how one moment can stick in your memory and be a significant catalyst in your life. But of course, not all moments are good. Most of us can think of a moment in our life that was devastating, an event that had a negative impact on us and could have wrecked our faith. Paul speaks of times like this in 2 Corinthians 4. All the dreadful things that can happen to us, Paul had experienced them personally, but he concludes with today's verse. This verse saved my life and my faith too. I was going through a very rough patch in my ministry and there seemed no hope. But then God sent a man and His word. Pastor Pat Furtaw came from Texas on a preaching tour and I asked him for prayer. He gave me this verse and explained.

Our affliction, the thing that we are going through, is defined two ways. First, it is a "light affliction". When we see it in the great scheme of things, we realise that it could be much, much worse. Our mind has amplified it to intolerable proportions. And second, it is "but for a moment".

"What is a moment?" he asked. It is not really even a increment of time. It is something that we let carelessly pass. He told me the secret of saying, "I couldn't care less." When people say things that hurt, we must let it slip off us like water off a duck's back. We must not hold on to it. We must not care. My goodness, the heartache that simple thought has saved me!

Now, there are people reading this who are going through the mill at the moment... Did you see that? *"...at the moment."* It is something that will pass; it is not forever. It is but for a moment. So be encouraged; it is not as bad as it seems and it will not last.

The second part of the verse tells us *why* it is happening. God has allowed it to happen because it is doing some good in us. It "is working for us a far more exceeding and eternal weight of glory". When you put it in God's scales, the thing that we are going through is vastly outweighed by the good it is doing in us both now and in terms of our heavenly reward.

I hope this helps you as much as it helped me.

137

Jesus turned around and said to her, "Daughter, be encouraged! Your faith has made you well." And the woman was healed at that moment. ... Then Jesus rebuked the demon in the boy, and it left him. From that moment the boy was well.

Matthew 9:22; 17:18 (NIV)

What do you notice in these verses? A woman who had been sick for twelve years and had spent all her money on doctors, to no avail, was healed by Jesus in a moment. A boy who was demon-possessed and so tormented that he would throw himself into the fire was set free by Jesus in a moment.

These two wonderful things happened *in a moment* – almost instantly. That is the power of Jesus. He can do things very quickly; He can change things in a moment! That's all it takes.

This never ceases to amaze me. Remember, too, the man who had been crippled from his mother's womb; Peter prayed for him and "he, leaping up, stood and walked and entered the temple with them – walking, leaping, and praising God" (Acts.3:8, NKJV).

In a moment all the muscles, tendons and ligaments were made normal, and he was able to walk and leap. Picture that – if you could see the muscles that were withered growing in front of your eyes! In a moment!

I have seen things like this happen: a withered hand suddenly healed, a birth defect of a useless arm and hand immediately begin to function, a leg grow two inches in front of a crowd of onlookers. Wonderful!

The message today is that Jesus can turn things around fast! It doesn't take physiotherapy or rehabilitation; it can happen in a moment. But the most wonderful thing of all is that a person can change from a sinner to a saint in a moment too!

138

"Yes, I am going to send you to the Gentiles, to open their eyes so they may turn from darkness to light, and from the power of Satan to God. Then they will receive forgiveness for their sins and be given a place among God's people, who are set apart by faith in me."

Acts 26:11 (NLT)

Our theme this week is 'moments' and today I want to talk about the most important moment of all: that is when someone asks Jesus into their life and gets saved. I am aware that for some people, becoming a Christian is a process; boiling water is a process but there is a moment when it starts to boil and there has to be a moment when someone passes from death to life, from darkness to light.

We sometimes lose sight of the power of salvation. Without a doubt it is the most powerful thing that can ever happen in someone's life. Consider Paul on the road to Damascus: one moment he hated Christ and would go to any lengths to destroy the church; the next moment he was a follower of Jesus committing the rest of his life to His service. We see what Jesus said to him in today's verse.

I have seen this happen to so many people – an instant transformation. It cannot be explained any other way but that it is a miracle from God. The English language cannot call it anything else but a Damascus Road experience.

I remember leading two Libyan lads to Christ on the street in Malta. Their faces changed as they prayed and then they both started jumping up and down shouting, "I'm clean, I'm clean!" They had never even heard about Jesus before that moment.

In Estonia a room full of people of all ages from eight to eighty were transformed in a moment by the power of God as they gave their lives to Jesus. The communist government had made sure they had never even heard the name Jesus in their lives before that evening.

In Texas a drug lord who protected his house with a lion and a Uzi machine gun wept in my arms as he repented and Jesus came into his life. It only took a moment.

When people experience Jesus fantastic things happen. It's hard to believe unless you see it – or experience it yourself.

And if you want to, pray this prayer right now:

Lord Jesus, I know that I am a sinner. I am sorry for all my sins. I ask you to forgive me. I believe that you died on the cross for me. I give my life to you. Come and live in me. Make me a new person. I promise that I will love you, follow you and obey you for the rest of my life. Thank you for saving me and giving me a place in heaven. Amen.

139

But when they departed from Perga, they came to Antioch in Pisidia, and went into the synagogue on the Sabbath day and sat down.

Acts 13:14 (NKJV)

The parish church in the picturesque Cornish village of Landulph has some surprises in its grounds. In the graveyard two men are buried that lived two hundred years apart but were strangely connected.

One is Theodore Palaeologus, a decedent of the last emperor of the Byzantine Empire from Constantinople in Turkey. He sought refuge in Britain and became an assassin – a hit man for the Earl of Lincoln, the Master of the Horse, the most hated man in Britain. Theodore married an Arundell from this village and died here in 1636.

Also buried here is a clergyman who rejoiced in the name of Francis Vyvyian Jago Arundell – a distant member of the same family from Launceston. He was appointed chaplain to the British Army garrison in Smyrna, Turkey in 1822. He was a keen historian and antiquarian and relished the opportunity to do some archaeology in Turkey, the home of many events from the New Testament.

During one of his expeditions he stumbled across some ruins which, after careful research, he realised were the ruins of Pisidian Antioch. Until then the site of this city was unknown, so much so that people even said it never existed. Once he had located this site it was much easier for the locations of Lystra and Derbe to be found by others at a later date.

Rev. Arundell, a Cornishman from Launceston, served God in many ways but this was his greatest gift to the church: proving the city's existence, and so the truth of Luke's account in Acts 13.

It's wonderful that there are so many ways to serve God. This chap's archaeology hobby turned out to be very useful to the Lord.

140

...and after the earthquake a fire, but the LORD was not in the fire; and after the fire a still small voice. So it was, when Elijah heard it, that he wrapped his face in his mantle and went out and stood in the entrance of the cave.

1 Kings 19:12-13 (NKJV)

In 1763 a twenty-three-year-old preacher, Augustus Toplady, was riding through a gorge in the Mendip Hills in Somerset when he was caught in an almighty downpour of rain. He dismounted his horse and found shelter in a large crack or cleft in the rockface. While he was sheltering there he began to hear God. (This reminds me of the way that God shelters me from the storms of life.) A line came to him: "Rock of ages, cleft for me..." And then another: "Let me hide myself in thee." Before the rain had stopped he had the whole hymn, which became a favourite around the world.

I'm sure that Toplady, as a preacher, would have thought of Elijah who also hid in a cave to escape a mighty storm. Both these men found that in the middle of a storm, an earth-shattering event, God spoke. It's often the way.

When the storms of life come and we feel afraid and vulnerable, we are at our most receptive. All our bravado and self-sufficiency is gone; we are a cowering child ready to hear the Father's reassuring voice.

This is why this hymn became popular. It struck a chord, it revealed a need and then it gave us the answer: the Rock.

141

For God has not given us a spirit of fear, but of power and of love and of a sound mind.

2 Timothy 1:7 (NKJV)

As I have been watching what has been going on in the world over the last few weeks and listening to people talk more locally, one thing has really stood out: confusion.

Did you know that Satan's principle weapon is confusion? The very first sin was wrought in confusion; Satan asked Eve, "Did God say?" and actually she didn't know whether God had said not to eat the fruit or not because she wasn't there at the time. She got confused.

Time after time through the Bible we see the enemy use this weapon of confusion as the first line of his strategy to bring people down. Remember what happened to the disciples when Jesus had been crucified? They didn't remember what Jesus had told them; instead, they were thrown into confusion. "This wasn't supposed to happen," they must have thought.

Confusion, as we will see this week, leads to a downward spiral of events in our lives which leaves us totally paralysed.

In our lives, if we think about it, if we analyse our ups and downs, confusion is always how things kick off. It is confusion that keeps us awake at night, confusion that causes us to question our salvation, our calling, our relationship with God.

The first step in our fight back is to realise where this comes from. 1 Corinthians 14:33 (NKJV) says, "For God is not the author of confusion but of peace…" If God is not the author or originator of confusion, the devil is. God is the author of the remedy for confusion, as we see in today's verse. A sound mind is the antidote to confusion, and here in Timothy we see that God has given us a sound mind!

You have one; you don't even have to ask for one, all you have to do is turn it on. How do you do that? When my mind is flooded with confusion by the intrusive thoughts of Satan, I have learnt to say out loud, "I have a sound mind! I reject this confusion. God has given me a sound mind." It works because all it was, was a trick.

Try it.

142

You put more joy in my heart than when their grain and new wine increase.

Psalm 4:7 (GW)

Some time ago when I was in Austria, I saw a pharmacy with a sign which, translated, said, "Dr Jesus' remedy shop." Isn't it great that the Lord has remedies for everything?!

Yesterday we saw that confusion is Satan's primary weapon. He always starts with confusing the mind, but God counters this by giving the believer a sound mind which we have to declare to get rid of confusion.

If we don't tackle the confusion, then phase two of the devil's strategy begins. Have you ever noticed that if you are confused, it makes you upset? One of the reasons for this is that the human mind works on a pigeonhole system; we like to organise our thoughts, and if we can't we get upset. So confusion of the mind leads to sadness of the heart.

Think of the times in the Bible when this happened: Moses, King David, Job, Elijah and the disciples.

But God has a remedy for sadness too: gladness, joy.

The Bible tells us over and over again that God has put joy in our heart. Romans 15:13 tells us that God fills us with all joy in believing. Psalm 30:11 (NRSV) says, "...you have turned my mourning into dancing, you have taken off my sackcloth and clothed me with joy."

So we counter the sadness the devil sows by claiming the joy that God has given. We need to say, "God has given me a joyful heart – I will not be sad."

143

So if the Son sets you free, you are truly free.

John 8:36 (NLT)

The thing about Satan is that he is not at all creative. The Holy Spirit is wonderfully creative, and human beings (made in the image of God) are creative too, but the devil isn't. Therefore he uses the same old tricks from generation to generation. That's why Paul says in 2 Corinthians 2:11 that "we are not ignorant of his devices", his strategies. If we know them, we can pre-empt them and win every time!

The Bible reveals this strategy to us in the lives of people who grappled with it.

Confusion of the mind leads to sadness of the heart, and sadness of the heart leads to bondage of the will. Have you noticed that when you are confused and upset, you become paralysed? You just stop. You stop reading the Bible, you stop praying, you stop fellowshipping, you stop doing all the things that really you know you should do. This is bondage of the will. I know this so well. It can come on quickly – in minutes – or over a period of time; you could say 'acute' or 'chronic'.

I remember once the Lord sent me to Sicily. I arrived on the boat from Malta but to my horror found that there was no-one there to meet me. My letter had not got through. Catania was a dangerous city and the docks were frightening. Confusion started. The devil said, "Did God really send you here?" I started to get upset, and though I was in my twenties, I confess to shedding a tear. The boat had just left the harbour. I had no money. I sat on my suitcase and was paralysed.

Then the Holy Spirit whispered in my ear, "Confusion. Sadness. Bondage." My goodness, I had fallen for it again!

God has a remedy for bondage and that is freedom, liberty! I started to say out loud, "I have a sound mind, a joyful heart and a free will."

God has also given us the desire and ability to have a will that is obedient. Philippians 2:13 (NKJV) says, "...for it is God who works in us both to will and to do."

The devil cannot win with his paralysis, binding our will; it cannot work any more but we must remember that and push through it to the liberty that God has given.

I hope this helps – try to remember it!

144

Remember the wonders he has done, his miracles, and the judgements he has pronounced.

Psalm 105:5 (NIV)

I'm talking about Satan's strategy this week and we have seen how confusion of the mind leads to sadness of the heart and sadness of the heart leads to bondage of the will.

Yesterday I told the story of my first trip to Sicily and how, when the devil sowed confusion, I became upset and paralysed. Bondage of the will leads to disruption of the memory. Somehow, when you are in this kind of situation, you forget all the times that the Lord has come to the rescue and the promises He has made to help!

I had been in situations like this before and the Lord had done miracles. When I confessed out loud my sound mind, joyful heart and liberty in Christ, I also confessed John 14:26 (NKJV): "But the Helper, the Holy Spirit, whom the Father will send in My name, He will teach you all things, and remind you of everything I have said to you."

The Holy Spirit has a memory role – He will remind us and activate the memory. Suddenly, I knew what to do. I asked God to help as He had so many times before. He told me to go to the telephone box nearby and phone the Italian pastor's number. I must admit, I argued a bit because I knew that the pastor did not speak English. But the Lord insisted so I borrowed a coin, dialled the number and spoke. God helped me to speak Italian! I was amazed.

The pastor was there to pick me up in twenty minutes. I had told him that I was an English missionary stuck at the port.

From then on I found I could understand most of what they said to me and I even started to pray in Italian in the meetings. Praise the Lord!

God knows how the devil will disrupt our memory, and so with the children of Israel He built remembering into their worship. I can't help thinking that remembering should be a part of our worship too.

We can overcome this part of the devil's strategy by reminding ourselves to remember!

145

... holding on to faith and a good conscience.

1 Timothy 1:9 (NIV)

Satan's age-old strategy for immobilising people is easily defeated by God's remedy if we are aware of what is happening. Confusion of the mind leads to sadness of the heart, and sadness of the heart leads to bondage of the will.

God has an antidote for all of these things, which we apply by stating out loud what it is and declaring that we have it.

We looked at bondage of the will yesterday – that leads to dulling of the conscience. If we have fallen for the devil's strategy to the extent that we are paralysed, then we notice that we start to behave differently. It's as though we say, "What the heck!" and start doing things and saying things that we normally would not. We return to our old ways. Do you recognise this?

Peter said, "I'm going fishing," Elijah held a pity party, the children of Israel made a golden calf and Samson broke all the rules. Some people might reach for the bottle or the dope, others might swear in temper, but most people just give up.

When we begin to feel tempted to behave differently and realise that our conscience has been muted, we must declare, "I have a sharp and active conscience!" Hebrews 9:14 (NIV) speaks about our consciences being activated: "How much more will the blood of Christ who through the eternal Spirit offered himself without blemish to God cleanse our conscience from dead works to serve the living God."

We know how well our consciences work when we become a Christian and how they become even sharper when we are filled with the Holy Spirit. We must prevent the devil trying to turn down the volume with this strategy.

I hope that this week's talks will be helpful to you as you go on with Christ. This revelation has been helping me for years.

146

Examine yourselves to see if your faith is genuine. Test yourselves.

2 Corinthians 13:5 (NLT)

The question that I will be trying to answer this week is, how do you get people to listen to you? This is particularly pertinent for Christians as we are commissioned by the Lord Jesus to be witnesses for Him, but of course everyone needs to be listened to about something.

To help us with this we are going to get answers from the life of probably the most popular speaker in the Bible: John the Baptist. It is interesting that John does not seem to have had any opposition – that is, until he upset King Herod. In fact, the Bible says that "all the land of Judea, and those from Jerusalem, went out to him" (Mk.1:5, NKJV).

There is no doubt he drew huge crowds from every sector of society and people not only listened to him but responded to his preaching and were baptised. It's quite strange how even today John the Baptist is a still a popular figure among non-Christians.

What was his secret? Well, he had several, but the first one that we will look at is this: he lived his message, or, as we would say today, he walked the talk. He had himself rejected the materialism that he preached against, and lived as a repentant man. He denied himself even basic comforts and his whole life was a protest and statement against sin.

Now, I'm not suggesting that we should go and live in the desert, but what I am saying is that if we want people to listen to our message, we have to live it out. We have to get rid of inconsistencies and contradictions because they will be judged as hypocrisy.

People want to see genuineness and realness, and when they do, they will listen.

The New Testament talks a good deal about being genuine – Peter and Paul speak about genuine faith and John speaks about genuine love.

147

"Man looks at the outward appearance but the LORD looks at the heart."
1 Samuel 16:7 (NKJV)

Yesterday we saw that, like John the Baptist, only people who walk the talk and live out what they believe will be listened to. Today's Bible verse is one that we all know but only half understand. Sadly, we use this verse very often as an excuse. I am glad that God sees my heart but that's only half the story. People look at the outward appearance. If I want people to see what is in my heart, I have to turn myself inside out – I have to let what is on the inside show on the outside.

John the Baptist wore a camel hair garment. It was a statement; he was saying something by the way he dressed, by the outward appearance. It was the simplest and cheapest of garments. When he said, if you have two shirts give one away, it was obvious that he had done this and that all he had was what he stood up in.

Our message is one of love and forgiveness so we must wear those garments. We must demonstrate those things in our lives. When we do, people will listen. They will want to listen even before we start talking! They will even ask us to tell them about our faith.

The first people who got my attention for Christ, as a lad, were Jack Mitchell, our local minister, and Arthur Blessitt, the man with the cross. What was it about them that spoke to me? Their smile. It was radiant. The outward appearance made me listen.

Man looks on the outward appearance and so we must make sure we appear right!

148

For the preaching of the cross is to them that perish foolishness; but unto us which are saved it is the power of God.

1 Corinthians 1:18 (KJV)

We are looking at John the Baptist, who was probably the most popular speaker in the Bible. If there is one word that describes John's ministry it is 'radical'. His preaching did not pull any punches... "But when he saw many of the Pharisees and Sadducees coming to his baptism, he said to them, 'Brood of vipers! Who warned you to flee from the wrath to come?'" (Matt.3:7, NKJV) Does that kind of message win friends and influence people? Well, yes it does. They took it. He was calling a nation, a religion and individuals to repentance, and not only did the crowds repent, they did something unthinkable for Jews: they got baptised.

Ritual washing is part of the Jewish religion but baptism was reserved for Gentiles. If a Gentile wanted to become a member of the Jewish faith, there were three things he had to do: be circumcised, offer sacrifices and be baptised. So by getting baptised by John, the Jewish people (even Pharisees and Sadducees) were really saying, "I am not worthy to be a Jew – I need to repent and be baptised to become a Jew all over again."

And they came in droves, listened, agreed and responded.

There is an idea around that to gather people we must be mild, accommodating and stroke their egos – that we should not be harsh, fiery or radical – but that is patently not true. To start with, people like to see someone with the courage of their convictions, someone who is enthusiastic and sold out.

Secondly, people want to hear the truth. It might not be palatable and it might offend, but there is something in them that it resonates with. There's an old saying, "The truth hurts," and it only hurts because we know it is the truth.

Thirdly, the power of God is in the truth. It is only the faithful preaching of the truth of the gospel that God endues with power.

So if we want to be listened to, we mustn't water down our message or present a sugar-coated version of it. Radical is good.

149

"I indeed baptize you with water unto repentance, but He who is coming after me is mightier than I, whose sandals I am not worthy to carry."

Matthew 3:11 (NKJV)

John the Baptist was an amazingly magnetic speaker; everybody wanted to hear him and nobody seemed to oppose him. We have seen that he lived his message, he had an appearance that was right and he was radical speaking the truth. Today I want to mention a very important thing when it comes to being listened to: humility. In John 3:30 he says, "He must increase, but I must decrease." (Jn.3:30, NKJV)

There is a great temptation in ministry to blow your own trumpet, especially if we are insecure in it. If anyone could be proud, it was John the Baptist. He was the first person to recognise Jesus, when they were both in the womb! He was Jesus' cousin. He was drawing huge crowds and they were being baptised. He effectively launched Jesus' ministry at His baptism and Jesus said he was the greatest man who ever lived! But he didn't boast. He always humbly pointed away from himself to Jesus.

There is a beauty in true humility. John's phrase, "He must increase, but I must decrease," is one of the most beautiful verses in the Bible, and the hymn that is based on it – 'Oh, the bitter shame and sorrow' by Theodor Monod, which says, "...less of self and more of Thee..." – is a moving masterpiece.

People don't like bragging. There is something about a sermon with too many I's in it that turns people off. And we know that God doesn't like it either! If we humble ourselves, not only will we be listened to but God Himself will do our PR.

Jesus' brother James said, "Humble yourself before the Lord and He will lift you up in honour." (Jas.4:10, NLT) So, if you want people to listen to you, don't point to yourself; point to Jesus.

150

"Whatever I tell you in the dark, speak in the light; and what you hear in the ear, preach from the housetops."

Matthew 10:27 (NKJV)

One thing everyone knows about John the Baptist is that he lived in the wilderness – the Judean wilderness, that is. This area is made up of barren, sand-coloured rolling hills, sometimes with deep gorges and cliffs. The place where he did his baptising in the river Jordan was twenty-five miles east of Jerusalem, a journey that would take over eight hours by foot. So people were very committed to the idea of going to hear him. It was downhill all the way there – but, of course, uphill all the way back!

There is something about wildernesses in the Bible. They are wild and lonely places, and places where you hear God speak. Countless times in the Old and New Testaments we see God speaking to people in the wilderness. These encounters between John and God are not recorded but it is obvious that John heard from God.

And this is another reason that he was listened to. We can talk till the cows come home about our own ideas and opinions and nobody will listen, but when you have heard from God – that's a different thing altogether!

Jesus' words to His disciples in today's verse are the secret of spiritual communication: say what God gives you to say. Don't rely on your own intellect; rely on the inspiration of the Holy Spirit.

Remember, John the Baptist was filled with the Holy Spirit from his mother's womb (nobody else can say that). Because of that he was used to hearing God's voice but he still needed to position himself to hear it. And that was in the silence of the wilderness.

So if you want people to listen to you, find a quiet place to hear God and then speak out what He gives you. It works.

151

SATURDAY, 26TH SEPTEMBER, 2020

"He who believes in Me, as the Scripture has said, out of his heart will flow rivers of living water ." But this He spoke concerning the Spirit...

John 7:38-39 (NKJV)

When you hear the name John the Baptist, does your mind immediately picture him? Mine does. His image, style – his branding, if you like – was so strong that we still know what it was two thousand years later.

Do you think John set out to create this style? I do. Wilderness home, camel hair garment, leather belt, strange diet of locusts and honey, direct way of speaking. He wasn't copying anyone, he was unique. He got people's attention by being creative. People were intrigued by this prophet-like figure and were drawn to go to hear him.

We have to learn the lesson that the Holy Spirit is infinitely creative and if we are filled with the Holy Spirit, He will guide us, like John, into creative ministry. People are not drawn to carbon copies, neither are they drawn to the same-old-same-old. The Holy Spirit's creative leadings will give us an image that will appeal to the audience where we are and will give us a freshness that is exciting.

The apostle Paul knew all about this. He would change his approach depending on the situation he was in. He ministered in synagogues, at ladies' picnics, in prisons, amongst politicians and philosophers, and in each setting he had a different approach. That's what he was talking about when he wrote, "I have become all things to all men so that by all possible means I might save some." (1.Cor.9:22, NIV) He even changed his name from the Hebrew form 'Saul' to the Greek form 'Paul' to make himself more accessible to the Gentiles to whom he was sent.

We can still be ourselves and not use pretence whilst being creative about the way we reach people for Christ. Just because Jesus is the same yesterday, today and forever, it doesn't mean that the church has to be!

Some things, like doctrine, must not change of course, but where the Holy Spirit is, there should always be creativity and freshness.

152

Rejoice always ... pray without ceasing ... in everything give thanks; for this is the will of God in Christ Jesus for you.

1 Thessalonians 5:16-18 (NKJV)

One of the most challenging effects of the pandemic has been on people's mental health. All of us have had moments of disappointment, distress and maybe even panic. Of course, this is totally normal and a valid human response even for Christians. But this week I want to look at three verses in the New Testament that I call 'faith and sanity preservers'.

Right at the end of Paul's first letter to the Thessalonians we find a bullet point list. It's as though there were other things he had to say but didn't have time to expand on them. The first three things on this list are: (1) rejoice always; (2) pray without ceasing; (3) in everything give thanks.

These three things are not suggestions or recommendations but imperatives – vitally important things which will keep the balance right in our lives, particularly mentally. I think one thing that the pandemic has done is to remove perspective. Obeying the Word of God in these three things will always keep thing in perspective.

A lot of believers are always anxious to know what God's will is for them. Well, here it is in black and white, the underlying, foundational will of God for us: rejoice always, pray without ceasing, in everything give thanks; *for this is the will of God in Christ Jesus for you.*

If Jesus is the Rock on which we build, the first three stones that we lay on that Rock should be rejoicing, praying and thanksgiving. As with many Christian practices, these have a double impact: they do something for God and they do something for us. Rejoicing blesses God as we praise Him for who He is, but it stirs up joy within us as we do it. Praying pleases God as we communicate with our Father, but it also helps us get things off our chest. Thanksgiving shows our gratitude to God, but it also reminds us of how blessed we are.

153

Rejoice always ... pray without ceasing ... in everything give thanks; for this is the will of God in Christ Jesus for you.

1 Thessalonians 5:16-18 (NKJV)

This week we are talking about 'sanity preservers' or how to keep your mind on an even keel. Our verse contains three things that will maintain this right balance. The first is a favourite of mine. If you are in a quiz where they ask, "What is the shortest verse in the Bible?" everyone will say, "Jesus wept," but it is equal first with this one: "Rejoice always." They couldn't be more different, could they?

The New Testament goes to great lengths to show us that rejoicing is the default position for the Christian. Whether we feel like it or not, we are commanded to do it. Since you can't command a feeling, we have to deduce that rejoicing is not first and foremost emotional. However, what we do know from experience is that feelings follow. Rejoicing will produce joy.

One of the main ways a Christian rejoices is by singing. This is something that the Lord spoke to me about on Sunday. He told me that heaven is hearing less singing from the church than it has for hundreds of years and it is making Him sad.

There was a time when there was no singing in churches, just chanting. In fact, 'Amazing Grace' was written as a chant not a song. But that was two hundred and fifty years ago. The church has become accustomed to singing and heaven requires of us rejoicing in song.

The current pandemic restrictions have banned congregational singing so what are we to do? Sing privately of course. Sing in your home as a family. Sing to God and make Him rejoice. Everyone knows that singing has a tremendously therapeutic effect, and singing praises to God has an even greater effect on our mental health.

Our church has a drive-in service every Sunday so we have not stopped singing. But as in the early church and the persecuted church, we have to find a way to sing. Can I encourage you in your quiet time, don't be quiet – sing! God is missing it!

154

Rejoice always ... pray without ceasing ... in everything give thanks; for this is the will of God in Christ Jesus for you.

1 Thessalonians 5:16-18 (NKJV)

If you look this verse up in some other translations you will see "rejoice always" is often rendered "always be joyful". The Greek word used in the original is *chairo* which means 'to be glad, to rejoice and to be well'. In the Greek world it was used as a greeting like *shalom* or cheers. People were saying, "Be happy!" when they met or parted. It's a great greeting and included in the final words of Paul's letter: be happy!

Do you remember that song a few years back, 'Don't worry, be happy'? It wasn't a Christian song but the title is certainly a Christian sentiment. I get a bit tired of preachers saying it's not happiness we need but joy. Ridiculous! We need both – if there is really any distinction.

If we are to be the light of the world, we need to have a cheerful demeanour – a sunny disposition. A Christian should light up a room and bring God's darkness-dispersing joy into a gloomy world. After all, we have got a lot to be happy about! We know Him whom to know is life eternal!

C.S. Lewis went as far to say, "It is a Christian's duty to be as happy as he can."

You might remember Demos Shakarian's book called *The Happiest People on Earth*. He wasn't the first to think of this moniker for Christians; Charles Spurgeon, the prince of preachers, wrote, "Those who are 'beloved of the Lord' must be the most happy and joyful people to be found anywhere upon the face of the earth."

I think that Christians have a lot of work to do in this area. This is not how most people view churchgoers. But friends, if ever this was needed, it is now.

Choose happiness!

155

Faith means being sure of things we hope for and knowing that something is real even if we do not see it [or feel it].

Hebrews 11:1 (ICB)

We have been looking at Paul's advice in Thessalonians for Christian living. He goes as far as to say that rejoicing always, praying without ceasing and in everything giving thanks, are God's will for us. One thing I know is that these three things have a major impact on our mental health.

Pray without ceasing... Now, that sounds daunting, doesn't it? "I can't pray all the time," you might say. But it doesn't mean to pray 24/7 like some prayer marathon. J.B. Philips has the best translation of this verse: "...never stop praying..." Now that makes much more sense – we can relate to that.

I'm sure, like me, you have had times in your life when you just stopped praying. There are many reasons that you might do that; we will ignore sheer laziness and look at more legitimate reasons. There is disappointment – it doesn't seem like you are getting answers; there is disengagement – it doesn't feel like anyone is listening; there is distraction – you are too busy; there is despair – things are so bad it seems like it's gone beyond your capacity to pray. I can talk you down from any one of these situations – there is an explanation and an answer for each – but we don't have time for that. Suffice to say, "Don't stop praying!" If you were a deep sea diver connected to your support ship by an air line, whatever happened down on the seabed, the last thing you would do is cut that air supply. That is what we do when we stop praying – we cut the lifeline. We are not of this world, we are in an alien environment, we belong to heaven. We are connected to heaven by prayer.

Prayer is also our comms line to heaven. Again, why would you cut communication at the very time you need it most? But we do. We give up. Listen, the only place that help is coming from is heaven, and even if prayer seems a one way street, at least it is a one way street and not a dead end. Whatever you feel like, however it seems, your prayers are getting through.

When Paul says, "...pray without ceasing..." or, "Don't stop praying!" what he means is, "Keep going, your answer will come." As someone who has been through this, I can say amen.

156

Cast all your anxiety on him because he cares for you.

1 Peter 5:7 (NIV)

We are talking about 'sanity preservers' – things the Bible tells us God wants us to do which also help our mental health. Yesterday we looked at "pray without ceasing" or "never stop praying" from 1 Thessalonians 5:17. There's an old saying, a problem shared is a problem halved. This works in two ways: (1) talking about things always helps, vocalising our problems helps put them into perspective and we get things off our chests; (2) when you share a problem with someone, very often they are able to do something to help you and so some of the weight is gone.

This is true when we pray too. Many times the problem isn't just halved, it is very significantly reduced and sometimes solved altogether.

The Greek word used for "cares" in today's verse is *melo*. This carries with it the meaning 'he is interested in you' – interested in your problems, interested in how you are doing, interested enough to do something about it.

I often find when I pray about an issue, before I have finished I have started to see the problem in a new light. That is Him! The Lord is giving me a clarity and a course. This is phase one in answered prayer.

Phase two is God's intervention, which is the thing that seems to take time often. Here we must understand that time is not a factor to God. His answer is not delayed because He is too busy or He has run out of something and is waiting for a delivery or because it will take a while to sort out.

There was a church in Finland that was praying for God to send them an evangelist because the one they had booked for the coming weekend had cancelled. God spoke to me and told me to go there a few months before that prayer had even been prayed! Time is not an issue to God. Isaiah 65:24 (NIV) says, "Before they call I will answer, while they are still speaking I will hear." We have to conclude that an answer delayed is entirely for our benefit. God will send it at the perfect time for us – the time when it will have done us (and will do us) the most good.

Jesus said to His disciples, "You do not realise now what I am doing but later you will understand." (Jn.13:7, NIV) Never stop praying.

157

For although they knew God, they neither glorified him as God nor gave thanks to him, but their thinking became futile and their foolish hearts were darkened.

Romans 1:21 (NIV)

This week we have been looking at how the three things mentioned in 1 Thessalonians 5:16-18 are designed to preserve our sanity and keep our lives on an even keel – rejoice always, don't stop praying, and today's: "…in everything give thanks…"

As we said earlier in the week, this is one of the foundation stones of the Christian life: gratitude. Gratitude is a tremendous bulwark against sin, especially greed, envy and covetousness. If you make a practice of thanking God for what you have, you will find that your desire for more will decrease. If you thank God for your car, you won't be hankering after a better one; if you thank God for your home, you won't be wanting a bigger one; if you thank God for your wife… you get the idea.

The word translated "thankful" here is the Greek word that we get 'eucharist' from. Eucharist means 'to show gratitude'. That is why communion is called eucharist and even saying grace is a eucharist. The Christian life has gratitude built in.

The ERV version says, "Whatever happens, always be thankful." I like that. It's easy to be thankful when everything is going right but important to be thankful when it isn't. God hasn't changed – just your circumstances.

Romans 1 sheds some more light on gratitude and the way it affects our mind. If you are not grateful to God, your thinking becomes warped. The word here means 'empty, futile'. You become literally stupid, ignorant and your inner self becomes weird. That is exactly what the Bible says here.

As we look around us today and see the futile and often idiotic behaviour of people, we can trace it right back to this. The less grateful we are to God, the more 'wacko' we become! For our own sanity we need to lead lives of constant thankfulness. Build it in to your devotional life; learn to say "thank you, Jesus" often; weave it into your conversation; live it!

158

Then they cry out to the LORD in their trouble,
And He brings them out of their distresses.
He calms the storm,
So that its waves are still.
Then they are glad because they are quiet;
So He guides them to their desired haven.

Psalm 107:28-30 (NKJV)

Most of you know that our church is called Souls Harbour. This is the name that the Lord gave to us back in 1987 when we planted it. The scripture basis for this name is found in Psalm 107. The psalm describes a storm at sea and the terrible fear and distress that it causes. A deep-sea fisherman once told me that no matter how experienced you are, every time there is a storm at sea you think you are going to die.

Of course, this psalm is using the storm at sea as a metaphor for the storms that we experience in life and how in the midst of them we cry out to the Lord. The storm that we are going through at the moment – the pandemic – is certainly having that effect, and I believe there are many, many people still to cry out to the Lord.

The wonderful thing is that the Lord always hears our cry and He always responds to a distress call. When the flare goes up, when the mayday is transmitted from our breaking heart, He never pauses to think, "Do they deserve help?" or, "Are they registered with my company?" That's not what you do at sea. The Law of the Sea dictates that if someone is in distress, you rescue them. That is the Law of Heaven also.

Aren't you glad that God is no respecter of persons? If He were, there would be nobody rescued at all! The Bible says, "God demonstrates His love for us in this: While we were still sinners Christ died for us." (Rom.5:8, BSB) His rescue mission is, by definition, for those who don't deserve it. There are no barriers to His love, no prejudice. Whether you are black or white, male or female, rich or poor, Moslem, Hindu or atheist, the lifeboat of His love is launched.

Listen, if you are in a storm right now, call out to Him – send out the S.O.S. on heaven's frequency.

159

Humble yourselves before the Lord, and he will lift you up..

James 4:10 (NIV)

There are several ports or harbours mentioned in the Bible and each one of them represents something. Joppa is one of those ports. Joppa was the harbour that Jonah set sail for when he was running away from God (or so he thought). God had given him a job to do: "The Lord gave this message to Jonah son of Amittai: 'Get up and go to the great city of Nineveh! Announce my judgment against it because I have seen how wicked its people are.'" (Jon.1:1-2, NLT)

We know nothing about Jonah – the book of Jonah begins with these words – but we can deduce that he had a relationship with God, he knew God's presence with him and he could hear God. We also know that God trusted him and obviously thought him capable of this great task. God had called Jonah to be a prophet.

But Jonah did not like the mission that God gave him so he rebelled. He didn't at this point try to reason with God or ask for an easier mission. The Bible says he ran from the Lord's presence. He went in exactly the opposite direction to the way God had directed him; Nineveh was due east and Tarshish due west.

The boat to Tarshish left from the port of Joppa and so Joppa is associated here with rebellion. It was Jonah's escape route. See what happens: "He went down to Joppa, and found a ship going to Tarshish; so he paid the fare, and went down into it, to go with them to Tarshish from the presence of the Lord." (Jon.1:3, NKJV)

When Jonah ran from God, he went down – down to Joppa, down into the ship, lay down to sleep, was thrown down into the ocean and then down into the belly of the whale. The message here is that rebellion takes you down – when you turn your back on the presence of the Lord, there is only one direction and that is downwards.

Being obedient to God's will for your life will have the opposite effect; it will always take you up.

160

WEDNESDAY, 7TH OCTOBER, 2020

Then they cry out to the LORD in their trouble,
And He brings them out of their distresses.
He calms the storm,
So that its waves are still.
Then they are glad because they are quiet;
So He guides them to their desired haven.

Psalm 107:28-30 (NKJV)

This week we are looking at some of the harbours in the Bible and what they represent in our lives. When the Apostle Paul was arrested for preaching about Jesus, he appealed to have his case heard by Caesar himself. As a Roman citizen, this was his right. Of course, for this he had to go to Rome. So he was put under guard on a ship from Caesarea in Israel. The journey was going to be long and dangerous because winter was fast approaching: "We moved along the coast with difficulty and came to a place called Fair Havens, near the town of Lasea." (Acts.27:8, NIV)

Fair Havens in Crete is exactly that, a very beautiful harbour with azure waters and whitewashed houses surrounded by wooded hills – a place you'd love to holiday. Most people are looking for a harbour like this for their souls. They want to indulge themselves with an easy life surrounded by beautiful things. They are attracted by the sensual pleasures that a hedonistic lifestyle offers. But there was a problem with Fair Havens. As idyllic as it was, there was no protection there from the elements. Once the winter storms began in earnest, the ship would be lost.

Many a soul has been enticed by the pleasures of this world that look so appealing, so comforting, such fun, but when the storms of life come, they find that there is no protection there. They are exposed and vulnerable – their very life is at risk.

I can't help thinking that many are in this position right now. The coronavirus pandemic is a storm that has engulfed the world. But still people are making for the harbour of Fair Havens: for the bars, the clubs, the nightlife where there is no protection. Fair Havens is so deceiving because it looks like it offers respite but in fact is the most dangerous place of all. Proverbs 14:12 (NIV) says, "There is a way that appears to be right, but in the end it leads to death."

Our verse of the week has the answer. Jesus said, "Come to me, all of you who are weary and carry heavy burdens, and I will give you rest." (Matt.11:28, NLT) That's the harbour for me!

161

I tell you, now is the time of God's favour, now is the day of salvation.
2 Corinthians 6:2 (NIV)

Paul was on his way to Rome to face trial, escorted by a centurion named Julius. The ship left Fair Havens because it offered no protection from storms. It was no place to overwinter. The crew favoured another Cretan harbour at the west end of the island called Phoenix which would be much safer. So that's where they headed. They never got there. They had left it too late and they got caught by the winter wind which was so bad it had a name: *Euroclydon.*

Phoenix would have been a great place to spend the winter in – safe, sheltered, sunny – but it wasn't to be. So Phoenix represents lost opportunities.

I remember a preacher saying, and I must only have been eight or nine at the time, "The road to hell is lined with lost opportunities" And that's exactly what lay ahead for Paul and his shipmates – a voyage that was a living hell.

Paul had sternly warned the captain and the ship's owner, "Men, I perceive that this voyage will end with disaster and much loss, not only of the cargo and ship, but also our lives." (Acts.27:10, NKJV) Paul was not a sailor, let alone a helmsman, but he had a check in his spirit warning him of the danger ahead. But nobody listened; they pressed on.

How many times in someone's life do they get an opportunity to change direction; how many times does God send someone or something across their path with the message of salvation? Yet, for whatever reason, they press on regardless.

I remember a dear school friend of mine who got into drugs. One day he overdosed and wound up in hospital – his skin had turned purple from head to foot. The doctor told me that it was a miracle he had survived. I pleaded with him by his hospital bed, saying "God has given you another chance. Turn to Jesus!" He said, "I'll think about it." Several years later the same thing happened again – this time I stood by his grave.

Lost opportunities. If you are reading this today and you have never given your life to Christ, this is an opportunity for you. Don't miss it. Pray with me right now. (Turn to the back of the book for the prayer you need to pray to give your life to Christ.)

162

Then they cry out to the LORD in their trouble,
And He brings them out of their distresses.
He calms the storm,
So that its waves are still.
Then they are glad because they are quiet;
So He guides them to their desired haven.

Psalm 107:28-30 (NKJV)

The Bible's account of Paul's voyage to Rome is unmatched in ancient literature – we learn more about seafaring in those days from it than from any other source.

The storm that Paul's ship endured was a nightmare; they did everything they knew how to survive. They undergirded the ship with ropes, they threw everything they could overboard to lighten the ship and for two weeks they battled, the two hundred and seventy-six people onboard eating nothing. There was no sun or stars to navigate by. All hope was lost. And then, after Paul had encouraged them with a message from God that they would all survive, they saw land – Malta.

Having been to Malta fifty times, I reckon I know it quite well. I have even been in a storm at sea in the old ship Ghawdex – which was terrifying. Traditionally, people have thought that Paul was shipwrecked at a bay named after him, but scholars believe now that it was at St. Thomas Bay. They have even found the wreck.

Although Malta has one of the best harbours in the world, it was useless to Paul's ship as it broke up before they even got there. But what does this harbour have to say to us today? St. Thomas Bay represents the place we are taken by the will of God. Strange isn't it, but we often find the will of God through a storm. Paul would never have gone to Malta. The ship would never have gone to Malta. But God used the storm to change their direction. Sometimes it needs a storm.

We can be so stubbornly set in our ways that nothing short of a storm is going to move us. Or we can be so intent on doing what we want to do that we don't listen to God and He is forced to resort to a storm to get through to us.

The storm that took me to Malta and changed the direction of my life was a head-on collision with a truck. I was running away from God's will and doing my own thing.

The storm that we are in at the moment is changing people's direction too. I believe, I hope, that it will change the direction of the church.

God speaks through storms. What is He saying to you?

163

God is our refuge and strength,
A very present help in trouble.

Psalm 46:1 (NKJV)

In 1987 we planted the church here in Camelford and after much prayer and discussion we decided on the name Souls Harbour. Many people over the years have commented on this name. It was taken, as I have said, from Psalm 107. We wanted our church to be a harbour for people, a place where they could find refuge and be replenished, a place where a refit could take place and damaged lives could be repaired – a place where a fishing fleet could be based too!

But when we look a little more deeply into this, we understand that the real harbour for the soul is God Himself. He is the one doing the repairs and replenishment. In fact, today's verse, which many people know well, is translated in some bibles, "God is our *harbour* and our strength." Yes, He is the desired haven that the psalmist is writing about in Psalm 107.

A fisherman friend of mine told me about being six miles out at sea one day in his little boat when a thick Atlantic fog suddenly rolled in. Without compass or phone he was completely lost. He didn't know which direction to make for, where the coast lay. Any false move could take him farther out to sea or onto the rocks. Fear gripped his heart. There was only one thing he could do: pray.

Within moments of finishing his prayer, the fog parted for a few moments forming a corridor to Port Gavern – his harbour. He pointed the boat in that direction and kept going to safety.

It is God's supreme desire that people would do just this: call out to Him and be guided into His arms that stretch out to us like welcoming harbour walls. There within the harbour of His love we will find all we need for life and godliness.

Every boat needs a harbour – everybody needs a saviour.

164

When I look at your heavens, the work of your fingers, the moon and the stars, which you have set in place, what is man that you are mindful of him, and the son of man that you care for him?

Psalm 8:3-4 (ESV)

One of the most amazing testimonies I ever heard was from John Michael in Peru. As soon as John Michael learnt to speak, they knew something was wrong; he had a terrible stammer. At school he didn't do well; he was mocked by the children and teachers alike; they called him 'Donkey' and he was treated as a special needs student. There was no respite at home either. His father would come home drunk every day and beat his wife and John Michael mercilessly.

One day, when he was in this teens, he had had enough. He decided to take his own life. He took a sharp knife, and he and his dog climbed up one of the high hills overlooking Cusco. He found a place and sat down, preparing himself for the act. Just then he saw a bright reflection as the sun hit something in the city below. At first he couldn't make out what it was but then he realised it was a church roof. "Hmm," he thought, "I wonder if there is a God…" So he prayed his first ever prayer: "God, if you are there, show yourself or else I will die today."

John Michael lay back on the ground and waited. Suddenly he felt hands – hands that gently reached under his body and lifted him up. Peace flooded his heart. There *was* a God! He quickly made his way back home. When he began to speak to his mother, she just stared at him. His stammer had gone!

He was just wondering how he was going to find out more about the God that he now knew existed, when there was a knock at the door. A stranger stood there. The stranger was looking for lodgings in the area. Being inquisitive, John Michael asked him what his business was. "I'm a missionary," the man replied.

"I've never heard of that," John Michael said. "What does that mean?"

"Well, it means I work for God," the stranger said.

John Michael grabbed his arm and pulled him inside. "Then you can answer my questions!" he said excitedly.

One question that he asked was, "Why is the sky blue?"

"I don't know the answer to that; you need study physics to answer that question," the man said.

"Then that's what I want to do," John Michael said.

Following this conversation he went to the local college and asked to study physics. When the principle asked him what exams he had passed, John Michael said, "None."

The principle laughed. "Well, that's that," he said. "Goodbye!"

"But there must be another way..."

"Well," the principal replied, "there is an entrance exam but I don't put down much hope. You would have to study hard." He gave John Michael a list of books.

For the next few weeks he spent all his time in the public library reading. The day of the exam came and he sat it. He passed with the highest marks anyone had ever achieved.

To cut a long story short, John Michael won a scholarship to a prestigious university in the USA and has a glittering academic career in nuclear physics, specialising in nuclear medicine and cancer research. But better that that, he remains a faithful disciple of Jesus and has founded orphanages in Peru to help children with no hope.

165

But God demonstrates his own love for us in this: While we were still sinners, Christ died for us.

Romans 5:8 (NIV)

Pat Furtaw was my best friend. We met in Houston, Texas in 1985 when I was on my first preaching tour there and hit it off immediately. As we swapped stories, we discovered that we had been saved within days of each other, filled with the Holy Spirit at the same time and even got married the same month.

Pat's story was incredible. He grew up on the streets of Flint, Michigan. An alcoholic father with a failed marriage left him to run wild. At eight he was smoking, at ten he was drinking whiskey and by the age of twelve he was doing drugs – pot and LSD. Sadly, at fifteen he began to shoot drugs into his veins. To pay for his habit he began to break into homes – six or seven a night. Always a man with a plan, Pat saw how he could make money by selling drugs, and when that worked, he started running drugs from Arizona to Michigan and employing a chemist at the university to manufacture synthetic drugs. He was seventeen.

Some of the stories that Pat told me about this time in his life made my stomach turn. I have no doubt that his life would had been cut short right then if God had not intervened.

Two things happened. One day his sister Michelle, who idolised him, walked in on him as he was injecting drugs. He felt so ashamed, it broke his heart. And then his best friend David returned from a visit to his uncle who was a pastor, having met Jesus and given his life to Him. David was so changed it blew Pat's mind and he surrendered his life to Jesus too.

He was in such a state physically that no churches would let him in. He was so on fire for Jesus he had to tell people, so he started to preach on the streets, often getting a captive audience by addressing people at a pedestrian crossing as they waited and then walking backwards still preaching as they crossed the road!

Eventually, a youth-oriented pastor in Houston, Cleddie Keith, took Pat under his wing and gave him the training he needed.

I met Pat when he was pastor of a tiny church in Shepherd, Texas. But God had greater things in store for him. After pastoring one of two other churches, Pat was called to Pasadena, Texas, where his church saw incredible growth. He became a much respected pastor in the area. When there was a disaster, like the earthquake in Mexico City or 9/11, Pat would be on the first plane out and put his formidable organisational ability to work, rallying the churches to spearhead relief.

One day he had a call asking him to open in prayer at the Texas Legislature in Austin. The official told him he could ride up on the plane with the then Governor of Texas – George W. Bush.

Pat had a saying, "God has a way of taking people from the bottom of the deck and putting them on the top." He knew all about that.

Pat went to be with Jesus sixteen years ago at just forty-nine years of age. I still miss him terribly.

166

"No weapon formed against you shall prosper, and you will refute every tongue that accuses you. This is the heritage of the servants of the Lord, and their vindication is from Me," declares the LORD.

Isaiah 54:17 (BSB)

I met Paolo when I was on a preaching tour in Sicily. The scenery was stunning as we travelled from town to town, passing through orange groves heavy with blossom and quaint hilltop villages, always with the volcano Mount Etna brooding in the background. But the most beautiful thing of all were the testimonies of what God had done in people's lives – amazing miracles.

It was in the town of Francofonte that I met Paolo. He smiled radiantly as he shook my hand and kissed me on both cheeks and then asked me if he could tell me his story.

A man of about forty now, he had met Jesus as a young man, maybe in his late teens, after attending a meeting with his friends. He was not prepared for the reception that he got when he returned home. When he told his mother what he had done, she was furious; as a Sicilian Catholic he had brought shame on the family.

From that moment on she tried everything in her power to get him to recant and give up his newfound faith. When all her persuasion, tears and threats failed, she tried something else. All over Sicily there were signs outside homes advertising the supernatural power of the occupant; these occultists, or 'magicians' as they called themselves, offered a range of services from love potions to curses. Paolo's mother started visiting them, first asking them to change him back and then buying curses to put on him. She would bring curses home and make Paolo stand there whilst she performed the incantation that the magician had prescribed. Paolo would just stand laughing, knowing that the blood of Jesus protected him.

Then it got serious. One day Paolo's brothers asked him if he wanted to go hunting with them. He excitedly agreed but when they got up into the mountains, his brothers kicked him to his knees and pointed the gun at him. Having spent all her money, his mother had commanded his brothers to take him out and kill him. Again the peace of God flooded Paolo's heart and he smiled at his brothers. "Do it," he said. "I will get to see Jesus today." His assurance was literally disarming and they couldn't do it.

His mother had run out of ideas. She never spoke to him again.

Years went by, Paolo estranged from his family but growing and enjoying life in God. Then one day he got a call. His mother was sick; in fact, she was on her deathbed and she was calling for him. When he got there, tears flowed down her face. She asked for his forgiveness for all that she had done. She realised that she was not ready to meet her Maker and asked Paolo if she could be saved.

Paolo knelt at her bedside and prayed with her the sinner's prayer. She met Jesus on earth just a few moments before she met Him in heaven.

167

I would rather be a gatekeeper in the house of my God than live the good life in the homes of the wicked.

Psalm 84:10 (NLT)

As I sat in the auditorium of Hedmarktoppen Bible College, Norway waiting to address the student body, he walked in. I knew there was something different about him as soon as I saw him – a six-foot-tall African with his nose in the air. I said to the person next to me, "Who does he think he is? The king or something?"

"Actually," they replied, "he *is* a king." Have you ever felt like you wanted the ground to open up and swallow you?

His name was Emanuel and he was the uncrowned king of a tribe in west Africa. Now, I had never met a king before, so after the meeting I made a beeline for him and shook his hand. He looked at me imperiously and said, "Would you like to go shopping?" Of course, I agreed. We went into the town and to a shoe shop where he bought some bright pink shoes.

Over a coffee I asked him to tell me his story.

He told me that his father had been king of a certain tribe which numbers over one million people. Sadly, his father had been charged with corruption and put in jail. The powers that be had then looked to Emanuel as the next in line. They had come to him and told him that soon he must be crowned. He was a young man and had never been to a coronation so he asked them what was involved. When they told him, he was horrified. The coronation ritual involved many witchdoctors and a pagan ceremony. You see, Emanuel was a Christian; some time before, he had given his life to the Lord Jesus Christ and he knew that he could have nothing to do with such people.

So he told the officials that he could not participate in a ceremony of that nature. However, if it could be made a Christian ceremony he would happily go through with it. They told him that it had to be done in the traditional way. To which he replied, "Then I cannot be involved. I will not be king."

"In that case," they said, "we will take you and tie you to a chair and do it anyway."

He had to make a quick decision. He knew he could no longer stay in that country and so Emanuel made an application for political asylum in Norway, which he was granted. He was soon on a plane – to Oslo.

Emanuel had to think of a new path for his life, so he sought the Lord and was directed to attend the Bible school at Hedmarktoppen. I asked him what he wanted to do when he had finished Bible school. He told me, "I think I want to work with children."

So the man who would be king now serves the King of kings. The Bible says, it is better to be the doorkeeper in the house of the Lord.

168

For I am convinced that neither death nor life, neither angels nor demons, neither the present nor the future, nor any powers, neither height nor depth, nor anything else in all creation, will be able to separate us from the love of God that is in Christ Jesus our Lord.

Romans 8:38-39 (NIV)

I will change the name of the person today for reasons that will become clear. Frida was another Bible college student in Norway. I could see her paying particular attention as my week of lectures on spiritual warfare progressed. At one point she came to me and asked if she could talk to me privately. I, of course, agreed.

That afternoon she poured out a tale so dreadful I was shocked and upset. Frida was the victim of child abuse. During her childhood and into her teens her father had sexually abused her, and as it escalated, satanic practices became involved. Frida had been party to the most horrific diabolical manifestations. What made it worse (if it could get any worse) was that the family were involved in their local church.

Frida had looked for some way out and eventually cried out to God and asked Jesus into her life. She instantly found the forgiveness and cleansing that she had sought – although she of course had nothing to be forgiven for in this. Jesus became her best friend and she learnt to lean on His love and grace daily.

She thought that would be the end of her torment, but Satan would not let her go that easily. She started experiencing very frightening supernatural manifestations. When she was out on a date with her boyfriend, she looked out of the car window and saw a wolf-like creature with burning red eyes circling the car. Sometimes when she was alone in her room, she would see a grey fog coming under the door into the room changing the atmosphere. You see, she had been so used to demonic manifestations that the powers of evil didn't bother to hide themselves from her. Even while in Bible college these things persisted.

After listening to her sad story, the Holy Spirit told me what was happening. I discerned what is called an attendant spirit – a demonic entity that comes and goes. It is not in the person but it troubles and oppresses them.

We prayed over her in the way that I had been taught by my pastor, Arthur Neil, praying very specific things to cut her off and to protect her from the attendant spirit.

When we looked up, her face had brightened, a peace had flooded her soul and she was set free. She never experienced any of those things again. Praise the Lord!

169

When Jacob awoke from his sleep, he thought, "Surely the LORD is in this place, and I did not know it." And he was afraid and said, "How awesome is this place! This is none other than the house of God, and this is the gate of heaven!"

Genesis 28:16-17 (NIV)

Manuel was a chef at one of Malta's classiest restaurants. Before that, he had been a chef in the British army and had even cooked for the queen. He and his wife were very annoyed when we put our gospel tent up in Fgura very close to their home. Each night, as the singing began, they would get hot under the collar and rant about it to each other.

Then one evening, as Manuel was returning home, he saw something. There were flames leaping out from the roof of the tent. He ran indoors shouting, "Call the fire brigade, call the fire brigade! The tent is on fire!"

His wife looked out of the window. "I don't see any flames," she said. "Just do it," he replied.

With that he left the house and ran over to the marquee. When he got there, he looked inside. There everybody was, calmly listening now to me preaching. Scratching his head in puzzlement, Manuel came inside the tent, stood and listened.

He was touched by what he heard. For the first time in his life he listened to the good news about Jesus and His love. When I had finished preaching to the crowd of one hundred plus people, I asked if anyone wanted to give their life to Jesus, repent of their sins and be born again. Manuel lifted his hand and came to the front for prayer.

After the meeting he shook my hand vigorously and told me what had happened. "Surely God is in this place," he said. And then he invited me for a meal – it was one of the best I ever had!

Manuel joined our church in Fgura and became one of the most faithful members. When he retired, he began to spend hours at the church doing all the odd jobs. He was such a lovely man.

170

So He said to them, "When you pray, say: Our Father in heaven…"

Luke 11:2 (NKJV)

Today I want to look at two of the most powerful words in the Bible. In fact, they are so strong that when Jesus said them, there must have been a communal gasp. The words were revolutionary and nobody had ever said them before in this context. In fact, they were illegal.

What were those words? "Our Father…"

The disciples had asked Jesus to teach them how to pray. It's a perennial question. Books on prayer are always bestsellers for that very reason.

I don't know if the disciples heard anything else the first time around because they were so astonished at the first two words: "Our Father…" The Jews were forbidden to even use the name of God – even to say the word 'God' – and here comes Jesus using the most intimate, familiar term to address the Almighty.

Maybe they were expecting Jesus to say, "When you pray say, 'Father of Jesus in heaven…' But "*our* Father", "*my* Father"… No way!

Yet here is the essence of Christianity: relationship – a relationship with God. Not only relationship in the sense of knowing someone personally (which is wonderful and great) but relationship in the sense of being related!

John in his Gospel explains it like this: "But as many as received Him, to them He gave the right to become children of God, to those who believe in His name…" (Jn.1:12, NKJV) Those that receive Him (Jesus) have the right to become God's children and so to call Him Father. Nobody else has that right – only those who believe in Him.

This is the relationship with God we enter into when we are born again – a father-child relationship. And it is on that basis that we can pray and make our requests known to God.[7]

This is huge.

So right now, use your right to say, "Father…"

---

[7] See Philemon 6:2

171

TUESDAY, 20TH OCTOBER, 2020

To Him who loved us and washed us from our sins in His own blood, and has made us kings and priests to His God and Father, to Him be glory and dominion forever and ever. Amen.

Revelation 1:5-6 (NKJV)

Yesterday we looked at the amazing privilege of being able to call God Father. This indicates the relationship we have with God through the Lord Jesus Christ. But as John said in his Gospel, Jesus "gave [us] the right to *become* children of God" (Jn.1:12, NIV). That tells us that we were not children of God before. So if we are not all children of God as human beings, then there is no such thing as the brotherhood of man.

Being a child of God makes us a family member with Jesus as our older brother. Just think for a moment what that means. You are a member of the royal family – Jesus is the King of kings, after all. Think what privileges you can enjoy as a royal!

I used to preach that royals behave differently to other people, but these days I'm not too sure. However, in this text from Revelation we see that we are made kings and priests – that this authority is coupled with holiness. You can't have one without the other.

In the older translations it doesn't say that we have the right to become "children of God", but to become "sons of God". This is not sexist – this points to another right, the right to inherit, to be an heir. In former times only sons could be heirs. Romans 8:16-17 (NKJV) says, "The Spirit Himself bears witness with our spirit that we are children of God, and if children, then heirs – heirs of God and joint heirs with Christ, if indeed we suffer with Him, that we may also be glorified together."

My goodness, what a lot to take in! Children of God, kings, priests, heirs... I think God wants you to see yourself in a whole new light!

172

For you did not receive the spirit of bondage again to fear, but you received the Spirit of adoption by whom we cry out, "Abba, Father."

Romans 8:15 (NKJV)

This week we are looking at the father-child relationship that we have with God as born-again Christians. This is not just a nice idea or a something to make us feel good; it is a legal reality. God has adopted us!

In ancient cultures adoption was a common practice and in law it was stronger than a blood relationship. That's because you chose whom you adopted. And you went through a legal process to do it. Funnily enough, adults were adopted more often than children and it was done to guarantee that there was an heir. The process was fascinating.

In a Roman court of law the person being adopted had to stand in front of the judge, a priest and witnesses, and publicly renounce his old family and their gods – then publicly accept the new family and their gods. He lost all his rights in the old family – he could no longer inherit anything from them or have any contact with them. All his former debts and obligations were cancelled and he became a full heir of his new father. He walked from the court not only with a new name but with a new identity – a new life.

This is what Paul was thinking about when he wrote today's verse. This is what happens in the law courts of heaven when we become a child of God. Our debts – or sins – are cancelled and our old life has no hold over us any more. We are given the name 'Christian' and become an heir of God.

For our part though, we must renounce the devil and our old gods, whatever they were, and have no more contact with them!

2 Corinthians 5:17 (NKJV) says, "Therefore, if anyone is in Christ, he is a new creation; old things have passed away; behold, all things have become new."

173

"If a son asks for bread from any father among you, will he give him a stone? Or if he asks for a fish, will he give him a serpent instead of a fish? Or if he asks for an egg, will he offer him a scorpion? If you then, being evil, know how to give good gifts to your children, how much more will your heavenly Father give the Holy Spirit to those who ask Him!"

Luke 11:11-13 (NKJV)

We are looking at our relationship with God our heavenly Father. It is often said that many people cannot relate to God as Father because either they did not know their father or their father was rotten and gave them no paradigm. To be honest, this is nonsense. Everybody knows what a father should be like, and the things that a father should do are written deep inside our psyche. And God is the perfect Father. He is the perfect paradigm of fatherhood.

In Jesus' words in today's verse, the implication is that earthly fathers are generally good but God is even better. If we as fathers know how to give our children good gifts, our heavenly Father will be even better at it and the gift will be what we need.

I was far from a spoilt child and my parents were not rich, but if I ever said I needed anything to pursue my education or interests, you could guarantee my dad would bring it home from work within a couple of weeks. I got a microscope, an astronomical telescope, a geologist's hammer and, best of all, a study bible. He supplied what I needed. He wanted to see me develop and grow. This is a father's instinct and it is an instinct given to him by God.

Fathers want the best for their children and will give them the best that they can afford. Your heavenly Father wants the best for you. He wants to give you what you most need for both your spiritual growth and your growth as a person. That happens to be the gift of the Holy Spirit. Why? Because it is through the Holy Spirit that we get access to a multiplicity of other gifts.

He's a good, good Father!

174

*Sing to God, sing praises to his name, extol him who rides on the clouds –
his name is the LORD – and rejoice before him. A father to the fatherless, a
defender of widows, is God in his holy habitation.*

Psalm 68:4-5 (BSB)

Yesterday I mentioned that some people say they cannot relate to
God as Father because they never had a father themselves. Did
you know that the fatherless are mentioned forty times in the
Bible? God has a special place in His heart for the fatherless.

But God is not a God of sentiment – of kindly thoughts. He is a God
of action and answers. When God looks at the fatherless, He says, "I can
do something about that – I can be a Father to them." He is a Father to
the fatherless.

A brilliant gospel song by Larry Norman has these words:

I was born about eighteen years ago
In a little wooden shack
I was born about eighteen years ago
On the wrong side of the tracks
And I never knew my father
And I never had a home
Well I don't know where I came from
And I don't know where I'm goin'

I was born to be unlucky
From my shoulders to my shoes
And I guess I'm stuck with my unlucky blues

After being rescued from a river by a preacher, the unlucky boy is
transformed by the knowledge of God.

Well, he told me things I did not know
I'm glad I did not die
'cause he told me God's my father
And my real home is in the sky

God will be a Father to the fatherless and He is a Father to all who
come to Him – a heavenly Father; a Father who can do what a father
does but in greater measure and dimension. He protects, provides,
prepares, disciplines, demonstrates and devotes Himself to them.

But most of all, our heavenly Father loves us. Who could love us more than the one who *is* love? The best known verse in the Bible tells us, "For God so loved the world that he gave his only Son, so that everyone who believes in him will not perish but have eternal life." (Jn.3:16, NKJV) And, "How great is the love the Father has lavished on us, that we should be called children of God!" (1.Jn.3:1)

175

And because you are sons, God has sent forth the Spirit of His Son into your hearts, crying out, "Abba, Father!"

Galatians 4:6 (NKJV)

When I was in Israel last year, I heard it for the first time: walking through the streets of Jerusalem on Friday afternoon as the Jewish people were scurrying about preparing for the Sabbath, which starts at sunset, a little voice crying out, "Abba! Abba!" I looked around and there was a little lad trying to get his father's attention. "Daddy, Daddy!" he was saying in Hebrew. Three times this word is mentioned in the Bible. Tears welled up in my eyes as all that I had learnt and been told was suddenly a reality – a heart crying out, "Daddy."

For me this is the most intimate thing in the whole Bible. There is no word that expresses our relationship with God in such a familiar way because it's the family way. But not only that, it's childish – or should I say, *childlike.*

To be honest, I have struggled with this over the years. My reserved English brain always wants to say "Father" but my heavenly heart needs to say "Daddy".

The Bible says that the Holy Spirit, the Spirit of the Son of God, of Jesus, has been sent into the hearts of every born-again believer, and He cries out, "Abba" (Daddy) to God.

Romans 8:15 (NKJV) says, "…but you received the Spirit of adoption by whom we cry out, 'Abba, Father'." The *Spirit* within us cries out and *we* cry out, "Abba!" Just like the child on the street of Jerusalem trying to get his daddy's attention.

The third place in the Bible where we read the word 'Abba' is at Jesus' lowest moment. As He sweated drops of blood in anguish in the garden of Gethsemane, Jesus said, "Abba [Daddy], Father, all things are possible for You. Take this cup away from Me; nevertheless, not what I will, but what You will." (Mk.14:36, NKJV)

Daddy…

176

"For I know the plans I have for you," says the LORD. "They are plans for good and not for disaster, to give you a future and a hope."

Jeremiah 29:11 (NIV)

One thing that seems to be in short supply at the moment is the future! Because of the pandemic, people are not planning ahead, not even looking ahead, because they don't know what lies ahead.

But God has always been a futurist. Some people would criticise Christianity for being retrogressive, backward-looking, but if it is, that is entirely the fault of the followers, not of the leader. The Bible is always pointing forward – urging us on.

Most of us are familiar with today's verse. The Bible is the only place that you can find real hope and a future. The promise here is to you. It is not to the world, it is to the individual. God has your future all mapped out and it is good.

The plans He has for the world are not good; they are for disaster.

Within the last twelve months, and largely due to David Attenborough, the world has caught up with the Bible that this planet has a shelf-life. The activist group Extinction Rebellion is peddling its message of doom with mass rallies on the streets. I had a confrontation with a member of this group at one of their protests. I told the man that the Bible had prophesied these things would happen. "That's why we must act now to stop it!" the man said. "You can't stop it," I replied. "The Bible prophesied it and it will happen. But Jesus came to rescue you and give you a future." He didn't know what to say.

In these days of doom and gloom, of bad news and heavy hearts, we must bring the message of hope. We cannot say, "Don't worry; it will all be all right," because it won't.

But we can say, "God promises you a bright future if you will turn and trust Him."

177

Now may the God of hope fill you with all joy and peace in believing...
Romans 15:13 (NKJV)

So, do you think you don't have a future? Many people are in that position right now. The events around us are so damaging to our hope for the future.

The politicians and their scientists have many people believing that they are probably not going to survive the pandemic. Race riots and increased violence everywhere are producing fear of what is ahead, and the 'save the planet' brigade are spreading their message of doom as we saw yesterday.

The incidence of mental health problems is understandably sky-rocketing. Of course, today with instant global news coverage we get all the world's problems served up on the hour. And we take the bad news onboard. Did you ever think that we were not meant to carry the weight of the world on our shoulders? We are not equipped for such emotional strain. That is God's job.

This is one of the primary reasons for hopelessness and stress. But wait. Two thousand years ago a man was hanging on a cross just outside Jerusalem. He hung there in agony waiting to die. His only hope was that the end would come soon. His future was numbered in hours, maybe minutes. Was there ever a more hopeless situation?

But then there was a commotion with the prisoner on the cross next to his. They were saying He claimed to be the Son of God. He turned his head and called out, "Remember me when you come into your kingdom!" The man on his left looked at him, smiled and said, "Today you will be with me in paradise."

He gave him a future. Right there, right then, when there was no hope at all, Jesus gave him a future.

It doesn't matter how grim your situations looks, with Jesus you always have a future.

178

Live wisely among those who are not believers, and make the most of every opportunity.

Colossians 4:5 (NLT)

When veteran missionary David Newington was staying with us some years ago, he told me about something that happened on a trip to India.

Each morning he left his hotel for a walk. Hundreds of people were swarming the streets on their way to work. He noticed that many of the people would visit a stall on the pavement for a few moments. He took a closer look. When they had paid their money, a little bird would hop off its perch, hop across the table and pick out a rolled-up piece of paper from a box full of them. Then it would return to its perch. The stall-holder would then give the scroll to the punter. When he got back to the hotel, he asked someone what this was all about. "Oh," they said, "that is their horoscope for the day. The bird predicts the future."

"Really!" David said. "But everybody was stopping there."

"Oh yes," said the Indian, "everybody in India wants to know their future."

John went back to his hotel room deep in thought. As a literature evangelist, he was always looking for opportunities. "Well, I can tell everybody their future too," he thought, "and my predictions would be 100% accurate. With Jesus in their life they are going to heaven and without Jesus in their life they are going to hell."

He began to write a leaflet. He went to the printers and got it printed. Then he went to the *Times of India* newspaper office and put an ad in the next day's edition: "Your Future Told for free – send stamped, addressed envelope to this address."

A couple of days later there was a knock at his hotel room door. "Post for Mr. Newington."

"Ah, someone replied," he thought. He opened the door and there were several men with sackfuls of letters!

He got a team together to put the leaflets in the envelopes and posted them out. In the coming days he received hundreds of replies from people who had read their future in the leaflet and given their lives to Christ! He started all of them on his new believer correspondent course.

The Bible tells us all our future. We need to let people know…

179

...but one thing I do, forgetting those things which are behind and reaching forward to those things which are ahead...

Philippians 3:13 (NKJV)

In Philippians 3:13 the Apostle Paul shares some wisdom with us from his personal 'life skills' file. "...one thing I do..." is like saying, "If there's one piece of advice I would give you..." From a man that's brimming with godly advice this must be important.

Forget the past and go for the future! That's his advice. It doesn't sound that profound, does it? But when you've been on the trail as long as I have, you will know that this is absolute gold.

Now, if you've been reading through these talks, you will know that I spoke on the importance of remembering the past. I'm not contradicting myself. What Paul is saying is, "Be selective about what you remember, what you think about, what you brood over."

The Greek word translated here "forgetting" means 'to neglect, to send into oblivion, to not care about'. We must take the pain, the hurt, the trouble of the past and send it to Room 101. That's easier said than done, you might say – the very nature of these things is sticky, stubborn.

Paul knew that the main thing affecting our future is our past. Bitterness, resentment, discouragement, conflict have a crippling effect on our ability to go forward. But we are not in this alone. In verse 13 of the previous chapter it says, "God is in us both to will and to do."

He will help us. He will set us free of the past so that we can launch enthusiastically into the future.

Ask Him to do it today.

180

...but one thing I do, forgetting those things which are behind and reaching forward to those things which are ahead...

Philippians 3:11 (NKJV)

Yesterday, we saw how the past, and more specifically the hurts and wounds of the past, needs to be jettisoned with the Lord's help so that we can fully enjoy the future God has planned for us.

Paul goes on to say that we should reach forward to those things that are ahead. Different versions of the Bible translate "reach forward" differently; some say "stretching" and some even say "straining"! Picture this in your mind: someone stretching forward to grasp something. What does that suggest to you?

It suggests eagerness, eagerness to grab hold of and embrace the future. It suggests joyful anticipation of what is ahead. Ultimately, it is saying, what God has planned for you is something to be excited about. Now, that is a lot different from the status quo at the moment when many people are dreading the future – at least the next few months. But the calling of the Christian is to be a futurist, to be a hope-giver. Our motto is, "The best is yet to come!"

Whatever the future holds, one thing we know: God is there in it, waiting for us. He is ahead making the path smooth, clearing the snares of the evil one, preparing the way, because He knows the plans He has for us – they are "plans for good and not for disaster, to give you a future and a hope" (Jer.29:11, NLT).

Bill Gaither wrote, "Because He lives I can face tomorrow, because He lives all fear is gone, because I know, I know who holds the future and life is worth the living just because He lives."

Come on – let's live this today!

181

...but one thing I do, forgetting those things which are behind and reaching forward to those things which are ahead...

Philippians 3:11 (NKJV)

It's sad that some people think their future is a *fait accompli*, that it is fixed and inevitable. Some think that they have made their beds and they must lie in them, and that they cannot change the outcome of their lives. Even some Christians are fatalists, thinking that the future is set in stone and whatever will be will be. People like this just walk passively through life, taking every blow and allowing circumstances to dominate them, thinking that this is the will of God.

But this is not true. We can change the future. First and foremost, by accepting the Lord Jesus Christ into our lives and being born again, we change our future. Our eternal future is changed from hell to heaven. Our path through life therefore is in an entirely different direction – 180 degrees different. And if you walk in a different direction there is a different view ahead. Just think how much different a view of heaven ahead is to a view of hell ahead. It is a new outlook on life entirely.

Secondly, we can change the future by either accepting God's will for our life or pursuing our own will. I can't imagine how dull and dreadful my life would have been if I had gone my own way and pursued my own ambitions. But I chose the will of God and my life has been exciting and satisfying.

Thirdly, we can change the future for others. Jackie Pullinger changed the future of thousands of drug addicts in Hong Kong by choosing to obey God and go there as a missionary. Dorothea Clapp changed the future from her living room by praying daily for a teenager who lived across the street. As a result of her prayers, he got saved – it was George Verwer, who would go on to form the biggest missionary society (OM) and change the world.

Your prayers, your obedience, your efforts today can change somebody's future – maybe even change the world

182

"I call heaven and earth as witnesses today against you, that I have set before you life and death, blessing and cursing; therefore choose life, that both you and your descendants may live; that you may love the LORD your God, that you may obey His voice, and that you may cling to Him, for He is your life and the length of your days; and that you may dwell in the land which the LORD swore to your fathers, to Abraham, Isaac, and Jacob, to give them."

Deuteronomy 13:19-20 (NKJV)

Our Prime Minister announced on Saturday that the whole country is in lockdown again. My first reaction to this was, "Oh, no! This is going to be terrible, especially with the dark evenings and winter weather." I could feel my mood falling – until I caught it. "No!" I declared. "I choose life – this is going to be great! Thank you, Jesus."

In today's passage Moses addresses the Israelites... "Choose life" has become the maxim of different organisations – not least the pro-life anti-abortion movement (God bless them). But its impact and implication is wide and appropriate to use every day in our Christian walk.

As Christians we have chosen life – and Life with a capital L. Abundant life, eternal life, the Jesus life. We must keep on choosing it and embracing the mindset that goes with it. Have a 'life' attitude.

Romans 8:28 (NKJV) says, "We know that all things work together for good to those who love God..." So let's get on with living life to the full.

The alternative choice has its own mindset and attitudes – we don't want to go there!

183

"I call heaven and earth as witnesses today against you, that I have set before you life and death, blessing and cursing; therefore choose life, that both you and your descendants may live; that you may love the LORD your God, that you may obey His voice, and that you may cling to Him, for He is your life and the length of your days; and that you may dwell in the land which the LORD swore to your fathers, to Abraham, Isaac, and Jacob, to give them."

Deuteronomy 13:19-20 (NKJV)

Yesterday we looked at the choice people have always had: to choose between life and death, between God's way and their own way. And we saw that choosing life is not only an action but an attitude.

Often people selfishly think that their choices are their own affair and that their beliefs and resultant lifestyle are nobody else's business. But that is where they are wrong. The seventeenth century poet John Donne famously wrote, "No man is an island." We do not exist sealed off from everyone around us; our choices have repercussions.

The Bible passage goes on to say, "…therefore choose life, that both you and your descendants may live…" The decision that we have taken to follow Christ affects everyone around us. Our behaviour is changed by our allegiance to and love for Jesus. Our descendants, starting with our children and grandchildren, are blessed because we walk with God; they have access to truth and a demonstration of faith because of us.

But it's not just that. Every single day we touch those around us – we touch them with our attitudes – even those we casually meet at the checkout or on the pavement. This is why it is important for us to "choose life" every day and to live out and radiate the Jesus life.

Today you will be life or death, blessing or curse to people you come into contact with, and at this time of lockdown with its super-sensitivity, mental health challenges and limited social contact, it is really vital that we bring Life and Blessing to those we *do* meet.

184

"I call heaven and earth as witnesses today against you, that I have set before you life and death, blessing and cursing; therefore choose life, that both you and your descendants may live; that you may love the LORD your God, that you may obey His voice, and that you may cling to Him, for He is your life and the length of your days; and that you may dwell in the land which the LORD swore to your fathers, to Abraham, Isaac, and Jacob, to give them."

Deuteronomy 13:19-20 (NKJV)

When we choose life, we choose love, we choose obedience and we choose closeness to God. In today's passage God is telling us that we must love Him, obey Him and cling to Him. It's quite an unusual word to use: "cling". It is translated from the Hebrew word *dawbak* which means 'to pursue and catch, to stick to and to be joined'.

A.W. Tozer wrote a Christian classic called *The Pursuit of God,* which I highly recommend, but we must not think of pursuing as a cat-and-mouse game where the cat might catch the mouse or it might not. *Dawbak* means 'to pursue and catch'. We have caught hold of God and He has caught hold of us; we must now hold on to His shirt-tails, as it were, and follow Him relentlessly.

We most often use the word 'cling' to describe a child who won't let their parent out of their sight. Have you had the experience of trying to drop a toddler off at kindergarten and having to peel them off you? No sooner do you get one hand dislodged than a leg wraps around you. The child is like an octopus. This is clingy, sticky human glue. Ruth is described with this very word as she refuses to be separated from Naomi.

Can you see what God is saying here? In the days in which we live it is imperative that we cling tightly to the Lord. Any degree of separation is one too many. We cannot allow anybody or anything to come between us and our Saviour. And while it is true that He holds us, it is our responsibility to stay close.

God will never try to prise us off Himself; it is the enemy who wants to do that. Make sure he doesn't get the chance. Cling to Jesus!

185

Love without hypocrisy. Abhor what is evil, cling to what is good.

Romans 12:9 (NASB)

We are talking about clingy Christianity! Yesterday we saw how God wants us to cling to Him. The New Testament re-emphasises this when Barnabas was sent to Antioch, where many Gentiles were being saved. He was commissioned to tell them to cling to Christ.[8] That's great advice.

Clinging to Christ involves clinging to something else too; today's verse tells us to "cling to what is good". Now there's a sermon!

Clinging is exclusive. By definition, you cannot cling to two things. To cling to one thing you have to let go of another thing. Again, I think of my little grandson who had to be peeled off my wife when he was delivered to kindergarten but then clung on to the teacher.

To cling to Christ and to what is good we have to abhor evil – let go of that which is not of Christ. When we first became believers, we had to let go of some pretty big stuff. Recently, we have seen several people delivered from drug addiction, for example, but as we progress in our Christian lives we still have to let go of what is evil to get a better hold of what is good, of Christ.

I could say with some certainty that everyone reading this today is struggling to let go of something. It may be a small something but if the Holy Spirit says, "Enough of that!" to you, you will have to let go. When you do, you will get closer to the Lord and you will experience blessing – both for your obedience and for removing something that came between you and Him.

Abhor what is evil. Cling to what is good.

---

[8] See Acts 11:22

186

I have chosen the way of truth, your judgments I have laid before me. I cling to your testimonies.

Psalm 119:30-31 (NKJV)

This week we have been talking about clingy Christianity and we have seen that the Bible tells us that we need to cling to God and cling to what is good. There is a third thing that we are instructed to cling to and we find that in today's verse. What does it mean? Does God have a testimony?! Well, yes, He does. He has a story of what He has done and it is all written down – the Bible. The Bible is God's testimony and we are told to cling to it.

The Word of God can mean two things: it can mean the Bible, but it can also mean Jesus – He is called the Word of God. This should tell us something about the Bible: we cannot have a fully functioning relationship with Jesus unless we have a functioning relationship with the Bible.

The Bible isn't just a storybook, it isn't just an instruction book, it isn't even just a holy book; it is a *living book*. And if something is living, it can give life too. The New International Version (NIV) of the Bible renders 2 Timothy 3:16 as, "All Scripture is God-breathed and is useful for teaching, rebuking, correcting and training in righteousness..." "God-breathed", often translated "inspired", is the literal and accurate translation of the Greek. But hold on a minute. When God created Adam out of the dust, how did He make him come alive? He breathed the breath of life into him and he became a living being. God's breath is the source of life.

When Jesus had risen from the dead and met the disciples once more, John says that He breathed on them and said, "Receive the Holy Spirit." (Jn.20:22, NKJV) That wasn't Pentecost, that was salvation. That's when they were born again and came alive to God.

Now, the Bible has that same capacity; God breathed it out and we can breathe it in and receive life, new life from Him. That is how salvation works, but we need to stay on that spiritual life support system, receiving the life-sustaining breath of God daily.

187

"Hear this, you kings! Listen, you rulers!
  I, even I, will sing to the Lord;
  I will praise the Lord, the God of Israel, in song."

Judges 5:3 (NIV)

A thousand years ago a Viking longship was sailing along the Cornish coast looking for settlements that they could go ashore and plunder. But when they came to the Isles of Scilly, just off Land's End, they got more than they bargained for.

In the ship was Olav Tryggvason, king of the Vikings. When the ship landed on Tresco, one of the islands, in 998, the king was greeted by monks of the priory that had been established there just fifty years before. We don't know exactly what transpired, but what we do know is that Tryggvason heard the good news about the Lord Jesus Christ and was so moved by the Holy Spirit that he knelt before the cross and gave his life to Him.

When the monks discovered he was a king, they realised that he could not be baptised by them or indeed by anyone except the primate of the land in his cathedral at Winchester. So they travelled together to Winchester where he received a king's baptism.

Now he was instructed in the faith and baptised, Tryggvason, or St. Olav as he was one day to become, set sail for his native Norway. This time he was taking home a treasure that far exceeded anything he had carried back before: the gospel.

The ship landed at Mosterhavn on the island of Bømlo (a place I have visited and preached many times) and Olav commanded all his subjects to become Christians, sharing the truths of the faith with them.

He didn't get everything right but he was the first to bring the Good News to Norway. Today you can see the oldest church in Norway at Mosterhamn, and Norway has enjoyed a thousand years of Christianity because of Olav Tryggvason, the missionary king!

188

And the boy Samuel ministered to the LORD...

1 Samuel 3:1 (BSB)

Let me ask you a question. What do you do in dark times when nothing seems to be happening? What do you do when there's no leadership and even heaven seems silent?

The Bible describes a time like this saying that the "word of the Lord" was rare and there "was no open revelation" (1.Sam.3:1, WYC). Corruption, sin and apathy had virtually closed everything down as far as the people of God were concerned, and the weird thing was, nobody seemed to care. Except, that is, for one little lad who can only have been ten or eleven years old. This young man was not satisfied. He wanted more. He wanted a living, vital relationship with God and believed that God wanted the same. He had been a miracle baby, and because of that his mother had dedicated the boy to God and, as soon as he was old enough, presented him to Eli the priest as a live-in helper. His name was Samuel.

Eli's place of worship, the tabernacle, was about the most uninspiring place you could find. Eli was old and virtually blind and his sons were stealing from the tabernacle and committing adultery with the women who served there. Grim. But young Samuel did not let any of this discourage him or dampen his enthusiasm to have a relationship with God. We can too easily be put off by what is going on around us, what other people are doing or aren't doing. And really, that is none of our business. Samuel wanted to get to know God personally and that's what mattered. That is always what matters.

The Bible says in 1 Samuel 3:1 (BSB), "...and the child ministered to the LORD before Eli." What a beautiful thing – the child ministered to the Lord. Do you know something? He was the only one doing it – maybe in the whole nation. But he was doing it. This is phase one in Samuel's secret of success – *he* ministered to the Lord. And we can employ this ourselves. It doesn't matter what other people are doing; we spend too much time and energy thinking about that. What are *you* doing? Samuel was ministering – he was a child but he was ministering. Serving, praying, singing, learning – doing things that pleased God and blessed God – that is ministering. Let's minister to God today.

189

One night Eli, whose eyes were becoming so weak that he could barely see, was lying down in his usual place. The lamp of God had not yet gone out, and Samuel was lying down in the temple of the LORD, where the ark of God was.

1 Samuel 3:2-3 (NIV)

Samuel was just a lad of ten or eleven when he decided that it didn't matter what everyone else was doing in the spiritually dark climate of the day, he was going to serve God. We can see the boy's devotion as he ministered to God in the tabernacle – the place of worship.

But look at today's verse; where did Samuel sleep? He slept in the temple, or holy of holies, where the ark of God was. Think about it. Think about everything you know about the ark of the covenant. That is where young Samuel chose to sleep. I don't think it was even allowed, but then, Eli the priest was almost blind.

Why in the world would Samuel sleep next to the ark of the covenant? Wouldn't it be spooky? Wouldn't it be dangerous? There is only one reason: that is where the presence of God was. In those days the manifest presence of God was in the holy of holies – more specifically, above the ark. This lad wanted to be as close to God as he could possibly get. I can read his mind: if God is going to show up, or speak or do anything, it's going to be here, so that's where I'm going to position myself. And as we know, it paid off.

This is phase two of Samuel's strategy: get as close to God as you can. Spiritual survival and success in dark times revolves around this.

The Bible says in James 4:8 (NASB), "Come close to God and He will draw close to you." You have to be intentional; you have to demonstrate your desire, your hunger, your longing for a closer walk with God.

Of course, we can't go and sleep in a church – God doesn't live in buildings any more anyway – but we can show Him our desire by spending time with Him in personal prayer and worship, in study and service, in being where He is – where His manifest presence is.

Collective worship is banned at the moment, but notice that private prayer isn't! Show God your heart for more of Him. Like young Samuel, get as close as you can and He will do the rest.

190

Now the LORD came and stood there calling as at the other times, "Samuel, Samuel."

1 Samuel 3:10 (NKJV)

If you are familiar with the story of Samuel, you will know that as the young lad slept next to the ark of the covenant, God spoke to him four times. The first three times he thought it was Eli calling him but then Eli realised that it must be God and told Samuel how to reply.

Notice what happened in today's verse. The Lord came and stood there. Now, when the Old Testament says something like this, we understand that it is a Christophany – an appearance of Jesus before He was born. Jesus is the only member of the Trinity that is able to come and stand. He is the part of the godhead that deals with people in this way.

So Jesus came and stood by Samuel and called him. His seeking had paid off. His hunger for God that made him sleep in the holy of holies was rewarded. He had drawn close to God and so God drew close to him.

But think about this. Three times Jesus had been there and Samuel didn't notice – he thought it was Eli the priest calling. I think this happens a lot. Jesus is right there and we don't realise it or recognise it. Jesus Himself said, "For where two or three are gathered together in My name, I am there in the midst of them." (Matt.18:20, NKJV)

People can go to church on a Sunday and go home again without acknowledging Jesus. People complain if nobody speaks to them, especially if the pastor doesn't greet them personally, but what about Jesus? What if nobody speaks to Him?! "I was there," He might say, "standing in the midst. You came in, you went out, you talked to everyone but you did not acknowledge Me."

I believe there are many times when Jesus is standing beside us and we don't realise it. But when we are in church, we know He is there – we must speak to Him, listen to Him, answer Him, worship Him personally.

Let's make this our practice.

191

Be doers of the word, and not hearers only. Otherwise, you are deceiving yourselves.

James 1:22 (BSB)

We have seen how Samuel ministered to the Lord when nobody else did, how he slept in the holy of holies to get close to God, and how because of that Jesus came and stood by him and spoke to him. How did he respond?

Well, he had to be taught how to respond. Eli the priest had obviously not forgotten everything he knew. He told young Samuel that if God spoke to him again, he should say, "Speak, Lord, your servant is listening." And so that is exactly what he did. And Jesus did speak to him.

Eli's advice was wise and we would do well to heed it. First of all, we need to hone our listening skills. Back in the nineties, my friend Matt and I wrote and ran a nine-hour course on effective listening skills which was taken up by a hundred and twenty churches around the UK. The first thing the course did was to show people what bad listeners they were.

Are we listening for God's voice? Are we hearing what He is saying to us? *Do* we remember what He has said? But the biggest question of all is, what do we do with what He says? There is a very important word in the answer Eli told Samuel to give: "servant". And I would say, God is not really interested in speaking to anybody unless that word is used. By saying "servant" you are telling God that what He says you will do.

Too often we want God to speak to us just for our own spiritual gratification – to give us a lift, a buzz, a blessing. Some people don't want God to speak because they are frightened what He might ask them to do! But God will speak to us if we are prepared to obey – to do what He asks of us.

God is a God of words. He does everything with words. Jesus is even called The Word! So if God is word-orientated, we should be listening-orientated.

192

Then Samuel told him everything, and hid nothing from him. And he said, "It is the LORD. Let Him do what seems good to Him."

1 Samuel 3:18 (NKJV)

The pre-incarnate Lord Jesus spoke to the boy Samuel at his bedside by the ark of the covenant. What He said was difficult – difficult to hear and difficult to do. He told Samuel that judgement was coming on Eli and his sons – on his sons because of their sins and on Eli for allowing it. The Lord told Samuel that he had to relay this to Eli.

All sorts of questions come into your mind; why ask a young boy to carry such a devastating message? Well, there is a simple answer to that: Samuel was the only one listening to God. But also, maybe it was a test to see if Samuel could be trusted to do this.

In the morning Eli asked Samuel what God had said. To his credit he told Samuel to give it to him straight. I think he knew what was coming. It says that Samuel was afraid to tell Eli but he did it. He told it like it was, hiding nothing, adding nothing – not wrapping it up or putting a spin on it, just faithfully conveying God's message.

This is an important message for the day in which we live. Sadly, people have played around with God's message to the human race – the gospel. They have added things to it and removed things from it. They have thought that this would make it more palatable, more acceptable, that it would help fill their churches and make them relevant. But the message of God is as unchangeable as God is Himself.

When Eli heard the message, he said, "It is the LORD." When people hear the true word of God, it always has a resonance, a ring of truth, a Holy Ghost stamp of approval – people know "it is the LORD".

Faithfulness is not just always being there; it is also conveying the truth of God in an unadulterated form.

193

So Samuel grew, and the LORD was with him and let none of his words fall to the ground. And all Israel from Dan to Beersheba knew that Samuel had been established as a prophet of the LORD. Then the LORD appeared again in Shiloh. For the LORD revealed Himself to Samuel in Shiloh by the word of the LORD. And the word of Samuel came to all Israel.

1 Samuel 3:19-4:1 (NKJV)

It is obvious that the Lord's hand was on Samuel from the beginning. He was Elkanah and Hannah's miracle baby and she dedicated the boy to God. But Samuel, too, made great choices, and pursued God even as child. We have seen how he ministered to the Lord, slept in the holy of holies, listened as a servant when Jesus came and stood by his bed, and faithfully carried the message of God.

What effect did all this have? Well, the prophecy that he brought to Eli and his sons came to pass. The Philistines invaded Israel and stole the ark of the covenant, which they kept for seven months. It brought such terrible trouble to the communities that housed it that they brought it back. Israel suffered for twenty years because of the Philistine invasion but during this time Samuel became a trusted and esteemed prophet. God used him to keep Israel focussed during this time.

At the end of the chapter we read today's lovely passage which tells us how God honoured Samuel. "None of his words fell to the ground." That is just about the best thing that could happen to a preacher or a prophet. Nothing they said was wasted. Every sermon hit the target. Every prophecy came to pass. God's Word was effective.

Every ministry is a partnership – we don't have to go it alone. It's not a do-it-yourself project! 2 Corinthians 6:1 says that we are co-workers with Christ. In Samuel's case God gave him what to say, he said it and then God took the words and, not letting them fall to the ground, disappear into the ether, go in one ear and out the other, made them find a home in people's hearts and minds.

We are co-workers with Christ; He gives us the words and if we are faithful with them, He will take them and make them count. We do what we can do and He does what we can't.

194

By God's grace and mighty power, I have been given the privilege of serving Him by spreading this good news.

Ephesians 3:7 (NLT)

Richard Wurmbrand was for many years the voice of the persecuted church. More recently, his bestselling book *Tortured for Christ* has been made into a film. He was born into a Jewish family in Romania in 1909. At an early age he became fascinated with the ideals of communism and so he went to Moscow to train as a Comintern agent. These agents were committed to bringing about revolution in their own countries and this is what Wurmbrand wanted to do. God, however, had other ideas. Six years before the Soviet invasion of Romania, Richard Wurmbrand was led to Jesus by a carpenter!

His life changed direction radically but he was still an activist! He set out to fearlessly and publicly oppose the communists in Romania in any way he could. By this time he had become an Anglican pastor.

His activities so annoyed the communist authorities that he was arrested and spent over eight years in prison, three of which were in solitary confinement in a permanently dark cell twelve feet underground. The sensory deprivation was made complete by the warders wearing felt shoes so there was no sound as well as no light. During this time Richard Wurmbrand spent his nights preaching sermons which he constructed each day. He found that he was also able to communicate with men in other cells by tapping out morse code on the pipework!

He was eventually released and forbidden to preach. He took no notice. Three years later he was arrested again and sentenced to twenty-five years. This time his punishment was torture. He writes in his book that one of the methods was to be beaten on the soles of his feet until all the skin was gone; the next day this was repeated until the bones were visible. In hideous amounts of pain he could no longer pray coherently so he put a prayer on his heartbeat, telling God that every time it beat, it would tell Him of Richard's love for Him.

Wurmbrand was released after five years following the payment of a $10,000 fee by a Norwegian mission.

As a lad of fifteen, having only been a Christian for a year, I had the privilege of meeting brother Wurmbrand at the Methodist Church in Truro. As he spoke, I remember wave after wave of emotion crashing over me. Some of the things he said have never left me. He said, "I would love to be able to stand up to preach to you tonight but have received so many beatings on the soles of my feet, I am unable to stand for too long."

What did meeting Richard Wurmbrand teach me? Well, many things, but above all else that our relationship with Christ is so precious and the imperative of preaching the gospel so important that no price is too high to pay for the privilege.

195

For with God nothing shall be impossible.

Luke 1:37 (NKJV)

Chris Panos is better known as 'God's Spy' after his autobiography of the same name became a global bestseller. I read it in 1981 and my life was never to be the same again. I had just entered full-time service as an evangelist but didn't have much idea where to start, when I somehow got a copy of it. When I had read it, the Lord clearly told me to telephone its author in Houston, Texas.

Chris Panos, a Greek American, has a story that would make anyone sit up and take notice. His worldwide exploits for God read like a Christian James Bond, with courageous forays into hostile territory behind the iron and bamboo curtains.

Chris had been a successful businessman in Houston when God spoke to him and called him to sell everything and become a preacher. He had no Bible school training but learnt to simply do what God told him to do and say what God told him to say. The Holy Spirit was then able to move him around the world at a moment's notice – political, spiritual and economic barriers disappearing as he walked in obedience. Brother Andrew wrote the foreword to *God's Spy* in recognition of Chris Panos' bible-smuggling successes, one of which was floating a million bibles up the Yangtze River in China!

He was used not only as a secret agent but as a Christian diplomat, meeting Mrs. Gandhi in India, Greek leader Archbishop Makarios and President George Bush.

Chris Panos is also known for huge crusade meetings, preaching to over two hundred thousand people in India on one occasion and leading over a million people to Christ in one year.

With a trembling hand I dialled the Panos number in Texas. I had never made an international telephone call before, let alone phoned anyone like this! To my surprise, Chris himself answered the call. I introduced myself and told him that his book had inspired me and that I had been called into God's work but had no idea of where to begin. He gave me one of the best pieces of advice I have ever had. He said, "David, all ministry is born in prayer and fasting. If you start fasting a day or two every week, God will tell you what to do." I did and God did!

On my first trip to the USA I arranged to meet Brother Panos. We met at a restaurant in the shadow of Houston Astrodome. The next time I visited America he invited me to stay at his home. He picked me up at the station in his shiny black Lincoln Continental. We arrived at his home to be greeted by his wife Ernestine. I found Chris always spoke his mind; he looked me up and down and said, "David, your clothes are garbage, come with me." He took me into his wardrobe and started pulling out his own suits. "You can have this one, and this and this..." When he finished, I had a suitcase full of designer suits, jackets and ties! "When you mix with influential people, you've got to look the part," he told me. And then he took me to the most exclusive restaurant in Houston, full of oilmen and politicians, one of whom had given him a charge card to use as he saw fit.

The next morning we had a prayer time. We marched up and down his lounge as he stormed heaven with his prayers. I had never heard anything like it!

What did I learn from Chris Panos? I learnt that nothing is impossible with God, no doors are closed if God wants to open them, and that if we will simply be obedient to the Holy Spirit's leading, we will succeed in a way that we never could by qualifications. One more thing: people won't mind you being direct as long as you have their best interests at heart and a generous spirit!

196

"Let your light so shine before men, that they may see your good works and glorify your Father in Heaven."

Matthew 5:16 (NKJV)

Arthur Blessitt has a whole page dedicated to him in the *2015 Guinness Book of Records* as he holds the record for the Longest Walk – forty thousand miles! However, he has not just been walking since 1969 but also caring a twelve-foot cross every step of the way!

Arthur was born in 1940 in Mississippi and grew up in Louisiana. He became a Christian at seven years old in an open air outreach meeting in a car park. When the Lord called him into the ministry, his father gave him some of the best advice I have ever heard to honour all men.[9] In the late sixties he found himself starting a Christian nightclub on Sunset Strip in Hollywood, reaching out to bikers, hippies and junkies. In 1969 God challenged him to take the large cross that he had made off the wall and start walking, carrying it. On Christmas Day, against doctors' advice as he had a brain aneurism, he set out carrying the cross from Los Angeles to Washington DC.

Along the way Arthur spoke to everyone he met and invariably led them to Christ. In fact, he testifies that he has led someone to the Lord every day of his life! In 1972 a film was made about him and it was while watching this film in the Methodist Church in Tintagel (January 1973) that I became a Christian.

Arthur has now carried the cross in every nation of the world and every populated island group. He has walked in Antarctica, North Korea,

---

[9] "Always let God fill your heart with love. Look at every person as though he were a member of your own family. Think of every man as your Father except that he may be lost and needs Jesus. Think of every woman as your Mother except that she could need Christ to change her life. Look at every boy and girl as your brother and sister and consider them as candidates for the Lord's blessings. Never insult a man or woman by look, word or gesture. Love everybody. The good have already earned your love. The bad may give you love when you least expect it. Don't look up at anyone, don't look down at anyone. Consider every woman a lady, every man a gentleman. If you do this you will never mistreat anyone or pass them by without telling them of God's power to save." Quoted from Arthur Blessitt (1971); *Turned On To Jesus.*

Yemen and though fifty-four war zones. He has been kidnapped, arrested multiple times (most times in the USA) and even stood in front of a firing squad! He has met and prayed with many world leaders, including Yasser Arafat during the civil war in Beirut.

There are obviously so many stories to tell that I cannot do justice to them here, but Arthur has written several books. (I recommend his first: *Turned On To Jesus.*) An amazing documentary film was made about his life in 2009 which was released in cinemas across America and is available on DVD now.

The first Christian book I read was *Turned On To Jesus* and it really set the pace for my Christian life. Ten years later I was to meet Arthur personally in Bristol. I heard that he was going to be speaking in a church in that city as part of a major outreach and so I decided to go and meet him and thank him for all that the Lord had done in my life through him. I wrote to him and told him I would come.

I arrived at the church early and told the pastor that I had come to meet Arthur. He showed me to the door of the vestry where he said Arthur was praying before the meeting. I opened the door but the room was empty. I looked again and then I saw him; he was prostrate on the floor, praying! I gave a little cough and said, "Hello, I'm David Flanders." He leapt to his feet said, "David!" and threw, his arms around me in a big Christian man-hug. It was one of the best moments of my life.

What have I learnt from Arthur Blessitt? Well, he is one of the most personable people I have ever met; he doesn't have to say anything, Jesus shines from his face and his smile could melt icebergs! I learnt from him that your face is your biggest billboard; you don't need T-shirts, badges, crosses, dog-collars; your face should say it all. Through him (and his dad) I learnt that you have to earn the right to talk to people about Jesus by the way you speak to them and treat them.

Arthur is a true pioneer and he is still walking!

197

Humble yourself before the Lord, and He will lift you up.

James 4:10 (NIV)

David Wilkerson was one of the most significant Christian leaders of the twentieth century. His story began the year I was born, when he moved to New York to try to reach the notorious drug-fuelled gangs causing mayhem on the city's streets. He was a fairly naive country preacher, but motivated by the love of God, he confronted the gangs and their leaders. When threatened with a switchblade, he spoke the famous words, "You can cut me up into a thousand pieces and lay them in the street, but every piece will still I love you."

The first blockbuster Christian film *The Cross and the Switchblade* was based on the great story of how David Wilkerson won these gangs (including Nicky Cruz) for Christ.

My life had been profoundly influenced by this film and the book. Wilkerson had become one of the most well-known Christian leaders in the world and founder of the Teen Challenge drug rehab ministry by the time I came into the ministry. When I was invited to New York as a guest at a missions conference, my first thought was maybe I could visit David Wilkerson's church in Times Square.

I absconded from the conference with a couple of friends one evening and made my way to the church. I sat in the converted theatre waiting for the service to begin. When an insignificant little guy came on to give the announcements, including a few thoughts on litter around the church, I took the opportunity of speaking to the huge black guy sitting next to me.

"When is Brother Wilkerson going to come on?" I asked.

He looked incredulously at me though the half-light of the theatre.

"What do you mean, sir?" he asked. "That's him!"

"Thank you," I answered sheepishly.

It was not that I had never seen a picture of him or that I was expecting Pat Boone (who had played him in the film); it was that I didn't expect him to come onto the platform with no fanfare and to talk about litter. He seemed more like the janitor than the pastor. After the service I was privileged to go backstage, shake his hand and have a short conversation with the great man.

What did I learn from meeting David Wilkerson? That God gives grace to the humble. Here was one of the foremost Christian leaders in the world but he came over as just an ordinary man. Not even litter was beneath him, and more to the point, neither was I!

Whatever our achievements, notoriety or the accolades given to us, God still expects humility from us. I have noticed this in all the great men and women of God I have met. That is why they are great!

198

And He said to them, "Go into all the world and preach the gospel to every creature."

Mark 16:15 (NKJV)

R.W. Schambach was known as the last great American tent evangelist. He was saved on a street corner in his native Philadelphia listening to a street preacher. After serving in the U.S. Navy during WW2 he spent five years working alongside 'God's General' A.A. Allen whose tent meetings across America were legendary.

Schambach went on to form his own ministry which used the same strategy of mass meetings across the U.S. and around the world, bringing hundreds of thousands to Christ and seeing people healed on a daily basis.

I first heard of R.W., as he was affectionately called, when browsing Finn Arne Lauvaas' huge audio library in Skudeneshavn, Norway. I copied every tape he had by the great preacher and listened time and again to each. I was so encouraged, my faith was boosted and my own preaching enhanced; R.W. was evangelism personified and I loved it! Over the years, whenever I was down or discouraged, I would get a Schambach tape out.

In 1998, on one of my annual trips to Houston, Texas, this time with my daughter Joanna, a pastor arranged for me to visit Lakewood Church. I don't know what my friend said to Lakewood, but when we arrived we were told we were guests of honour and shown to the roped-off GOH section of the huge auditorium, in front of the platform. Early in the service the Guests of Honour were introduced and asked to stand as our name was called. I wept as I heard who else was in that section. I turned to Joanna and whispered, "You have no idea what company you are in; these people are responsible for millions coming to Christ." Then I heard the last name called: R.W. Schambach! My heart leapt. I couldn't believe it. God had arranged for me to meet one of my heroes.

A little later in the service there was a prayer time and people were asked to come to a certain part of the auditorium to be prayed for. I said to Joanna, "I'm going to get Schambach to pray for me!" And I left my seat. I walked the five or six rows forward and approached him. As I got close, a burly man intercepted me. "What do you want?" he asked.

"I want Brother Schambach to pray for me," I answered.

He bent over and spoke to R.W. who nodded and rose from his seat. I told him how God had blessed my life through his ministry (with the above details) and that I would really like him to pray for me.

He smiled and, in his usual style, grabbed my head and nearly pulled it off my shoulders! "Dear God!" he began his usual shouted/screamed prayer, and God's power began to flow.

After the meeting we were invited to meet Pastor Joel and the whole Osteen family but that was nothing compared to what had happened to me earlier. When we got back to Dale Dailey's house, we had another surprise. The service had been shown live on TV and they had recorded it. I had been unaware that a TV camera had come and recorded my encounter with R.W. and it had been transmitted! I still have the video.

What did I learn from R.W. Schambach? I learnt that the gift of 'evangelist' is an extremely powerful tool in God's hands. Maybe that's because winning the lost is so close to God's heart. The shame is that there are so few seeking that gift these days.

199

So we make it our aim to please Him, whether we are at home in the body or away from it.

2 Corinthians 5:9 (NIV)

Reinhard Bonnke will go down in history as one of the greatest evangelists that has ever lived. Certainly the numbers of people that he has preached to would be rivalled only by Billy Graham. He was born in Königsberg, Germany in 1940, the son of a soldier. When he was nine he gave his life to Christ at his mother's knee and soon after received a call to preach!

Bonnke attended Bible school in Wales. A remarkable thing happened when he went looking for the veteran evangelist George Jefferies in London. The aged man asked him in and prayed for him, passing on his mantle. The very next day he went home to heaven. After pastoring a church back in Germany for seven years he felt a strong call to Africa. He joined a missionary society and was sent to work in Lesotho. God had bigger things for Reinhard than that posting though. He began to feel confined by the organisation and sank into depression because of the meagre results he was seeing. At this time God gave him a dream on four consecutive nights: he saw a map of Africa covered in the blood of Jesus and heard the message, "Africa shall be saved!"

Believing wholeheartedly that the Lord was calling him to a different kind of evangelism, he resigned from the Mission. This was not popular with his bosses and one in particular tore him to pieces! Nevertheless he bought an eight-hundred-seater tent and took it on the road.

Immediately he began to see much greater results and needed bigger and bigger tents! This culminated in Bonnke commissioning a thirty-four-thousand-seater tent – which was the world's largest mobile structure. However, after very little use the tent was destroyed by a storm. It was then that Bonnke decided to forget tents and go fully 'open air', and right away the numbers grew to over 150,000 people a night!

The phrase "From Cape Town to Cairo, Africa shall be saved" became Reinhard Bonnke's battle cry, and for over thirty years that is exactly what has happened: over seventy-nine million recorded decisions (worldwide), as well as similar numbers of healings and deliverances across the continent. I have no doubt that Reinhard Bonnke's ministry is largely responsible for turning the 'dark continent' into arguably the most Christian continent.

I met Brother Reinhard when our group of churches invited him to do a one-night outreach in Torquay. During the day there were seminars and the rally was in the evening. I was inspired by the teaching in the afternoon which was about Elisha being apprentice to Elijah and receiving Elijah's 'mantle' by sticking close by him.

The theatre was so packed in the evening that bus-loads that had come from as far away as Birmingham could not get in. We made a little extra room by us pastors sitting on the stage. As brother Bonnke took the stage, he shook hands and greeted us all. After he had preached he invited the sick to come forward for prayer. Many did, including one or two pushed out in hospital beds. As he left the platform with his assistants to pray for the sick, I followed on. When he prayed for people, I joined in. None of the other pastors had come. After a few minutes he turned around and said to me, "Brother, what are you doing here?" To which I replied, "Just doing what I was taught to do this afternoon and sticking close to the man of God!" What could he say? He just smiled and let me carry on.

What have I learnt from Reinhard Bonnke? As well as 'if you teach people to do something, you shouldn't be surprised if they do it', I have learnt that organisations can sometimes restrict the ministry that God has given us – we need to be careful of that and to obey God regardless. People don't see us or know us the way God does, and only He knows the true purpose He has for us and so only He can tell us that purpose.

200

...your rod and your staff, they comfort me.

Psalm 23:4 (NIV)

In these difficult days we are living in, people are looking for a little comfort – not the easy chair or warm bed kind of comfort but reassurance for the soul.

Psalm 23 tells us, "...your rod and your staff, they comfort me." Admittedly, sticks are not the first thing I think of when I want to be comforted. So, what does this mean? This statement is still against the background of "Though I walk through the valley of the shadow of death"; it goes on to say, "I will fear no evil for you are with me; your rod and your staff, they comfort me." (v.4, NIV)

The greatest comfort possible, the best comfort available to a human being, is the presence of God – "You are with me." If God is with us – not in a general way but in a specific way because we have invited His presence – then we need fear nothing, least of all death itself. But how is He with us? It is His Holy Spirit who abides with us and in us, and He is called the Comforter. If you are believer I'm sure you have experienced the comfort of the Holy Spirit. I know I did in a big way when I was in hospital last year.

But where do the rod and the staff come in? To find out we must think of the shepherd. "The Lord is my Shepherd," the psalm begins, and Jesus said that we are His sheep. Sheep don't need to be afraid when the shepherd is around, and the Middle Eastern shepherd had two tools of the trade: a rod, called a *shaybet;* and a staff, called a *mishaynaw.*

The rod was a short stout stick with a knob on the end that hung from the shepherd's belt. We would call it a shillelagh. This was a weapon. It was used for defending the sheep against wild animals and more likely against thieves. The sheep were safe with a shillelagh-wielding shepherd.

The staff was a long, thin stick, sometimes with a crook on the end. This was used on the sheep to protect them from themselves, if you like – to guide and to herd them.

The rod and the staff in Psalm 23 are pictures of the ministry of the Holy Spirit's work in our lives – the comforter. We will explore this further tomorrow.

201

'I am the good shepherd. The good shepherd lays down his life for the sheep.'

John 10:11 (NIV)

This week we are looking at the verse in Psalm 23 that says, "Even though I walk through the valley of the shadow of death I will fear no evil for you are with me, your rod and your staff they comfort me."

When I was a little boy in Sunday school, I remember there was a large framed picture of Jesus on the wall. It was a lovely picture but the impression of Jesus it gave me was that He was a bit of a cissy. The prayer my mum used to pray with me when I went to bed was, "Gentle Jesus, meek and mild..." – this reinforced that image.

When I came to know Jesus personally, I found that was only one side of His character. I discovered Jesus was a fighter. I found that He was the bravest, strongest, most resolute man that had ever lived. And what is He fighting for? He is fighting for you – and me.

Yesterday we saw that the rod mentioned in the 23rd Psalm refers to a shillelagh, a fighting stick or truncheon that the shepherd used to defend the sheep. We need fear no evil because Jesus is fighting for us – fighting to defend His sheep; fighting to protect us from that which would steal, kill and destroy; fighting because we are precious to Him.

Why are we so valuable to Jesus? Because we cost Him everything. He fought for us and won. The greatest fight in history was waged on the cross. Jesus fought for us with every ounce of strength He had. He shed His blood and in death won the victory, setting us free from the clutches of evil. There is no doubt that Jesus is a fighter. The implication of today's passage is that the good shepherd fights, and fights to the death, for the sheep.

And guess what? He is still fighting for us. The Holy Spirit has been sent to us to defend us and protect us. He is the One who comes alongside. Jesus said, "I will ask the Father and He will give you another advocate to help you and to be with you forever." (Jn.14:16, NIV) Do you know what an advocate is? Someone who fights for you.

202

[Jesus said,] "Behold, I have given you authority to tread on serpents and scorpions, and over all the power of the enemy, and nothing shall hurt you."

Luke 10:19 (ESV)

We have already seen that the rod – *shebet* or *matteh* in Hebrew – was a short, stout fighting stick that hung from a shepherd's belt. This humble instrument was to have regal connotations as it became over the years a symbol of power and authority. The rod – a stick with a knob on the end – was to be cast in metal and become the sceptre, a part of a monarch's paraphernalia. We see this demonstrated in the story of Esther where Xerxes had a golden sceptre, and today the Queen's sceptre is one of the crown jewels – the Koh-i-Nor at its head being the largest diamond in the world but topped with a jewel-encrusted cross recognising the supreme authority of God.

But let's get back to the Bible. Remember Aaron's rod. That is where all this started. That rod became a symbol of power and authority in the hands of Moses. It showed Pharaoh and everyone else that God was with Moses. It was not just human power and authority that it symbolised but spiritual. It was the rod of God.

Now in Psalm 23 it tells us that we need not fear evil, even in the valley of the shadow of death, because God is with us and His rod and His staff comfort us. Do you begin to see the significance? We can relax and rest easy even in the darkest days because of His power and authority! The rod speaks. It says – however big the problem, however strong the demon, however bleak the prognosis, however bad the news – *God trumps the lot!* His power is supreme, He is in charge, and if you are on His side, you win! End of...

Friends, we can endure a lot if we know that eventually we win. But more than that, we can live in the victory now. The wonderful thing is – and it's almost too wonderful to grasp – that the Lord Jesus Christ has chosen to share His authority with us, to put a rod in our hands, as we saw in today's verse.

203

All we like sheep have gone astray, we have turned every one to our own way.

Isaiah 53:6 (NKJV)

The shepherd's staff was long and thin, sometimes with a crook on the end, sometimes a simple wispy stick. It had many uses as a tool of the shepherd's trade, one of which was rescue. The crook is designed to fit around a sheep's neck so that it can be pulled away from danger.

Again I can remember in our Sunday school room when I was small, there was a framed picture on the wall of Jesus the shepherd with His crook, leaning over a cliff edge rescuing a sheep. It might have been the painting 'The Lost Sheep' by Alfred Soord. As a boy, I had no idea that the sheep represented me. I had no idea that I needed rescuing – but I did, we all do.

When I was fourteen, I was suddenly confronted with the realisation that I was lost, and it was a shock. You know, sheep don't realise that they are lost until it's too late. They don't set out to get lost any more than we do. They are just so focussed on eating grass, their eyes are blind to where they are going. Around here on the North Cornwall coast, sheep often have to be rescued from the cliffs because in pursuit of the next clump of grass they walked off the cliff. Then they are stuck on a ledge and there they would stay unless help came.

No wonder Jesus compared human beings to sheep. That sounds just like us – that was me at fourteen. Very often the valley of the shadow of death is somewhere we took ourselves. I have met so many people stuck in a predicament of their own making.

Jesus, though, is the Good Shepherd, and we do not have to fear because He has a staff, a method of rescue designed to fit us. Two thousand years ago Jesus died on the cross to affect our rescue.

What a comfort to know that Jesus has a rescue plan for us. Don't try to save yourself – surrender to Him!

204

Even though I walk through the valley of the shadow of death I will fear no evil for you are with me, your rod and your staff they comfort me.

Psalm 23:4 (BSB)

The staff that King David talks about here is the stick the shepherd used for managing his sheep. Yesterday we heard about how he rescues the sheep; today we look at herding the sheep. Sheep are not the most compliant of animals – that's why you need a sheepdog! But there's no evidence to suggest that they had sheepdogs in Bible days.

The shepherd usually led the sheep. They learnt to follow him because he always took them to good places to eat and drink – but there is always one that needs some persuasion. Sheep bruise very easily so you have to be gentle with them. Therefore the shepherd would use his staff to give them a gentle prod.

The psalm is, of course, referring to us as sheep and God as the shepherd. Do you ever need a gentle prod? I do.

In the Bayeux Tapestry, which depicts the Norman conquest of Britain in 1066, there is a picture of King Harold prodding one of his soldiers in the back with his sword. Underneath are the words "King Harold comforteth his troops". 'Comfort' can mean 'encourage' as well as 'sympathise'.

God uses the staff of the Holy Spirit to encourage us, to motivate us, to say, "Come on, let's get to it!" When this pandemic is over, God's people are going to need a lot of prodding, I think!

God also uses the cattle prod of the Holy Spirit on those that He is herding towards salvation. Remember Jesus' first words to Paul on the road to Damascus: "It is hard for you to kick against the goads." (Acts.26:14, NIV)

When the Holy Spirit prods, you don't kick against it. Respond to it, move in the direction that God wants you to go. It's the best kind of motivation there is!

205

"However when He, the Spirit of truth, has come, He will guide you into all truth…"

John 16:13 (NKJV)

Yesterday we spoke about the shepherd's staff being a motivator and how the Holy Spirit motivates us and gets us going. Once we are motivated into action, God has to steer us in the right direction. Can you imagine a Bible shepherd walking along a path with his sheep? Sheep are prone to wander and some sheep (known around here as 'breakers') seem determined to leave the flock and go it alone. The Bible shepherd would reach out with his staff at the first sign of one of his sheep leaving the flock and the path, and nudge it back in.

The Holy Spirit is God's staff of guidance for us. He has many, many ways of nudging us back onto the right path: reminding us of what Jesus said; illuminating a scripture; preaching; prophecy; words of knowledge; conviction of the heart; and so on.

Guidance seems to be a perennial problem for Christians, which is strange seeing God has so many ways of doing it! I think, as a pastor (which is Latin for 'shepherd'), it is not that God cannot make Himself clear but that His sheep don't like what they hear. Sheep, after all, have their own agenda.

What we must realise is that Jesus is a good shepherd. He never takes the sheep anywhere that is not good for them. He laid down His life for the sheep so He must have our best interests at heart. We belong to Him; we are the sheep of His pasture; we must follow. Like Peter said, "…to whom shall we go?" (Jn.6:68, NIV)

I have found in nearly fifty years of following Him that His way is the best way.

Do yourself a favour and trust the Shepherd. Follow Him.

MONDAY, 30TH NOVEMBER, 2020

"I tell you the truth, anyone who will not receive the kingdom of God like a little child will never enter it."

Mark 10:15 (NIV)

I often hear people say, "Oh, to be young again…" or, "It's no joke getting old." Did you know that the Bible contains the secret of eternal youth? Well, it's true, and it doesn't suggest a trip to Shangri-La!

Most believers know the verse in Psalm 103 that says that "your youth is renewed like the eagle's" (Ps.103:5, NIV). There is a lot more to this than meets the eye, and Psalm 103 has the key. But let me just ask you: do you really want to be young again or to be eternally young?

Youth has its own issues – it is not the best time of your life, as most teenagers would agree. And do you think that the Bible is promising some kind of a beauty therapy to get rid of wrinkles, hair loss and snoring? Obviously not.

So, what is it about God's promise of a restored youth that is so appealing? Well, age can be the enemy of faith, as we see in today's verse, spoken by Jesus.

Childlike faith. Jesus is not saying you have to become a child or that adults can't have that kind of simple, trusting faith. He is saying that grown-ups need to have faith *like* a child. The older we grow, the more the enemies of faith start invading our thinking: cynicism, prejudice, worldly wisdom, common sense, fear of failure and stuck-in-your-ways-ness.

This is why the most common age statistically for someone to become a Christian is thirteen, and it gets progressively harder to win someone to Christ the older they get.

But what if you are a Christian? Do the enemies of faith I have mentioned affect us? Yes they do, and that is why God wants to renew your youth – to give them their marching orders!

207

Praise the LORD, O my soul; all my inmost being, praise his holy name.
Praise the LORD, O my soul, and forget not all his benefits – who forgives
all your sins...

Psalm 103:1-3 (NIV)

Whilst the Bible does not say that God will get rid of your wrinkles or hair loss, it does say that He will renew your youth! Quite something! How old is old? People say different things. Some say you are as old as you feel, others say age is only a number. There is no doubt though that if you perceive yourself to be old, it will have a big effect on your faith and your service to God. Of course, in the light of eternity we are all just babies!

When we give our lives to Jesus, He promises to renew our youth. How is this possible; how does He do it? The verses above that lead up to this amazing promise in Psalm 103 give us the answer.

The first step in our rejuvenation comes through forgiveness. Sin is the original ager. It was only because of sin that Adam began to age. All around us we can see the aging effects of sin in people's lives – even written on their faces. Apart from the aging effects of drugs, alcohol, nicotine and gluttony there are aging consequences from less obvious sources.

Guilt is an ager and so is worry. They can trigger diseases like diabetes and can even cause tooth decay. Guilt causes sleeplessness and that has a knock-on effect, not only to our physical wellbeing but also our mental health. People often turn to drink and drugs to self-medicate – to give them respite from their guilt and worry.

But Jesus' solution is much better: be forgiven. When you repent of your sins and ask God to forgive you, something happens that is almost indescribable. That weight that you were carrying suddenly lifts. It takes many people by surprise. It can even be a physical sensation.

Without guilt and worry in your life you will not only feel younger, you will *look* younger too!

God promises, "...your youth is renewed as the eagle's..." and it's true.

208

Praise the LORD, O my soul; all my inmost being, praise his holy name. Praise the LORD, O my soul, and forget not all his benefits – who forgives all your sins and heals all your diseases ... so that your youth is renewed like the eagle's.

Psalm 103:1-3,5 (NIV)

My wife and I had a fantastic time when we visited Israel. There was a problem though. My digestive system rebelled, with the usual consequences and a lot of pain. I had to resist the wonderful hotel food and eat plainly. I had suffered with IBS for many years and had been taking tablets every day.

Towards the end of the trip we visited a congregation on Mount Carmel for their main service of the week – it happened my old friend Eric Benson was preaching. At some point in the meeting someone said, "I want to pray for the sick. Everybody put your hand on the part of your body that needs healing." This is quite a common practice, for those of you who don't know. I put my hand on my side where the pain always was. The person on the platform prayed for healing.

Later that day I realised that I hadn't had any symptoms – I stopped taking the tablets. The next day was the same and the day after that. Now, eighteen months later, I have never had the pain or any of the other symptoms – praise the Lord! I was healed on Mount Carmel!

It is a fact that illness and disease has an ageing effect on the human body. Even comparatively mild but persistent illnesses like IBS can get you down and induce premature aging. I can testify that God has healed me on many occasions and we see people healed in our church on a regular basis. Our oldest member went for an operation to remove a tumour in her bladder a few months ago. When she got into the hospital, the surgeon scratched his head and said, "Why are you here?" Following prayer the tumour had vanished.

Part of God's youth-restoring package is healing – believe me, it's real!

209

...who redeems your life from the pit...

Psalm 103:4 (NIV)

We are looking this week at God's promise to renew our youth in Psalm 103. We have seen so far that forgiveness of sin and healing are both ways in which our youth can be renewed. We need that spiritual and mental youthfulness to stave off the very negative effects that we can be prone to as we get older.

Today we are looking at verse 4. "The pit" literally means 'grave'. He buys you back from the grave. Amazing! So many of us are in an early grave in our thinking. Some are so afraid of everything, they see disaster everywhere.

Let me ask you a question: why do we send young people to fight our wars? The answer: because young people see no danger, have less fear and are not so prone to worry.

Alex Quinn, a young friend and member of our church, is a racing driver. In fact, he came fifth in the Formula Renault Eurocup Championships in Europe this year, which is usually a stepping stone to Formula 1. Alex's dad was a racing driver too but in rallying. However, now he cannot be a passenger in a car that Alex is driving around a circuit – he can't handle it.

God often requires of us courage, boldness, fearlessness in our Christian walk, but age militates against them. We get wary of dangerous situations, frightened to step out in faith, worried about change. I catch myself sometimes thinking the thoughts of the aged, seeing myself in an early grave! I need my youth renewed. I need it renewed so I can be brave.

One of the best examples of this was Jack Mitchell. He was the first man of God to have an influence on my life when I was a little boy. Jack lived into his nineties, and I asked his son David (also a pastor) one day, "Does your dad take any meetings these days?" "Yes," David answered, "but only youth meetings!" That's what you call renewed youth!

Most of our fears and worries are imagined. The sixteenth century French philosopher Michel de Montaigne famously said of worry, "My life has been full of terrible misfortunes most of which never happened."

Let God renew your youth – we need to be brave.

210

...who redeems your life from the pit and crowns you with love and compassion...

Psalm 103:4 (NIV)

In Psalm 103 we are told the things that God does in us so that our youth can be renewed – and it needs to be renewed because age is an enemy of faith. Over the last few days we have seen what God needs to remove from us. Today we see what He needs to add to us to complete this process.

"...crowns your life with love and compassion..." My goodness, that sounds wonderful, doesn't it? We might say, "And to top it all He gives us love and compassion," but the Hebrew word used for "crown" here also means 'to surround' (as in, a crown surrounds your head).

This is saying to us that God extends love and compassion towards us and fills us with love and compassion too. We need that. As we get older, we can get more crochety, less patient with people, more critical. Because we become set in out ways, we start to think that we are right and everybody else is wrong. We can have the attitude, "You made your bed, now you must lie in it." We need an injection of love and compassion. Our attitudes need rejuvenating.

You never saw an old person stamp their feet and say, "It's not fair," did you? The young have a sense of fairness, an idealism about the world, a belief that it can be a better place. Old folk tend to be world-weary and resigned to the status quo.

We often lose sight of the fact that Jesus was a young man. We are called to be like Jesus. That means we have to have His attitudes and His outlook (which incidentally never change). If Jesus lives in you, then everything you need you already have; it's just a question of moving aside and letting His youthful mindset and demeanour shine through – a mindset, a heart-set, of love and compassion.

God has been doing this work in me over the last year or so and I'm so glad.

211

...who satisfies your mouth with good things so that your youth is renewed like the eagle's.

Psalm 103:5 (NIV)

We have seen that God will remove from us things that make us age, like sin and sickness. Also, that if we are to be youthful, we need to deal with fear and worry in our lives and allow God to give us courage and boldness though the Holy Spirit. Yesterday we saw that our attitudes need to be rejuvenated too.

There's an unusual turn of phrase in today's verse: "who satisfies your mouth". That is the way the King James Bible renders this. Let me ask you a question: what are the two things that we put in our mouths? Yes, food and words. One goes in and the other comes out.

If we feed on the good things that God provides, we will be satisfied. This will be at a deep level. The aching void within us, the search for significance, the longing for reality will be met. This is one of the most fundamental keys to happiness and lightness of Spirit – to be content, satisfied. Paul said, "Now godliness with contentment is great gain." (1.Tim.6:6, NKJV) We can only truly rest when we are content. We need to learn that.

But what about the other thing in our mouths – our words? Just as what goes in must be of God, what comes out should be of God as well. The Bible goes to great lengths to tell us how important what we say is. One such is, "Let no corrupt word proceed out of your mouth, but what is good for necessary edification, that it may impart grace to the hearers." (Eph.4:29, NKJV)

But what we say is also important for us personally – it not only *reflects* our attitude but *affects* our attitude too. The Bible says we should "encourage ourselves in the Lord"; we should speak life, speak positively and not negatively, and the best thing of all, speak the Word of God.

Old people say, "It can't be done." Young people say, "I can do that." Old people talk about the past. Young people talk about the future. Hmm... What about you?

212

And he stretched it out, and his hand was restored as whole as the other.

Mark 3:5 (NKJV)

I don't know about you but I am always losing things, usually my keys! But some of us have lost things that are a lot more important and significant than that – things that change our lives, things that cripple us and make us less than we were and less than we could be.

The story of Jesus is the story of restoration. He is able to intervene in our lives and to restore what we have lost. He is very good at it.

In Mark's Gospel we read a touching story about a man who had a withered hand. It was unusable and useless. Jesus saw him one day in the synagogue, standing near the back hiding himself and his disability as usual. But Jesus called him forward. Then Jesus said the worst thing that He could possibly say: "Stretch out your hand." I wouldn't mind guessing that the man was tempted to hold out his good hand! But he knew what Jesus meant. In that simple act of obedience, he was healed. Jesus restored the lost use of the hand – a miracle, life-changing, wonderful; praise the Lord!

But hold on a minute. If we are not careful, we will miss something here. Read it again: "...and his hand was restored as whole as the other." It became like the other one, his 'good' hand. You see, I went to school with a boy who had lost his hand in a tragic accident. But what happened was that his remaining hand became a super-hand. He was top of the class in woodwork and metalwork and he could swim better than anyone I knew; in fact, Nicky would swim out to sea harpooning fish. That's what often happens. The other hand compensates and becomes a super-hand. Well, in this story Jesus made the man's crippled hand "as whole as the other", just like it. He walked away with two super-hands! I would love to know what that man did with those hands!

The point here is that when Jesus restores something, He doesn't just put it back as it was; He makes it better than it was, better than it ever could have been.

When we take something to Jesus to be restored, even our very lives, He makes it better than it ever could have been.

213

Therefore, if anyone is in Christ, he is a new creation; old things have passed away; behold, all things have become new.

2 Corinthians 5:7 (NKJV)

Mary Magdalene was one of Jesus' devoted followers. We don't know exactly when she met Him but we do know the circumstances. In Luke 8 we read that He had cast seven demons out of her. She must have come to Jesus in distress and asked to be set free. You don't become the home of seven demons by playing tiddlywinks; her life must have been in a real mess, and the activities that she had been involved in would have been either very evil or very sinful.

When God was thinking about who to use to be the first person to see the risen Lord Jesus on resurrection day, He chose Mary. *Boom* – that is restoration! Do you remember yesterday I said that when God restores something, He makes it better than it ever could have been? Mary Magdalene was not just forgiven and set free, but her innocence was restored.

Restored innocence. I have seen the most remarkable things in my life – remarkable restoration in people's lives.

My old friend John, on his search for the truth, had read so widely about alternative religions and philosophies that he was a walking encyclopaedia on everything from the Bhagavat Gita to I Ching. Then one day he was wonderfully saved. Jesus came into his life and changed everything. People at work still asked him questions about those false religions but he found he couldn't answer them. God had wiped his memory; it was all gone, his innocence had been restored.

I held the hands of a sixteen-year-old murderer in Exeter prison as he wept and repented of his sin and was born again. He was still guilty of the crime but his innocence was restored. A male prostitute and heroin addict who had seen it all in Malta ran to the front of the marquee to be saved – his innocence was restored.

I could go on.

It is so wonderful to see innocence restored. People think they have to live with what they have done and pay for it with their guilt, shame and fear for the rest of their lives. They don't; Jesus is still in the restoration business.

214

Peter replied, "Even if all fall away on account of you, I never will." "I tell you the truth," Jesus answered, "this very night, before the cock crows, you will disown me three times."

Matthew 26:33-34 (BSB)

His disciple Peter always seemed to be getting it wrong. Sometimes it was out of enthusiasm, sometimes he just did things his own way. The most well-known failure was when he denied knowing Jesus not once but three times, and to make it worse, Jesus had predicted it publicly.

It was at the end of the Last Supper meal that Peter had proclaimed the words in today's verse. Peter felt sure in himself that this would never happen – he even tried to prove it by attacking one of the men arresting Jesus in the garden and cutting off his ear with a sword. But before the night was over he did deny Jesus and everyone knew he did. At that moment Peter, the apparent leader of the disciples, lost his credibility. He had failed miserably, even when he had been warned.

Put yourself in Peter's shoes. He was not only utterly miserable and angry with himself for his failure, but so ashamed and embarrassed at his loss of credibility. How could his friends ever respect him again?

Actually, we don't really have to think too hard about this to empathise with Peter because we have all been there. We have all let Jesus down. We have all denied Him by not speaking up when we should have or by saying or doing things that made a nonsense of our pledge of allegiance to Him.

But something happened. Following the resurrection Jesus met the disciples by the sea. He cooked them breakfast and then, after that meal, He turned to Peter and asked him, "Do you love me more than these?" "Yes, Lord," Peter said, "you know that I love you." Jesus said, "Feed my lambs." Three times Jesus asked him, three times Peter replied yes, and Jesus assigned him the duty of feeding His sheep – teaching the others, leading them. Jesus had restored his credibility and done it before his peers – He did it beautifully.

If we lose our credibility, it is a mistake to try to get it back ourselves. If we just keep on loving and serving Jesus, He will restore it and do it beautifully.

215

And Jesus said to him, "Today salvation has come to this house, because he also is a son of Abraham; for the Son of Man has come to seek and to save that which was lost."

Luke 19:9-10 (NKJV)

We have seen how Jesus restored a man's hand and made it better than it had ever been, how Mary Magdalene had her innocence restored and Peter his credibility as a leader. Today we look at someone who had lost his reputation.

Zacchaeus was one of the most selfish people Jesus met. His love of money had turned him into a cheat, a thief and an extortioner. Money had certainly not bought him love or even friendship. We don't read about a wife or children, and he had no friends among the people of Jericho – they despised him. His reputation was in the gutter. But Something within Zacchaeus was crying out for help. Sin, the Bible tells us, only brings pleasure for a season; after that, people start looking for a way of escape. It's obvious that Zacchaeus was risking further humiliation: he climbed up into a sycamore fig tree in an effort to at least see Jesus.

What he didn't know was that Jesus was actually coming to Jericho especially for him. We know what happened: against the advice of a jeering crowd, Jesus went back to Zacchaeus' house with him. Meeting Jesus had a profound effect on the tax collector. He decided to start paying back the money he had stolen and cheated his neighbours out of, giving them back four times the amount he had taken. He also told Jesus he would give half his money to the poor. We don't know what the result of all this was but we can guess.

Zacchaeus not only repented but made restitution for his sin and the tide of public opinion turned. His reputation was restored.

It's a fact of life that people are often known for their lowest moment and a good reputation can be impossible to get back. But with Jesus nothing is impossible; He came to seek the lost, save the lost and give them back their reputation.

216

Aristarchus my fellow prisoner greets you, with Mark the cousin of Barnabas (about whom you received instructions: if he comes to you, welcome him), and Jesus who is called Justus. These are my only fellow workers for the kingdom of God who are of the circumcision; they have proved to be a comfort to me.

Colossians 4:10-11 (NKJV)

This week we are looking at the power of God to restore – to restore our bodies, our innocence, our credibility, our reputation. Today we look at confidence.

There's a particular young chap in the New Testament that I have always had soft spot for and that is John Mark. He was just a little boy when he first met Jesus but he witnessed some of the most important events in His life: the last supper, the crucifixion and the resurrection as well as the day of Pentecost. When Paul and Barnabas set out on their first missionary journey maybe fifteen years later, they had a problem. What if people asked them if they had seen the events they were talking about themselves? They would have to say no. Perhaps it was Barnabas' idea to take his cousin Mark with them because he could testify as an eye witness.

All went well at first, but when they got to Perga in Turkey something went wrong. John Mark deserted them, causing Paul and Barnabas to have a big fall out. He really messed up and we are not told why he did this. Paul and Barnabas had to continue alone.

For John Mark the adventure was over; he couldn't hack it, he had failed. Things like this have a profound effect on our confidence. The temptation is to say, "Well, that's the last time I do anything like that." As a child I was embarrassed in front of the whole congregation and vowed never to speak in public again! How many people are there out there like that?

Discouragement results in exactly what it says on the tin: a loss of courage, a loss of confidence. I can imagine this was John Mark's experience. We hear nothing of him for a long time. Tradition says that he went off to Egypt for a while and founded the Church of Alexandria.

But lo and behold, his name crops up in Colossians 4:10-11 (today's verse). Ten years later John Mark is taking care of Paul in prison in Rome and Paul calls him his fellow worker and someone who has been a comfort to him. He was restored. But the greatest proof that his confidence was totally restored is that when you open the New Testament the second book is called *Mark*. You see it is *his* Gospel. Not only did he get his confidence back but God honoured him.

217

Restore us, O God; make your face shine on us...

Psalm 80:3 (NIV)

This week, more than usual, I have sensed that the Lord was speaking to specific people through the talks. Today the feeling is stronger than ever. God is saying "I want to restore you."

There are two different things that He wants to do and the first is found in Psalm 51:12 (NIV): "Restore to me the joy of your salvation and grant me a willing spirit, to sustain me." There may be people reading this today who have lost their joy – the joy that God gave them when they were saved; the joy that has kept them going over these years. God wants to give it back to you. This psalm is a prayer that King David prayed and so it shows us that even someone who is "a man after God's own heart" can lose their joy.

Losing joy is just the beginning though. When your joy is gone you become indifferent to the things of God; you just go through the motions of the Christian life with no enthusiasm and gradually good habits begin falling away – you end up in the wilderness. King David saw his predicament and asked God for help: "Restore me; restore the joy." The request has to come from you. Ask God to restore you now. Ask Him to give you your joy back, and wait for it. When it returns, the other things will come back too. As David said, he wanted a willing spirit back too, a desire to serve God fully, to get involved in the work of God. He knew that that would keep him on the right track.

The second thing I felt God saying is from Joel 2:25 (ASB): "And I will restore to you the years that the locust have eaten." Maybe there is someone reading who fell away from God many years ago. You haven't really done anything about your faith for all that time and you wondered if you even had faith any more. But God has somehow engineered it so that you read this today and He wants to speak to you. He wants to say that it's not too late and it doesn't matter what has taken place in the intervening years; it is what you do now that is important. He will forgive you, restore you and welcome you back. In fact, the rest of your life will be so blessed that it will make up for all the years you were away from Him. That is what restoring the years that the locust has eaten means.

Don't procrastinate. Don't delay. God has spoken to you today. Pray now.

218

So then, just as you received Christ Jesus as Lord, continue to live your lives in him, rooted and built up in him, strengthened in the faith as you were taught, and overflowing with thankfulness.

Colossians 2:6-7 (NIV)

This week our theme will be 'the power of gratitude'. One of the first things an infant is taught is to say thank you. So, from the earliest age we know that it is good to be grateful. Gratitude is the response to kindness, whether from others of from God.

Billy Bray is a legend among Christians here in Cornwall. A simple tin miner who lived two hundred years ago is still talked about often. He was a dynamic little man who built three churches, saw hundreds accept Jesus and had an unconventional preaching style. But the thing that marks him out was his gratitude. When God answered his prayer or blessed him in any way, Billy would dance. He would shout, sing and dance in gratefulness to God on whom he depended for everything. Whether it was a new pair of boots or funds to put a roof on one of his chapels, he would dance.

St. Ives, the now popular tourist resort, was then a fishing village called Down-Long. When Billy visited there, the people were on the point of starvation because there had been no fish that season. He was holding a meeting in the chapel and prayed for God to send shoals of fish. Suddenly a cry went up from the harbour as the boats began to return packed to the gunwales with fish. The men and women toiled all night, the men going out time and time again and the women gutting and salting the fish. In the morning there were eight thousand barrels of fish and Billy was sent home with a large donation to finish his chapel. He praised the Lord and danced all the way.

I can identify with this story because my forefathers came from the tiny Cornish fishing village of Port Loe. But can I identify with the gratitude? When reading about Billy Bray last night, I wondered about my own response to God's kindness – it isn't the same as his.

I am reminded of the line from the harvest hymn, "Accept the gifts we offer for all thy love imparts, and, what thou most desirest, our humble, thankful hearts."

Colossians 2:7 (NASB) tells us that we should be "overflowing with gratitude". Billy Bray certainly was – I should be too.

219

Because, although they knew God, they did not glorify Him as God, nor were they thankful, but became futile in their thoughts and their foolish hearts were darkened.

Romans 1:23 (NKJV)

I have found that gratitude is a powerful shield against temptation and sin. It's not just a question of feeling grateful but of expressing it to God. If I continually thank God for what He has given me, greed has nowhere to go. If I thank Him for my car, my TV, my home regularly, then it stops me wanting a new one. The secret is to see everything you have as a gift from God and to be grateful.

I told someone this once and they replied, "But I worked for that, I earnt the money to buy it!" to which I replied, "But who gave you the health and strength to work?" Society has come so far down the entitlement path that people think they deserve the blessings they have. The Bible teaches the opposite. Thank God we don't get what we deserve. Thank God for grace!

Ingratitude is the mother of sin. Lucifer was not grateful to be an archangel, in charge of heaven's worship – he fell. Adam was not grateful for the paradise that he lived in and unbroken fellowship with God – he fell. Judas Iscariot was not grateful for being chosen as one of the twelve disciples – he fell. When you are ungrateful and don't recognise that all good gifts come from God, then a special kind of delusion takes over.

Do you see the role of ingratitude in today's verse? The words for "futile" and "foolish" here mean 'morally wicked' and 'unintelligent'. Now where have I seen that before?

But the converse must also be true: that if we glorify God and are thankful, our thoughts will be productive, righteous and clever. Gratitude has the power to make you more intelligent. I have seen that happen so many times.

Praise the Lord!

220

Don't criticize one another, brothers. He who criticizes a brother or judges his brother criticizes the law and judges the law.

James 4:11 (HCSB)

One of the most precious gifts that God has given us is each other. Months of isolation this year have shown us that what we most missed about church was each other. Hopefully this realisation will remain with us for a long time. We need each other. Not only are human beings by nature gregarious, but God's plan is to put us in fellowship in churches.

The grand plan of God cannot work without the *koinonia* – the assembly, the church – people of one heart and one mind working together in unity.

The sad thing is that so often churches can be full of criticism. I was preaching about this in a church once and said, "Too often we pull everything apart over Sunday lunch, especially the preacher." A voice rang out from the congregation, "We do that, don't we, Daddy!"

Paul adds the other side of the coin in 2 Thessalonians 1:3 (NIV): "We ought always to thank God for you, brothers and sisters, and rightly so, because your faith is growing more and more, and the love all of you have for one another is increasing." We ought always to thank God for each other. I wonder when we last did that? You see, if we are grateful for one another and express that in our prayers, we will find it much more difficult to criticise. And if we don't criticise, then there will be more unity among us. Gratitude brings unity.

Gratitude also has the power to create. We all need encouragement, and if someone thanks us (shows gratitude for what we have done), then we will not only be ready to do it again but to do more. Our faith and our ministry will grow and develop, as Paul said, because gratitude has created an atmosphere in which we can thrive.

Why not make a list of people that you are going to show gratitude to today?

221

One of them, when he saw he was healed, came back, praising God in a loud voice. He threw himself at Jesus' feet and thanked him – and he was a Samaritan. Jesus asked, "Were not all ten cleansed? Where are the other nine? Has no one returned to give praise to God except this foreigner?" Then he said to him, "Rise and go; your faith has made you well."

Luke 17:15-19 (NIV)

Ten lepers met Jesus outside a certain village. It wasn't uncommon to see a group of lepers – they were forced to live together because of their condition. What was uncommon though is that they approached Jesus and the disciples and shouted to Jesus to have mercy on them. They obviously knew who Jesus was and that He could help them and maybe even heal them.

He shouted back to them, "Go and show yourself to the priests." What did that mean? Well, in those days if you wanted a certificate of healing – an all-clear, if you like – you had to get it from a priest. It was only then that you could return to your family and start living a normal life again. Of course, this never happened with leprosy.

The lepers were overjoyed; it was a promise of healing. And the Bible says, "As they went they were cleansed." (Lk.17:14, NIV) Can you imagine the emotion, the joy, the relief that they felt? Their life sentence had been cancelled, they were free! They couldn't wait to see their wives, their children, their families – just a quick trip to the priest and they'd be there. However, one of them, when he saw he was healed, stopped in his tracks, turned around and went back to Jesus. He wanted to say thank you.

This episode shows us clearly that the Lord Jesus appreciates gratitude. He 'called out' the nine who had not said thank you and blessed the one who did. I wonder which of the lepers I would have been? I can identify with the nine who were so ecstatic about their healing and so anxious to be reunited with their family that they didn't think to go back to Jesus and say thank you.

Gratitude effects our relationship with God. Throughout the Bible we see people who gave thanks and people who didn't, and it was always the latter that came worse off in the end.

Every day we enjoy a plethora of God's blessings on our lives – how often do we count them and go to Jesus to say thank you?

222

Be anxious for nothing, but in everything by prayer and supplication, with thanksgiving, let your requests be made known to God.

Philippians 4:6 (NKJV)

We are looking at the power of gratitude this week and we have seen how gratitude improves our thinking, has the power to create, brings unity and develops our relationship with God.

Today I want to look at how gratitude enhances our prayer life. Of course, one of the key things that we should do when we pray is express our thanks to God. I have always found it a little odd that there is no thanksgiving in the Lord's Prayer, but elsewhere the Bible is full of prayers of gratitude and it urges us to give thanks.

In today's verse Paul is saying that when we ask God for things, we should at the same time thank Him for what we have already got and for what He has already done. You see, thanksgiving builds our faith. It is so easy to forget all the answers to prayer that we have had. Some people keep a prayer journal and that's not a bad idea. I go back to my diaries and old newsletters sometimes and I'm amazed! God did such incredible things but I have forgotten so many of them.

The Hebrew faith has a pattern of prayer which mentions the great things that God has done before any new requests are made. It goes something like this: "Thanks be to God who brought us out of the land of Egypt and delivered us from Pharaoh. Who opened up the Rea Sea and brought us into the promised land." In fact, Rabbis today still teach that Jews should say a hundred blessings – that is, thanksgivings – a day!

When we include thanksgiving in our prayers, it of course encourages us and gives us faith to ask again, maybe for bigger things. But also, it shows God that we are grateful for what He has done and that we don't take anything for granted. Nobody likes ingratitude – least of all God!

Why not try to thank God for a hundred things today?

223

The person without the Spirit does not accept the things that come from the Spirit of God but considers them foolishness, and cannot understand them because they are discerned only through the Spirit.

1 Corinthians 2:14 (NIV)

Most people have no idea what our Christian faith is all about. There are many reasons for that but one is found in today's verse. One of the things that we are so used to as believers is being in the presence of God. People who are unspiritual would just frown or roll their eyes if we spoke to them about this or tried to describe it. New believers are blown away by the amazing feeling of peace and joy and elevation that comes with being in His presence.

As followers of Jesus, going to church is not a chore or a duty but a delight! The psalmist says, "I was glad when they said to me, 'Let us go into the house of the LORD.'" (Ps.122:1, NKJV) And one of our best known Bible verses tells us, "Enter his gates with thanksgiving and his courts with praise; give thanks to him and praise his name." (Ps.100:4, NIV)

The way that we enter this awesome state is with gratitude, giving thanks for Jesus, for salvation, for His blood that has made this access possible, for His grace that makes us comfortable, for His love that makes us accepted, for His Spirit that brings us in.

If we could only show people what the presence of God is like, there would be a queue around the block trying to get in. But we can't. The only thing that we can do is to show people the results of being in His presence, what it does to us and how grateful we are for it.

Colossians 3:17 (NIV) hints at this when it says, "And whatever you do, whether in word or deed, do it all in the name of the Lord Jesus, giving thanks to God the Father through him."

A friend of mine has a lovely habit: when anything good happens or someone shares good news, he says, "Thank you, Jesus." People who hear him begin to see that all good gifts come down from above and that we should be grateful.

Let's all adopt a lifestyle of gratitude. Thank you, Jesus.

224

For unto us a Child is born, unto us a Son is given; and the government will be upon His shoulder. And His name will be called Wonderful, Counselor, Mighty God, Everlasting Father, Prince of Peace. Of the increase of His government and peace there will be no end, upon the throne of David and over His kingdom, to order it and establish it with judgment and justice from that time forward, even forever. The zeal of the LORD of hosts will perform this.

Isaiah 9:6-7 (NKJV)

We usually regard Easter as the season of passion; we refer to it as the passion of Christ. But can I suggest that Christmas could well be called the passion of God? That familiar reading from today's passage concludes with the words: "The zeal of the LORD of hosts will perform this". That word "zeal" could equally well be translated 'passion'. The passion of God will perform this.

We can't imagine God's passion, His drive, His enthusiasm, but we can see it demonstrated in the Christmas story framed by the king of texts: "For God so loved the world that He gave His one and only Son." (Jn.3:16, NIV)

Passion. Can you grasp that God was so passionate about the human race, so passionate about you, that He sent His only Son to die in your place? But He did. God never does mediocre things. He is never half-hearted, He is always passionate – motivated by loving zeal; and the nativity was conceived, literally and figuratively, by His zeal.

Tonight in the western sky, just after sunset, we will see something that hasn't happened for eight hundred years: a great conjunction of planets. Jupiter and Saturn will appear as one planet. I hope the sky will be clear. But the newspapers are saying, "Is this the star of Bethlehem?" I don't think so but maybe it is a sign. One thing is for sure: that God in His passion caused an unusual and unpredictable astronomical event two thousand years ago that made the magi look up, pack up and mount up, and follow it to Bethlehem. That's passion.

If God is passionate enough about us to send His Son to be my Saviour, He is passionate enough to put a 'star in their sky' to let them know. Maybe that star is you: "...so that you may become blameless and pure, 'children of God without fault in a warped and crooked generation.' Then you will shine among them like stars in the sky." (Phil.2:15, NIV)

225

Who, being in very nature God, did not consider equality with God something to be grasped, but made himself nothing, taking the very nature of a servant, being made in human likeness.

Philippians 2:6-7 (BSB)

It's usually about now that we start raising our eyebrows as we think about the cost of Christmas. The real cost of Christmas is however incalculable – the cost to Christ. We tend to think that the price that Jesus paid for us is confined to Easter, to His sufferings and death on the cross. But today let me show you another cost.

When we talk about Christmas, we often highlight the fact that God became a man and dwelt among us and that He humbled Himself and was born as a little baby in a stable. But you must go back a further nine months to appreciate the full story: the miracle of Emmanuel.

Did you know that all the cells of the human body are invisible to the naked eye except for one? The human egg. This single cell is just visible, but you have to have good eyesight to see it as it measures 0.1 of a millimetre or 0.0039 of an inch.

When the Holy Spirit overshadowed Mary and she conceived, the eternal God, the maker of all things, the King of kings, became a single cell. Just 0.1 millimetres across! A fertilised egg planted inside Mary's body. Jesus.

The cost of Christmas is inestimable.

The Greek word that is translated "made himself nothing" in today's verse is *kenosis* which means 'to empty oneself'. My favourite hymn catches this thought when Charles Wesley writes concerning Christ, "Emptied himself of all but love and bled for Adam's helpless race." Jesus, the third person of the trinity, who was accustomed to the unparalleled splendours of heaven, emptied Himself of glory and became a man, a baby, an embryo, an egg.

Coming into this world was not a shock to Him as it would be to an alien; this was the world that He created, this was the world that He loved and these were the people that He was committed to. He had visited before but now He came to rescue a fallen race. Hallelujah! What a Saviour!

226

...and it happened that when Elizabeth heard the greeting of Mary, that the babe leaped in her womb and Elizabeth was filled with the Holy Spirit.

Luke 1:41 (NKJV)

Yesterday we went back nine months from Christmas and saw the miracle of the incarnation in a new light. As someone commented, "Our God contracted to a span, incomprehensibly made man." Jesus humbled Himself and became a single cell.

Today I want to go further back to the miracle of John the Baptist's conception. Zacharias, a temple priest, and his wife were not able to have children, but an angel visited Zacharias and told him that Elizabeth would conceive and their son would "be great in the sight of the Lord and shall drink neither wine nor strong drink. He will be filled with the Holy Spirit, even from his mother's womb." (Lk.1:15, NKJV)

Six months later the pregnant Mary visits Elizabeth who is her cousin, and Elizabeth is filled with the Holy Spirit. Then in verse 61 we read, "Now his father Zacharias was filled with the Holy Spirit and prophesied."

There are two things I want you to notice here. The first is that when you have a job to do for God, you need to be filled with the Holy Spirit; He is the great enabler.

Secondly, think about this: yesterday we saw how Jesus emptied Himself to come to earth and be born as a man; here we see that Zacharias, Elizabeth and John were all filled – filled with the Holy Spirit. The wonderful thing about our faith is that it is about being filled! Filled with the Holy Spirit, filled with joy, filled with hope, filled with faith, filled with love... Filled.

Jesus emptied Himself so that we could be filled. False religion talks about emptying ourselves; true faith talks of being filled – and filled with good things too. The purpose of Christ's coming is so you can "know the love of Christ which passes knowledge; that you may be filled with all the fullness of God" (Eph.3:19, NKJV).

227

He is the image of the invisible God, the firstborn over all creation. For by Him all things were created that are in heaven and that are on earth.

Colossians 1:15-16 (NKJV)

This week we have been thinking about the fact that Jesus, the third person of the Trinity, became a speck of life in a young woman's womb so that He could be born as a human being here on earth.

It is reasonable to ask, why did Jesus not come in all His glory? Why didn't He come the first time like He is going to come the second time when He comes in the air and every eye will see Him? Why did He have to be so ordinary, so humble and for thirty years live a life that was undistinguishable from anyone else – except for His lack of sin? Surely if He had demonstrated His glory to everyone like He did to the disciples on the mount of transfiguration, everyone would have accepted that He was God in the flesh.

There are many reasons why it had to be the way it was. He had to live as a man to know what life was like for us from the inside – so that now He can empathise with us. He had to be a man so that He could show us how to live – nobody else has ever been able to do it. He had to be a man so that He could die for our sins – the only substitute for humanity was a perfect man.

But the main reason that Jesus had to be a man and could not come in glory was because of faith. If you see someone riding on the clouds, shining like the sun, wielding supernatural power over the earth, you will say, "Oh, that's God." It would be so obvious that it would require no faith.

Jesus always has to be accepted by faith because it is by faith that we are saved. He could easily have got all the priests on His side by just telling them that He was born in Bethlehem. They knew what the prophets had foretold: the messiah would be born in the city of David. However, Jesus chose to let them think He was from Nazareth. If they were to accept Him as the Son of God, they had to do it by faith. Some did.

And today it is still the same. The only proof you will get that He is who He says He is will come after you have accepted Him by faith.

To accept Him by faith you have to speak to Him, pray. You have to say something like, "Lord Jesus, I come to you in faith, believing you are really there. I ask you to forgive my sins and come into my life. Reveal yourself to me; open my eyes, Lord Jesus." Nobody has ever prayed that prayer in faith and been disappointed.

228

"I am coming to you now, but I say these things while I am still in the world, so that they may have the full measure of my joy within them. I have given them your word and the world has hated them, for they are not of the world any more than I am of the world."

John 17:13-14 (NIV)

As we approach the new year, I thought I would talk about new beginnings. Of course, we all know that the transition from December 31st to January 1st is the same as the transition of any other day in the year, but it is useful to us, and I think useful to God, to have a season of taking stock, of self-examination and of planning.

One thing I like to do is to ask myself the question, how much have I grown in the Lord in this last year? Sometimes I have to admit, "Not much. Actually, I can't quantify any growth or improvement at all." This year, however, it is different. 2020 has been a challenging year and continues to be so, but the effect that it has had on my spiritual life has been nothing but positive. What about you?

One thing that has made it positive for me is this: my daily talks. It has not only brought a great discipline into my life as I sit down every morning for an hour to pray, study and write and then go somewhere to film, but it has brought joy. There really is nothing like being 'in the Word', as they say, which means immersing yourself in the Bible, consistently and constructively, daily.

In John 17 we have a transcript of the prayer that Jesus prayed in the Garden of Gethsemane. As we see from the passage, the Word of God brings joy – lasting and satisfying joy that is the king-pin of the Christian life.

When we bought our church building, which was built in 1846, I took my father-in-law, a master craftsman, to survey it. We popped our heads up into the attic and he let out an exclamation: "That's the strongest kind of roof you can have!"

"Why is that?" I asked.

"Because of the king-pin," he said. Every truss is not just a triangle of wood but has a central pin – the king-pin to stabilise it, see."

Let our new beginnings of the coming year have that king-pin to stabilise our lives, and as we leave the old year, let us, as Isaiah 55:12 (NKJV) puts it, "go out with joy".

229

"I have given them Your word; and the world has hated them because they are not of the world, just as I am not of the world."

John 17:14 (NKJV)

Jesus said ten things in His Gethsemane prayer for His disciples that lead to the fullness of joy that is mentioned in verse 13. Yesterday we saw that He had given them the Word of God which washes, refreshes and builds our faith.

The second thing is mentioned in the same verse: "...they are not of the world, just as I am not of the world." What a remarkable statement! And this applies to all believers – you are not of this world. Wow!

It is a wonderful thing that should bring us great joy to know that we are not of this world, because this world is bad. If you do even a cursory study on what the Bible says about this world, you will be overjoyed that you are not part of it.

It says the whole world lies under the influence of the evil one, Satan, and he is its ruler; that it is a dark, corrupt world which is deceived; and that it will be judged and will pass away.

But Jesus said we are not of this world. Thank God that by giving our lives to Jesus and being born again, we are made citizens of heaven and, as such, removed from the darkness and deception of this world and brought into His glorious light.

If in Bible days you were a Roman citizen, there were many privileges and you were exempted from certain things. The passport that you carry guarantees the protection of your country too, and if you have a diplomatic passport, you are not subject to the laws of the country you are in. In the same way we have a heavenly passport. We are not of this world. We are protected by heaven and exempted from the judgement that will come upon the world. We are free! That should give you reason to rejoice!

The even more wonderful thing is that this heavenly citizenship is available to absolutely everyone. No one needs to try to sneak across the border at night – they are invited in by the King!

Yes, we are *in* the world, but we are not *of* the world. Reason to be joyful number two.

230

"I do not pray that You should take them out of the world, but that You should keep them from the evil one."

John 17:15 (NIV)

We are taking for our reference point this week Jesus' prayer in Gethsemane. It is still Christ's prayer for your life that you may have the full measure of joy within you. In the rest of the prayer He tells us ten things that should not only bring us joy but maintain that joy as a lifestyle. Today we look at number three, which is found in John 17:15.

There is a thought here that we could be taken out of the world once we are saved – as a friend of mine says, we are 'heaven-ready' – but that is not Christ's desire. Without believers the world would be left without a witness. The testimony of His followers, you and me, is absolutely central to the fulfilment of God's plan here on earth. "How will they hear without a preacher?" (Rom.10:14, NASB)

So, Jesus' prayer is to keep us here but keep us under His protection. Not isolated, but implicated while insulated. We are in the world but insulated from evil, protected, kept by God. The word "keep" here is used in the terminology of English castles. The most secure place in the castle is called the keep. And the most secure place in the universe is where we are: in God's keep. Colossians 3:3 (NKJV) says, "…your life is hidden with Christ in God."

Many people will be entering into 2021 in fear. I won't and I hope you won't either. There is no need for fear when you are being kept by God. Whatever happens to us physically, it does not alter the fact that we are being kept. Evil cannot touch us. What a great reason to be joyful!

231

New Year's Day, 2021

"Sanctify them by Your truth. Your word is truth."

John 17:17 (NKJV)

As we enter the new year, let's do it with the "full measure of joy" that Jesus spoke of in His prayer in Gethsemane. In that same prayer He gives us ten reasons to be joyful. We have looked at the first three: we have received the Word of God; we are not of this world; and we are protected from the evil one. Today we look at number four, which is found in verse 17.

Jesus prays that we might be sanctified. A modern translation puts it, "Make them pure and holy." (TLB) The last thing most people in the world we live in seem to want is to be pure and holy, and they would certainly not see how this could possibly be a source of joy! People who do not belong to Jesus seem to want to revel in the impure and the unholy; as we watch our TVs we see illicit sex, violence and swearing becoming the norm. The underlying truth is that a younger audience will not watch any drama without these elements liberally and gratuitously scattered with them.

Sadly, some churches are giving their assent to the lifestyle that this culture reflects, thinking they have to move with the times. But God still calls for purity and holiness. We say that "Jesus is same yesterday, today and forever" and this is part of the sameness.

There is very good reason for Jesus' prayer that God would help us to be pure and holy – because He knows where the other lifestyle leads. The Bible says in Hebrews that sins' pleasures only last for a while. The hedonistic lifestyle comes with a heavy price tag: guilt, shame, broken relationships, addiction, depression and despair.

In Christ our sins are forgiven; we are made right with God. We enter into a lifetime of continual refinement, being made holy and receiving all the wonderful things that God showers upon us. Holiness brings lasting joy. Psalm 16:11 (NKJV) says, "You will show me the path of life; in Your presence is fullness of joy; at Your right hand are pleasures forevermore."

Let us today determine to enter the new year knowing joy because we say yes to purity and holiness.

232

"As you have sent me into the world, I also have sent them."

John 17:18 (NKJV)

Not many people realise that Jesus' prayer on the night of His arrest gives us a blueprint for a joy-filled life. He did pray, however, that we might have the full measure of His joy at the beginning of the prayer. We have reached number five in the ten reasons to be joyful and this is found in verse 18.

Now, we all know that the apostles were sent – that's what 'apostle' means. But Jesus is praying for all believers, so that means you and I are sent too. We are sent by Jesus to take the good news about Him to everyone. His final words on earth were, "Go into all the world and preach the gospel to every creature." (Mk.16:15, NKJV)

Now, some of you are scratching your head and thinking, "How can this be a reason to be joyful? It fills me with dread." Well, let me tell you. First of all, it says something about what He thinks of us. He trusts us. God trusts you. What an amazing revelation! If that doesn't put a smile on your face, I don't know what will.

Years ago in Texas I was travelling in a car with a pastor who had picked me up and was taking me back to his church for several days of meetings. He turned to me and said, "I'm sorry but I am not going to be there. I have to go away on business." The look on my face said it all; I was dismayed. "It's OK, David," he then said, "I trust you." Tears started pouring down my face. It was a seminal and joyful moment in my life.

I am so glad that Christianity is not a passive but an active faith. There is something to do and God trusts us to do it. All of us are sent and all of us can do it. He equips us and gives us the strength to take the good news to those around us in many different ways. You don't have to be a preacher but you do have to share God's love and the message of hope in your own way. Pray about how you are going to do this in the year ahead. There is great joy in it for you!

233

"And for their sakes I sanctify myself, that they also might be sanctified through the truth."

John 17:19 (NKJV)

This week we are going to continue to pursue our study on the reasons Jesus gives us to be joyful in John 17; or, more correctly, that we might have the "full measure of His joy". There are ten reasons and we are up to number six, which is found in verse 19

This is not an easy verse to understand and it raises more questions than it answers, but I am going to take it the way that it speaks to me. For Jesus to say that He sanctifies Himself – that is, makes Himself holy – is perhaps a humble way of saying that He *is* holy. Certainly, as man He had the potential to sin but did not, so He kept Himself holy even though he was "tempted in every way, just as we are – yet he did not sin" (Heb.4:15, NIV).

Jesus knows what sin is better than anyone, for three reasons:

1. Sin is breaking the laws that He Himself made.
2. He was tempted in every way to sin.
3. He made Himself responsible for every sin ever committed – on the cross.

But He Himself was pure, sinless and holy – and kept Himself that way so that He was able to pay for our sins with His perfect life.

This should give us double joy because not only did He sanctify Himself so that we could be forgiven, but also He knows what it is to be human and so can identify with our struggles. He knows how we feel.

There are many tales of gods masquerading as humans and kings dressing up as peasants. Shakespeare has Henry V walking incognito among his men the night before the battle of Agincourt. But these are myths, stories, fiction. Our God walked among us experiencing pain, loss, temptation and, on the cross, guilt and shame. And because He did, He won the victory over these things for us so that we could be holy too.

Hebrews 2:11 (NLT) says, "So now Jesus and the ones He makes holy have the same Father. That is why Jesus is not ashamed to call them his brothers and sisters."

234

"I am praying not only for these disciples but also for all who will ever believe in me because of their testimony."

John 17:20 (NLT)

Let's continue to find reasons to be joyful from Jesus' prayer in Gethsemane. Today is number seven and it's found in verse 20. It is a wonderful thing that Jesus prays for us. On earth, here in the Garden, He was praying to the Father just like we do, but now He is with the Father, He speaks to Him face to face and the Bible tells us He ever lives to make intercession for us.[10] He is speaking to God all the time about us. That's a reason to be joyful! What could be better than Jesus praying for you?

But let's look at the second part of the verse. He says He is not only praying for us but for all who will believe because of us. This presumes success. Our testimony will work. We will be effective. People will be saved because of us.

I am sure that many Christians have a defeatist attitude, not believing that anyone could be saved through them. This needs to change. Here Jesus is saying that He is praying for us and for all those who will come to know Him through us. As we set out today, let's set out with this mindset: who is going to believe in Him because of me today?

Remember how powerful your testimony is; your story is a lifesaver. Your smile and joyful attitude will make people warm to what you have to say.

Your reason to be joyful today is because your testimony is guaranteed to make a difference to people's lives.

---

[10] See Hebrews 7:25

235

...that all of them may be one, Father, just as you are in me and I am in you.
May they also be in us so that the world may believe that you have sent me.

John 17:21 (NIV)

We have reached number eight of our reasons to be joyful taken from John's Gospel chapter 17: "My prayer for all of them is that they will be one." One of the greatest joys of my life has been experiencing this – the friendship and brotherhood of all believers. From Finland to Peru, from Israel to Arkansas, I have met many followers of Jesus – thousands, tens of thousands in my forty years of travelling ministry – and I can say unreservedly that we were one. I have never been rebuffed, excluded or felt like an outsider.

Now, I am not a believer in ecumenicalism; that is man's attempt to do what the Holy Spirit does supernaturally and it is not the same by a long way. The secret of the togetherness, the *koinonia*, is in this verse. Jesus says to the Father, "...just as you are in me and I am in you, so they will be in us." We experience this mystic unity because Jesus lives in us. In the same way as John the Baptist leapt inside his mother's womb when he met Jesus who was in Mary's womb, so our spirits leap when we meet someone who has Jesus in them.

It never ceases to amaze me how such a diverse group of individuals can come together in a local church and be one. There is no division because of age, colour, intelligence, wealth or anything else – this is the only place on earth where true unity exists. Brotherhood without bias. Wonderful and amazing.

Jesus continues in His prayer with this: "...and the world will believe you sent me..." Because of this togetherness, the love that binds us together, the world will believe in Jesus. But how could the world ever know about it unless they experience it? In fact, the world thinks that the church is divided not united.

As far as I can see, the only way that people will believe in Jesus because of our fellowship is if they come in and are welcomed and accepted without question. I am so glad that everyone who comes through the doors of our church is treated exactly the same: welcomed and loved. What could be more of a witness to the reality of Jesus in us than this?

236

...I in them, and You in Me; that they may be made perfect in one, and that the world may know that You have sent Me, and have loved them as You have loved Me.

John 17:23 (NKJV)

We are nearly at the end of our study of reasons to be joyful from Jesus' prayer in John 17. Remember, Jesus asked at the beginning of the prayer that we might have the full measure of His joy. In verse 23 we see the ninth reason to be joyful – and this is a big one: God loves us as He loves Jesus. One translation goes as far as to say that God has loved us *as much* as He has loved Jesus. I can't think of a bigger reason to be joyful than that God loves me. Years ago, we used to wear badges and have bumper stickers that said "God loves you" – but what if we had one that said "God loves me"?! Would that be wrong? It would certainly be a talking point!

Jesus is praying here that the world may know that God loves us. Of course, God loves them too but they are not yet plugged in to that love and have not received the benefits of it. But we have. What does that look like?

In the current climate of a worldwide pandemic, knowing that God loves each of us as a son or daughter gives us great reassurance. We can endure a lot if we know that God loves us. And of course, we know that nothing can separate us from that love. When we are feeling down, or afraid or threatened, we should just say to ourselves, "Ah, but God loves me," and smile. We need to tell ourselves that every day. It will frustrate the plans of the evil one who wants to undermine our faith and confidence.

The love of God is a safe place. It is where we belong. Write "God loves me" on a Post-it note and stick it on your mirror!

237

"Righteous Father … I have made you known to them, and will continue to make you known in order that the love you have for me may be in them and that I myself may be in them."

John 17:25-26 (NIV)

Reason to be joyful number ten is that Jesus is in us. He makes Himself known to us so that He can be in us. Stop just a moment and consider how amazing that is!

I'm sure that when we tell people that Jesus lives in us, they think that we are saying something like, "My dad died but he will live in my heart forever," or, "Sam's grandfather will never be dead as long as Sam is alive." We have these winsome sayings meaning that we hold people's memory very dear or we are so like our predecessors. But of course, this is not what we mean at all when we say that Jesus lives in us. He really lives in us!

Our bodies are His temple. The presence of God on earth used to reside in the holy of holies in the temple in Jerusalem, but when Jesus died, the temple veil was ripped from top to bottom, not so much a symbol that we could go in but that He had come out! The Bible tells us that God "does not dwell in temples made with hands" (Acts.17:24, NKJV). And Paul tells us in 1 Corinthians 3:16 (BSB), "Do you not know that you yourselves are God's temple, and that God's Spirit dwells in you?"

I remember in a youth meeting once I rather vividly said to the teens, "I wish I could just open my chest and let you see Jesus – He lives in there!" One girl who gave her life to the Lord that night came up to me after the meeting and said, "It was when you said that thing about opening up your chest that the penny dropped." She had gone to church all her life but never been presented with the reality of Jesus living in us.

What a reason to rejoice and to keep rejoicing: Jesus, the King of kings, lives in here!

238

"I have given them Your word; and the world has hated them because they are not of the world, just as I am not of the world. I ... pray that ... You should keep them from the evil one. ... Sanctify them by Your truth. ... As You sent Me into the world, I also have sent them into the world. And for their sakes I sanctify Myself, that they also may be sanctified by the truth. I do not pray for these alone, but also for those who will believe in Me through their word; that they all may be one, as You, Father, are in Me, and I in You; that they also may be one in Us, that the world may believe that You sent Me. ... that the world may know that You have sent Me, and have loved them as You have loved Me. ...The world has not known You, but I have known You; and these have known that You sent Me. And I have declared to them Your name, and will declare it, that the love with which You loved Me may be in them, and I in them."

John 17:14-26 (NKJV)

Our series 'reasons to rejoice' has lasted for two weeks, so I thought it would be good today just to recap. This is a really important message just now, as the mood of the nation, if not the world, has plummeted because of coronavirus and political upheaval.

It is wonderful that we have a whole prayer that Jesus prayed recorded in John 17. In that prayer He shows that He is concerned that we have the "full measure of His joy". And as the popular advert goes, "Not just any joy but His joy!" Then He prays that joy into us and I believe He is still doing that today. Here are the routes by which His joy comes:

- "I have given them Your word." The Bible is one of the greatest sources of joy. Reading it daily will make it the king-pin of our lives.
- "...because they are not of the world, just as I am not of the world." It brings great joy to know that we are not part of the world's problem but part of the answer.
- "...keep them from the evil one." How wonderfully reassuring that God is protecting us from evil. The other Lord's Prayer also mentions this. What a joyful relief!
- "Sanctify them by Your truth." We need to remember that in *His* presence is fullness of joy. Looking elsewhere for it will take us farther away from it.

- "I also have sent them." God trusts us with His message of salvation – what a joy to be trusted by God!

- "And for their sakes I sanctify Myself…" Jesus kept Himself holy so that He could make us holy by dying for us on the cross. This is the greatest source of joy of all.

- "…also for all who will believe in Me through their word…" God promises fruitfulness – what we do and what we say will work! Be joyful that you are part of His plan; your testimony is guaranteed to make a difference.

- "…that they also may be one…" The joy of fellowship and real friendship with others because of Jesus is unique and precious.

- "You … have loved them as You have loved Me." God loves us as much as He loves Jesus so rejoice that this is the bottom line – this is where you live.

- "…and I in them." "Christ in you, the hope of glory." (Col.1:27, NIV) This really is the be all and end all!

As Christians we are plugged into a source of great joy that sustains us whatever the circumstances. It's about time everybody knew what joy we have and how to get it.

239

Then He spoke a parable to them, that men always ought to pray and not lose heart...

Luke 18:1 (NKJV)

I would dare to say that our witness is more needed right now than at any time in our lives. So it is vital that we stay strong in the Lord and do not give up or lose heart ourselves.

In the New Testament the phrase "do not lose heart" or "do not give up" is mentioned in five places and there are five different things that will prevent us doing so. That's what I am going to be talking about this week.

The first is found in Luke 18:1 and Jesus is speaking. The parable He tells is about the persistent widow and how because she kept on pestering the judge with her requests, he finally gave her what she wanted. I don't want to look at the parable but just at this verse: "...men always ought to pray and not lose heart..."

If we pray, we will not lose heart, we won't give up. You see people quit when they are consumed by the problem, when everything gets on top of them. Prayer prevents this. When we pray, our eyes are taken off the situation and put on Jesus – off the problem and onto the solution. Prayer brings perspective. It helps us see the bigger picture. Sometimes when we pray, God allows us to see things from His vantage point.

It's the old 'Peter walking on water' illustration: when Peter looked at Jesus, he was fine, he could walk on water; but as soon as he looked at the waves, the situation, he began to sink.

People should always pray and not give up, Jesus says. When I was in hospital some time ago, during the long-disturbed nights fear and worry were stalking me like wolves around my bed. I found prayer was like lighting a fire – it scared the wolves away. I stopped thinking about myself and put my eyes on Jesus in prayer. It works!

Don't give up, my friend. Pray!

240

Therefore, since through God's mercy we have this ministry, we do not lose heart.

2 Corinthians 4:1 (NIV)

Today we look at a verse in 2 Corinthians. I love this letter because the apostle Paul is so candid about his life in ministry. All ministers can relate to it big time. By far the biggest temptation that those in ministry face is to give up. Even Jesus was confronted with this when "certain Greeks" tried to see Him. We can see by His reply in John 12 that they were offering Him a way out. Even the Pharisees speculated that He would go to Greece in John 7 to avoid what was coming.

Life in the ministry can be hard, lonely and discouraging. We get frustrated and disappointed so often and the evil one takes full advantage of this. "Give up," he whispers. You know who that is!

In our verse today we see that Paul tells us that we must not lose heart because God in His mercy has given us a job to do, and if God trusts me with anything, I've got to keep at it. He kept at it for me to the cross – praise the Lord! – so how can I quit?

But also, we do not lose heart, the verse says, because we have a ministry. The bottom line of ministry is that people depend on us. We are a vital link in God's supply chain. It would be easy to say that no one is indispensable but that is not a hundred percent true – to some people you *are* indispensable. They rely on you and God has chosen you to meet their need; it can be a very personal thing.

I know sometimes the pressure becomes almost unbearable, but this might mean that you are not doing it right, not spending time with your Source, not resting, not reading, not having a day off.

When I feel like giving up, I sing myself a little hymn that I took to heart as a teenager: "Oh Jesus, I have promised to serve thee to the end…"

End of story… Don't give up!

241

Therefore we do not lose heart. Even though our outward man is perishing, yet the inward man is being renewed day by day.

2 Corinthians 4:16-17 (NKJV)

We are looking at things that the Bible tells us will encourage us not to lose heart or give up. George Fox, the founder of the Quakers, died three hundred and thirty years ago today, and I thought I'd tell you something about him. He has a local connection here in North Cornwall because he was imprisoned here in Launceston Castle for eight months. What was his crime? His hair was too long. That happened to be a charge that they could arrest him for – his real crime was preaching the gospel.

When he had his day in court, he refused to remove his hat, and so the judge, after hours of heated discussion, threw him into Doomsdale. This was an underground cell in the castle reserved for murderers awaiting execution. This cell was never cleaned, and the human waste was ankle deep. It was impossible for him and his friend to sit down or sleep. Some sympathisers in the town threw in some straw to help; George burnt a little of it to cover up the stench in the pit. The jailer was so annoyed by this that he tipped more sewage in on their heads.

After some time many friends travelled from all over the UK to Launceston to visit him, and so he was moved to a better cell and allowed out to exercise in the castle grounds. George was such a well-known person that many locals came to catch a glimpse of the famous man. Of course, being the man he was, he used the opportunity to preach to them.

He is recorded as saying that his imprisonment was "of God" because many passed from darkness to light and Satan's power to God through it. He noted that in Cornwall, "a very dark county", "the Lord's light and truth broke forth" and "a great convincement began".

After eight months Oliver Cromwell came to hear of Fox's imprisonment and commanded his release.

Feel like giving up? George Fox's story illustrates well our verse today. We don't give up because our eyes are on the advantages!

242

And let us not grow weary while doing good, for in due season we shall reap if we do not lose heart.

Galatians 6:9 (NKJV)

This verse describes something that is familiar to most of us who have been on the trail for a while: doing good can tire you out! I don't mean *being* good... Being good is much easier than being bad and doesn't take such a toll on you either. But *doing* good can be tiring.

There are several reasons for this. One is if you are doing good in your own strength rather than being empowered by the Holy Spirit.

Another is if you are doing things which are not your ministry. When I do things that are right in line with my specific ministry, I find that I don't get tired – in fact, just the opposite!

The third reason is the "flog a willing horse syndrome" – that is, because you are such a nice person and a have a servant's heart, you can't say no and so you get put upon to do far more than is good for you.

This tiredness will eventually lead you to the conclusion that you ought to quit, give up. Don't do that! Ask yourself today if any of these are true of you and try to change things.

Another reason, and maybe the one that the apostle Paul is thinking about here, is that we get tired of doing good when it doesn't seem to be making any difference. Specifically, we think we ought to have seen more fruit or at least *some* fruit by now! We can't be blamed for thinking that.

What Paul says is that the reaping of the fruit will come in due season. The word that is used for that in Greek is a strange word but in essence it means that every situation is different and that the reaping is very specific to each task. We will reap – that is one hundred percent guaranteed – but we are not permitted to know when that will be. It might not be until heaven.

David Livingstone is one of the most famous missionaries that ever lived. Guess how many people he saw saved? *One.* But a hundred and fifty years after his death, hundreds of thousands of people have been saved in places that he gave names to.

Don't give up – you will get your reward.

243

Therefore I ask that you do not lose heart at my tribulations for you, which is your glory.

Ephesians 3:13 (NKJV)

We are looking at five great reasons not to lose heart and give up. There is no doubt that Paul went through tremendous tribulations to bring the gospel to Turkey, Greece and beyond. Shipwrecks, beatings, imprisonments, rejection, to name a few! He tells the believers in Ephesus not to lose heart and give up because of this. What a terrible thing it would be if after all that Paul had gone through, those that had benefitted from his ministry simply gave up.

We can apply that of course to ourselves. There have been two thousand years of sacrifice to get the gospel to us and to get the Bible to us so that we might be saved and live lives that are pleasing to God. Men and women have been misunderstood, mistreated and martyred that we could be where we are today and enjoy all the spiritual benefits that we do.

We can think of people who died to make this possible, but let's bring it home. Who led you to Christ? Who has been your father or mother in the faith? Who has encouraged you? Who has fed you? If we lose heart and give up, all these things that they did – for our glory – will have been wasted. We cannot give up when such a high price has been paid to get us where we are. Now, we don't have to live our lives in debt to these people; just keep going! It is reward enough for them just to see us standing firm in our faith.

I cannot tell you what joy it is to me to see those that I have led to the Lord over the years still standing, not giving up. I'm sure that you too get real satisfaction by seeing those that you have invested your time in, your life in, growing in Jesus. No wonder Paul said, "For what is our hope, our joy, or the crown in which we will glory in the presence of our Lord Jesus when he comes? Is it not you?" (1.Thess.2:19, NIV)

Having said all that, we must not forget that the person who has paid the highest price to get you where you are is God Himself!

Don't give up!

244

We can rejoice, too, when we run into problems and trials, for we know that they are good for us – they help us learn to endure. And endurance develops strength of character in us, and character strengthens our confident expectation of salvation. And this expectation will not disappoint us. For we know how dearly God loves us, because he has given us the Holy Spirit to fill our hearts with his love.

Romans 5:3-5 (NLT)

This week we have been looking at great reasons not to quit. It's good to know that God anticipated that we would feel like giving up and put these five verses in the Bible to encourage us not to. Remember, Jesus knows how we feel; He has been through it all and now wants to strengthen us. We feel like giving up when circumstances get to much for us. Or at least we *think* they are too much for us. They aren't. You are much stronger than you think you are. I have cried out to the Lord on more than one occasion, "I thought you said you would not test us beyond that which we are able to bear!" And He said, "That's right." I realised that I was able to bear it with His help; it was just my puny 'flesh' saying, "Give up."

We go through these things for a reason. Paul, whom we have seen had more than his fair share of trouble, found the answer and conveyed it to us in today's passage. There is a saying that you can't make an omelette without breaking some eggs. It is evident that you can't make a strong Christian without putting them through trials. That's the way God chooses to do it. If we just became strong overnight, it would not be real – it would lack experience and understanding, it would be theoretical strength and not practical.

Jesus had to go through the things that we go through so that He was able to empathise with us.[11] What makes us think that we do not have to go through things so that we can empathise with others?

Paul says here in Romans, trials teach us to persevere and that builds character, which in turn makes our salvation that much more real to us. One of the Christian greetings that I love most, a relic from the seventies' Jesus Movement is this: "Keep on keeping on."

So God bless you – keep on keeping on!

---

[11] See Hebrews 4:15

245

He also spoke this parable: "A certain man had a fig tree planted in his vineyard..."

Luke 14:6 (NKJV)

Everybody knows Jesus was a great storyteller. His stories were called parables – that means that they had a spiritual meaning behind them. One story recorded in Luke 14 begins like this: "A certain man had a fig tree planted in his vineyard..."

"So what?" you might say. That's because you don't know much about fig trees. A fig tree will grow anywhere. Figs grow on waste-ground, on rubbish dumps; they don't need cultivation, they are wild. On the other hand, vineyards are highly cultivated and treasured patches of ground – especially in the Middle East where this story took place. A vineyard would be surrounded by a wall and really looked after.

Why on earth would a man plant a wild fig tree in a cultivated garden? It's like planting a bramble in a rose garden. There is only one reason: because he loved figs.

This opening statement of Jesus tells us something very important. You see, the fig tree is me and you – wild, thriving on waste-ground, untamed. But Jesus loves us. He loves us so much He wants to plant us in His garden and take care of us. So many people think that they are unworthy, wild, too far gone to be accepted by God, but that's where they are wrong. He loves them, He loves you and wants the very best for you. He wants to dig you up from the poor ground that you are planted in and put you in the very best soil – to water you, feed you, tend you, protect you; to bring the best out of your life.

I know that this is true because it happened to me. I'm not a Christian because I was brought up that way but because God saw a wild kid, loved him and transplanted him into His garden. And He wants to do the same for you.

The offer is there. All you have to do is say yes.

Pray this: "God, I know I'm wild and sinful. Please forgive me and come into my life today. I give myself to you to be planted in your good soil. Thank you for loving me so much. Amen."

Now tell somebody what you have done.

246

But if we walk in the light as He is in the light, we have fellowship with one another, and the blood of Jesus Christ His Son cleanses us from all sin.

1 John 1:7 (NIV)

A friend of mine, Eric, who lives in Israel, had Covid a few weeks ago. As soon as he recovered and was cleared by the doctors, he had a phone call from the government asking him if he would give blood. Because he had conquered Covid, he had the antibodies in his blood that would help cure others.

Many people are mystified when Christians talk about 'the blood of Jesus' and that the wine in the communion service represents Jesus' blood. But this is exactly what they are talking about: an antidote. Sin is a disease that the whole human race is infected with. It is a spiritual disease, but it has a huge impact on our lives. It also has consequences – it prevents us from going to heaven. Heaven is a sin-free zone and so no carriers can be allowed in.

The thing is that God loves us and wants us in heaven, every one of us. So to make this possible, He sent Jesus into the world. His role was to be sin-free all His life and then as a perfect human being to be infected with the sin-disease right at the end of His life when He was dying. This would then create an antidote – in His blood – that would cure sin for everyone.

Just like the antidote for Covid being in Eric's blood because he conquered Covid, so the antidote for sin is in Jesus' blood because He conquered sin and rose from the dead. We need to be spiritually injected with Jesus' blood, if you will, to be cured.

That is what happens when somebody accepts Christ and asks Him to come into their life. They are saved. All their sin is forgiven, they are totally cleansed and they are also given lifetime protection against it. Because of this wonderful new beginning and the thrill of having Christ in them, they find that they want to keep sin out of their lives from then on.

This vaccine is immediately available to everyone now. Ask for it by praying, "Lord God, I am sorry for my sins, please forgive me. Inject me with the blood of Jesus. I want Him to come into my life; cleanse me and keep me from this moment on."

Now tell someone.

247

"Why are you interfering with me, Jesus, Son of the Most High God? Please, I beg you, don't torture me!"

Luke 8:28 (NLT)

Yesterday I had a phone call with a friend who was quite distraught. One of the things that I said to her was, "But you don't know what tomorrow will bring." There is a saying, "What a difference a day makes!" and that is nowhere truer than in a report of Jesus' encounter with a man who lived on the eastern shore of the Sea of Galilee.

This man had many demons. These demons tormented him so much that he had left society to live off-grid in a graveyard. He was so violent that the locals had tried to chain him up like an animal but he broke even the strongest chains. He lived naked and filthy among the tombs, cutting himself with stones. People had learnt to avoid the area.

But one day Jesus arrived. Jesus had travelled miles across the water to get to this fellow. When the man saw Jesus, he ran to Him and fell down in front of Him crying, "Why are you bothering me, Jesus, Son of the Most High God? Please, I beg you, don't torture me!" He had never met Jesus before but the demons – spiritual beings – recognised who Jesus really was. Jesus commanded the demons to come out of the poor guy and they did immediately, and entered some pigs nearby which promptly ran into the water and drowned.

The pig herders ran back to their village in fright, telling everybody what had happened. People went to see for themselves. "And they saw the man who had been possessed by demons sitting quietly at Jesus' feet, clothed and sane." (Lk.8:35, TLB) An instantaneous and remarkable change – washed, dressed, hair combed, sane and sitting at Jesus' feet, asking to become a disciple. Jesus sent him off to tell his story and he did, through the whole region.

What a difference a day makes. Things like this still happen today. Maybe your situation isn't so bad as the guy in the Bible, but hey, if Jesus can do it for him, He can do it for you. I could introduce you to hundreds of people who could tell you the same story because it happened to them.

Being a follower of Jesus isn't about a set of rules or accepting there is a God; it's about meeting someone who will instantly transform your life and having Him walk with you through the rest of it.

Pray this: *"Lord Jesus, I want to meet you, to know you. Please forgive all my sin and transform my life. You died for me – I will live for you. Amen."*

248

But God demonstrates His love for us in this: While we were still sinners, Christ died for us.

Romans 5:8 (NIV)

Barabbas was a contemporary of Jesus but he couldn't have been more different. Whereas Jesus took the path of peace and love, Barabbas took the path of violence and hatred. He was a terrorist by today's definition, a killer of Romans. He had been caught though, and tried and sentenced to death by crucifixion. He waited in his condemned cell for the soldiers to come to take him to his execution on the Friday of the feast. There seemed to be a huge disturbance in the city; he could hear it through the barred window. Jerusalem was crammed with people but this sounded like a baying mob. Then he heard something that made his blood run cold. They were shouting his name. "Barabbas!" they cried. "Give us Barabbas!"

Then he heard heavy footsteps and the jangle of keys. The door swung open and a soldier stood there. "Right! Get out and get lost!" the soldier said.

Barabbas was incredulous. He thought it was some kind of cruel joke. "What are you talking about? I heard them shouting my name!"

"They were shouting for your release, you fool!" the jailer replied. "You are free."

Barabbas stumbled out of the fortress and into the streets, trying to make sense of what had happened. Then he remembered that it was customary to pardon one prisoner on a feast day and release him. "It must have been me," he thought; there was no other explanation.

The crowd was surging out of the city following the condemned men to the Place of the Skull where the executions took place. He didn't know whether it was the crowd that took him there or a morbid desire to see the spectacle.

He stood there. Three crosses. Three men nailed to them.

He recognised two of them; they had been in the cells with him. But the one in the middle, who was that? He turned and asked someone. "Oh, that's the preacher guy from Galilee. Jesus," they said. "I don't think He did anything bad; He just upset some people."

Then the shocking truth hit Barabbas like a sword through his heart: "That cross was made for me. I deserved to die – you didn't." Had he said it out loud? An innocent man was dying in his place; he was forgiven, free, because someone had taken his place.

I don't know whether Barabbas really saw Jesus on the cross, but I would like to think that he did and that he realised the significance. But I have stood where he stood and had the same realisation. I said, "Jesus, You died for me – I will live for you." And I have.

What will you say to the man who died in your place?

Say it now.

249

Jesus answered and said to him, "Most assuredly, I say to you, unless one is born again, he cannot see the kingdom of God."

John 3:3 (NKJV)

In one of the most famous chapters in the Bible, Jesus was approached by a leading intellectual, a man called Nicodemus. His reputation was so important to him that he came to see Jesus under the cover of darkness. He wanted to know how to get to heaven – something that, whether we own up to it or not, we all want to know.

What Jesus said to him took him completely by surprise. He had expected to be given a set of rules; he was used to laws to keep. He might have thought Jesus would say, "Do good, be kind, give to the poor." But no, it was this: "Be born again."

It was such a shock that Nicodemus' brilliant mind was thrown into confusion and he said a very childish thing: "How can a grown man get back into his mother's womb and come out again?!"

Jesus had to explain. He told Nicodemus that there were two kinds of birth: a physical birth – being born of water; and a spiritual birth. It was this second, spiritual birth that He had been referring to when He said, "You must be born again."

Nicodemus was mystified. "What do you mean?" he asked.

Jesus told him that He Himself had come down from heaven and would return there and that to be born again one had to put one's faith and trust in Him. This spiritual birth would be so incredible, it would be like coming out of the dark and into the light. What's more, whoever puts their faith in Jesus is no longer condemned by God but forgiven and therefore will see the kingdom of God – heaven.

We know that Nicodemus did put his faith in Jesus.

So folks, there is only one way to heaven and this is it – putting your faith in Jesus. When you do, you will experience a tremendous awakening. Well, you would, wouldn't you? You just got born again!

Pray this: *"Lord Jesus, I put my faith in you. Forgive my sins and come into my life today. I want to be born again. Thank you for giving me a place in heaven. Amen."*

250

Rejoice in the Lord always. I will say it again: Rejoice! Let your gentleness be evident to all. The Lord is near. Do not be anxious about anything, but in every situation, by prayer and petition, with thanksgiving, present your requests to God. ... Finally, brothers and sisters, whatever is true ... think about such things.

Philippians 4:4-6,8 (NIV)

I'm sure even the best of us are experiencing some challenges in our thinking in the current situation. With more and more gloomy news, our mental health is a big issue. The 'go-to' place in the Bible for help with this is Philippians 4. Here God gives us seven things to think or meditate on which are medicine for our mind. They will lift our thoughts, our mood and our outlook.

Before those seven things though, we must prepare the mind in two ways. Philippians 4:4 says, "Rejoice in the Lord always." I would interpret that as, "Don't stop praising the Lord, whatever happens – the best way to do that is to sing and be grateful."

The next verse says, "Don't worry about anything; instead, pray about everything." (Phil.4:6, NLT) Easier said than done, I know, but it's better to spend your time praying than worrying, if you can. Try to develop the habit of turning worry into prayer every time it rears its head.

With prayer and praise in place, we can start on the seven medicines; and the first of these is, we are advised to think on are things that are *true.*

Wow, that is very topical! Truth is a big issue and there is a war on for truth. Many people just don't know whom to believe any more. From politics to pandemic, from science to social media, truth is in very short supply. As one voice raises its head to proclaim, "This is the truth," so another shouts, "No, it isn't – the truth is this."

God anticipates this. After all, the first conversation recorded on earth was exactly this. So, for your own mental health, stop trying to work out who is telling the truth and instead think about things that you know are true – a hundred percent true – and that is what God says. Paul says in Romans 3:4 (BSB), "Let God be true and every man a liar."

So try to fill your thoughts with scripture. There are many ways of doing this, but can I suggest that you take one verse or statement from the Bible each day and think about it whenever you have a moment?

Satan is very quick to grab moments and to flood your mind with anxiety when it is in neutral. So beat him with this.

Today's 'true thing' that you think about could be this verse: "Let God be true and every man a liar."

Truth is medicine for the mind – God's truth.

251

And the peace of God, which transcends all understanding, will guard your hearts and your minds in Christ Jesus. ... whatever is noble ... think about such things.

Philippians 4:7-8 (NIV)

This week's devotions are about medicine for the mind – that is, the seven things that God tells us to think about to bring peace and positivity to our minds. What an incredible thought, that God's peace will guard our minds if we get these few things right.

Yesterday we looked at concentrating on things that we know to be true – in other words, the things God says. Today we will take the next one, which is "whatever is noble". Another word for "noble" is 'honourable'. Think about things that are noble and worthy of honour.

To be honest, I do not think many of us practise this at all. You see, the human mind is drawn to the opposite: to dishonour and ignoble things. If you don't believe me, take a look at today's newspaper. What sells papers? Crime, cheating, lying, fighting – people, parties, companies, nations behaving in dishonourable ways! We can't get enough of it.

Look at the TV schedules; full of programmes about murder, adultery, sin. It is obvious what people want. But here in Philippians, God advises us not to think about these things.

Let me make a confession. Up to a couple of years ago I used to read novels when I went to bed. I used to tell myself that I needed it to switch off before I went to sleep. Most of those novels were action-packed thrillers. One day God challenged me. Why was I wasting my time on such rubbish? So, I began to read biographies of Christian people – mostly missionaries, it has to be said. These books are full of what? Honour. Stories of wonderful noble and worthy people. It has done me so much good, I can't tell you – and gives me lots of sermon illustrations too!

Let me encourage you today to spend less time filling your mind with dishonourable things and instead concentrate on the noble, the honourable, the worthy – it is medicine for the mind, and who knows, it might just rub off!

252

...whatever is just ... think about such things.

Philippians 4:8 (NKJV)

Our minds are getting bombarded with unfamiliar things these days. We don't know how to deal with these thoughts because we have no experience of them. What we do know is how to protect our mind, because God has given us a prescription in Philippians 4. He says there are seven things that we should think about that will keep our mind healthy. Paul lays these out in his letter to the church in Philippi. The first three things are "whatever is true, whatever is noble" and today, "whatever is just".

Are you noticing that all these things are in the positive? God knew the value of positive mental attitudes before the word 'psychologist' was even invented! As fallen human beings, though, we are much more inclined to dwell on the negative. And it's always so refreshing to meet someone who has a bright and sunny outlook. I think all believers should be like that, don't you?

People all around us seem to concentrate on what is unjust, unfair, biased. False religion is one of the most unjust and biased things around. Indeed, many people around the world get their prejudices from religion. Political correctness and 'cancel culture' are taking people on a roller-coaster ride in pursuit of the unfair and biased.

This is where Jesus and His teachings stand out. He was called "the Just" (Acts 3:14, KJV). Jesus taught equity, justness, impartiality. In a culture that was very deeply prejudiced Jesus demonstrated the opposite. He said that "God loved the world so much that He gave His only Son so that *whoever* believes in Him should not perish but have everlasting life" (Jn.3:16, NKJV). No barriers of race, sex, culture or anything else. He embraced the leper, spoke to the Samaritan, included the Gentile, called the tax collector, helped the Roman, forgave the thief, ate with the cheat, honoured the women, healed the beggar. If ever there was a just one, Jesus was he.

Think on these things: whatever is just.

253

...whatever is pure ... think about such things.

Philippians 4:8 (NKJV)

Medicine for the mind is this week's topic and Philippians 4 is our inspiration – seven things that God advises us to keep thinking about to ensure a healthy mind. Number four, that we are going to talk about today, is particularly current. We are encouraged to think about things that are pure. If you said this out loud in a crowd, you would be guaranteed a laugh. Purity is so out of fashion that it is alien to most people.

The word translated "pure" here is the Greek word *hagnos;* it means 'clean', and can also be translated 'innocent', 'modest' or 'perfect'. Interesting.

God is asking us to focus on what is clean, not dirty; what is innocent, not corrupt; what is modest, not explicit; and what is perfect, not spoiled. This is quite an ask in a world which has gone so boisterously in the opposite direction. It would be naive to think that our generation is any different from those before in the area of sex and more specifically lust. What is different is opportunity.

Today's generation has become drunk on all that is available, especially on the internet. What people don't realise is how bad this is for them. God does not tell us to think about what is pure and wholesome for nothing. Feeding your mind on the impure and explicit will generate all kinds of 'diseases' of the mind and the soul: guilt, shame, lying, discontentment, strife, frustration, broken relationships, self-hate and so on.

It is hard to avoid the impure but that doesn't mean we shouldn't try! As Christians we must steer clear of this devilish trap which will ensnare us very easily if we are not careful. Once caught, it is impossible to escape without help.

Think on whatever is pure. The Song of Solomon in the Bible is full of sexual imagery, but it is pure because it is the eros of a relationship and a marriage. Pure thinking is exactly that.

If you are having trouble with impure thoughts, a great solution is to start thinking about the purest thing of all: Jesus. Say His name. Jesus.

Caroline Noel's poem 'At the name of Jesus' has this helpful verse:

In your hearts enthrone Him; there let Him subdue
All that is not holy, all that is not true,
Crown Him as your Captain in temptation's hour
Let His will enfold you in its light and power.

254

...whatever is lovely ... think about such things.

Philippians 4:8 (NKJV)

We are discovering God's medicine for the mind: seven things to think on that will have great results. Today we are considering whatever is lovely. Remember this?

All things bright and beautiful,
All creatures great and small,
All things wise and wonderful,
The Lord God made them all.

That was the first thing that came into my mind as I asked the Lord about this text this morning. Google this – or maybe you know the words by heart. This is exactly what Philippians is talking about. Think about lovely things.

My dear friend Lesley Gomez commented earlier in the week that she follows photographers of birds and flowers on Instagram because Jesus said, "Look at the birds of the air," and, "Look at the flowers of the field," in Matthew 6. She finds this is medicine for the mind. That's it. I had wondered why there were so many pictures of birds, flowers and kittens too on the internet. People have discovered God's medicine.

Some guys listening to this will be rolling their eyes perhaps. It does sound a bit twee, but it obviously works. I only live a few minutes from the sea; on the next page is my favourite view, which I go to look at once a week – it does me good. Why? Because it is lovely, and thinking about or looking at lovely things is medicine for the mind.

God made the natural world and gave us the appreciation of its beauty; we don't have to be told what is lovely. But more than this, this natural beauty speaks to our spirit. Romans 1:20 (NLT) says, "From the time the world was created, people have seen the earth and sky and all that God made. They can clearly see his invisible qualities – his eternal power and divine nature." And Psalm 19:1 (BSB) says, "The heavens declare the glory of God..."

So look at some lovely things each day and let them speak to you and be medicine for your mind.

Trebarwith Strand

255

...whatever is admirable... think about such things.

Philippians 4:8 (NKJV)

We call some people 'strong minded'. I'm not entirely sure what that means, but the fact is that the human mind is fragile and needs to be taken care of. With a car you have to be careful to put in the right fuel and even the right oil to avoid damage to the engine. With the mind you have to put in the right thoughts. Our heavenly Father well knows this and has given guidance on its maintenance.

During the pandemic here in the UK, there is a stand-out news story that lifted the spirit of the nation, and that is the coverage of veteran Captain Tom Moore. This ninety-nine-year-old thought he would raise some money for the NHS by walking, with his frame, the length of his garden a hundred times. He raised thirty-nine million pounds. It is an inspiring story; even the Queen came out of isolation to knight him. It did us all good.

That is what God means when He tells us to think about the admirable – and I would say that that is usually people. There are so many people to admire: heroes, veterans, athletes, performers, men and women of God past and present. Thinking about these lifts the soul, refreshes the mind.

We have a terrible habit of finding fault. I'm sad to say, I think it's a British thing that we try to burst the bubble of our heroes. I get fed up with programmes on TV that try to expose them and tell us they are not quite as virtuous as we think they are. We know that. Nobody is perfect. But let's think about the positive, the admirable and lift our mind.

In church life, too, we can all too easily be fault-finders, sin-hunters, nit-pickers when God has called us to be encouragers, nurturers, builders-up – not breakers-down. Look for what is admirable in someone and encourage it! The more the admirable is recognised in someone and praised, the more it will flourish.

256

...whatever is excellent... think about such things.

Philippians 4:8 (NKJV)

We are going to finish what we started last week in looking at medicine for the mind from Philippians 4:8. Today we are taking the penultimate of these: "whatever is excellent". Actually, the word used in the original here literally means 'manliness'. And if you would permit me, I would like to speak about this first, as it is a something I care about. The world's idea of a Christian man is a wimp, a cissy. The media pedal this stereotype relentlessly and, I think, illegally. You won't find many wimpy men in the Bible – I can only think of one. Christian men are courageous and I think we should show it more. We have Jesus as our example; He was the bravest man that ever lived and the epitome of manliness. For us, men becoming more like Jesus is about developing quiet strength.

Although the word "excellent" literally means 'manliness', it had come to mean 'a stand-out talent' at the time this was written. So the Word of God is encouraging us to think about amazing abilities and achievements.

Do you remember when Susan Boyle stepped onto the stage of *Britain's Got Talent?* There was nothing about her that prepared us for what was to come. As soon as she started singing, the nation held its breath, the judges were dumbfounded and it seemed the world stood still. Her remarkable voice has taken her around the world, she has sold nineteen million albums and won a string of awards as well as three Guinness World Records. That's talent, that is excellent. But how does it make you feel?

This kind of excellence and achievement makes us feel good. There is something uniquely uplifting and inspiring about the moment when a fabulous ability is discovered, and it is this feeling that the *Got Talent* franchise relies on. But God got there first. He told us to think about such things to keep our mind healthy and inspired.

I'm sure that Susan Boyle's humble and unassuming nature made her talent shine out all the more. Think about it.

TUESDAY, 1ST FEBRUARY, 2021

...whatever is praiseworthy... think about such things.

Philippians 4:8 (NKJV)

Number seven is "whatever is praiseworthy". Can you think of anything praiseworthy? I hope the first thing that you thought of was Jesus!

Some years ago when I was reading this verse, I suddenly realised that everything on this list can be said of Jesus. Jesus is the truth, Jesus is noble, Jesus is the Just One, Jesus is pure, Jesus is lovely, Jesus is admirable, Jesus is excellent and He is worthy of all our praise!

So when we are told to think on these things, we can just think about Jesus. All the other things that I have talked about are important too, but Jesus should be central in our thoughts. In fact, our thinking should always be in the light of our relationship with Him and coloured by His presence with us.

Another verse says, "And let us run with endurance the race that God has set before us. We do this by keeping our eyes on Jesus, on whom our faith depends from start to finish." (Heb.12:1-2, NLT) Keeping our eyes on Jesus means keeping Him in the forefront of our thinking. There is nothing more health-giving for the mind than having Jesus there. The things that are enemy intruders will have short shrift if they are confronted with Jesus thoughts. Fear, anxiety, temptation, discouragement will slink away! Praise the Lord!

Isaiah 26:3 (KJV) says, "You will keep him in perfect peace, whose mind is stayed on Thee." Sometimes people are told that they have a fixation on something. That is exactly what this verse tells us will bring us perfect peace: a fixation on Jesus.

So today, think about Jesus and how these seven things describe Him.

258

Do not be deceived: God cannot be mocked. A man reaps what he sows. The one who sows to please his sinful nature, from that nature will reap destruction; the one who sows to please the Spirit, from the Spirit will reap eternal life.

Galatians 6:7-8 (NIV)

One of the most fundamental laws of nature is that you reap what you sow; whatever seeds you plant, that's what crop you will get. The Bible tells us that this in not just true agriculturally but sociologically and spiritually too – it is an all-pervasive law of the universe.

How does it work? Well, if you are friendly to others, they will be friendly to you. If you treat people with respect, then you will be respected. Sounds obvious really, but it's not quite as simple as that. God has engineered it so that it is not necessarily the ones that you have shown respect to that will respect you back. It's not just 'what goes around comes around'. There is an external and unseen factor at work: the law of God.

Again, if you show generosity, God will make sure that you receive generosity back from somewhere else.

Another aspect of sowing and reaping is that you always reap more than you sow, and usually a whole lot more! In farming this is the whole point, of course, and it works in life as well. So it is very important what we sow in life because there will be a lot of it coming back in our direction!

Today's passage is powerful but true. Look around you and see it at work in the lives of others. In Hosea there is a verse which says, "...sow the wind and reap the whirlwind." (Hos.8:7, NIV) Sowing the wind is obviously sowing nothing. But you don't get simply nothing back; you get a lot of nothing – the whirlwind, a destructive force.

It's coming up to the time of year when gardeners start thinking about what they are going to plant. I think it would be a good time for us to consider that too.

259

...bringing every thought into captivity to the obedience of Christ...
2 Corinthians 10:5 (NKJV)

We are looking at sowing and reaping. Yesterday we established that we reap what we sow – that is a universal law of God – and that you get back more than you sow too.

Have you ever thought, though, of what has been sown into your life? We always make this about us doing the *sowing,* but we don't think about what has been sown into us – what we are *growing!*

Everybody's life is a field, and however good our intentions, things get sown in them that we didn't plant. The people that we rub shoulders with sow things unwittingly in our lives. Have you ever thought, "My, I sounded just like so-and-so then!" A seed has been sown – and it grew. We get attitudes sown into our lives which grow and bear fruit. Sometimes it's not the kind of fruit we want at all.

Jesus spoke about an enemy sowing weeds among the wheat. So, if you notice something growing in your life that you don't like – a desire, a bad attitude, a prejudice, a critical spirit – you must take action before it a) bears fruit or b) spreads through you to somebody else.

Here's what to do.

1. Try to identify where it came from. The most common source is from a person you mix with. So either stop mixing with them, or be very much on your guard in their presence and don't listen or put up with any of those seeds being transmitted through their conversation.
2. Repent before God. Ask Him to forgive you for allowing this seed to grow in your life and to remove it in Jesus' name.
3. Plant a good seed there instead. If the bad seed was criticism, go out of your way to praise and encourage others. In other words, do the opposite. Paul spoke about this in today's verse.

Thoughts are seeds – have a look at them before you let them get planted in your life.

260

Don't let anyone look down on you because you are young, but set an example for the believers in speech, in life, in love, in faith and in purity.

1 Timothy 4:12 (NIV)

We have looked at sowing and reaping as an immutable law of the universe, God's law, and how to deal with things that have been sown into us that were unwelcome. Today I want us to consider what we are sowing in other people's lives. Most of us have no idea what influence we have over others. The more time you spend with someone, the more you are influencing them – sowing seeds in their life. Some people will get more of the seed too because they look up to you; they are, if you like, following you. Children, grandchildren, students, people who respect you are all taking in your words, looking at the way you live and copying you, sometimes intentionally. That is how sowing works.

It is therefore incredibly important that we are a source of good seed. Actually, Jesus went further than that. He said, "The field is the world, the good seeds are the sons of the kingdom..." (Matt.13:38, NKJV) You *are* the good seed if you belong to Him! He sowed into you and now you sow into others. Quite a responsibility, quite an honour!

Paul taught his protégé Timothy this lesson in today's verse. He even told people, if they wanted to know how to live for Christ, to imitate him! Not many of us would be willing to tell somebody to copy us – but they are already.

A tomato has the characteristics of the plant it came from, back to the very first tomato – there has never been a break in the chain. Its seed carries those characteristics on. In my life are characteristics that have been sown into me by the Christians I have followed – I am passionate about passing those on (the good ones, that is). I'm thinking of Jack Mitchell, Ken McCleod, David Chaudhary, Arthur Neil, Stan Hyde. There's a little bit of all of them in me.

Have a think about whom you have followed and what you are passing on.

261

Peacemakers who sow in peace reap a harvest of righteousness.

James 3:18 (NIV)

Today we are looking at a less well-known verse on this subject – not an easy verse to understand. There are two great Christian principles at each end of the verse – two things that are very high on God's list of priorities: peace-making and righteousness. We know that righteousness, or us being right with God, can only be achieved because Jesus bought us peace with God through His blood. We are now commissioned to be peacemakers – to take this message of reconciliation to the world; in other words, to sow peace. Peace with God. The harvest of this will be righteousness. Sow peace, reap righteousness.

But this verse is saying something else as well. It's saying something about the way we go about it. "Peacemakers who sow in peace…" James, Jesus' own brother, is telling us that peace has not only to be a message but a lifestyle. How can we sow peace if we don't practise peace?

Peace is endearing, attractive and fascinating. One of the most wonderful things about Jesus was His serenity. People are magnetised by that. Two people that stand out in this way are Gandhi and Mother Theresa – two of the most influential people of the twentieth century. Gandhi, as far as we know, never became a Christian, but he was the first to say that Jesus was the greatest influence on his life. Mother Theresa lived for Jesus.

In these days of great uncertainly, turmoil and even despair there is a great work that can be done by calmness, tranquillity, peace. Sowing peace will, I believe, produce a great harvest of righteousness. That kind of peace is readily available to all who follow Jesus – it is a fruit of the Holy Spirit.

This weekend let's have a go at calmness. Get before God in a prayerful and receptive way and let Him fill you with His peace. By its very nature, it is not something that can be rushed.

Romans 15:33 (NIV) says, "Now the God of peace be with you all. Amen."

262

...be still, and know that I am God.

Psalm 46:10 (NIV)

On Saturday I left you with a thought (a task, really): have a go at calmness. Today I felt it was worth pursuing this theme and so my talks this week are going to be about being still.

Today's well-known verse is from the psalm that starts, "God is our refuge and strength, a very present help in trouble." (NKJV) Read it through.

"Be still, and know that I am God." What an incredible statement! People through countless generations have found great comfort and help in that advice. It has been a turning point in people's lives and, I'm sure, saved lives too. The principle behind this phrase is that often we need to relax, stop trying so hard to fix things and let God do His stuff.

The Hebrew word translated "be still" is *raphah* (pronounced raw-faw). It's a very vivid and explicit word meaning 'to cease, let alone, leave, stay still'. It could be used of sinking down into a comfortable armchair or being secure in the knowledge that you are safe.

John Greenleaf Whittier describes it beautifully in his hymn 'Dear Lord and Father of mankind':

Drop thy still dews of quietness
'til all our strivings cease.
Take from our souls the strain and stress,
And let our ordered lives confess
The beauty of His peace.

Many people would say, "Well, it sounds nice but it's easier said than done." The fact is that it can't be done unless you know God, unless you know how big He is and how much He cares for you. The psalmist paints a picture of calamity and against this backdrop the power, the greatness and the involvement of God.

It's one thing to know how big God is but quite another to know that He is interested in you, in your day, in your struggles and that he is ready, willing and able to help.

He is saying, "God is bigger than all your troubles so relax. Be still."

263

...stand still and see the salvation of the LORD, who is with you...
2 Chronicles 20:17 (NKJV)

Yesterday we saw that it is only when you know God that you can be still, especially in a crisis. I believe that in times of trouble those who really know God shine. Their stillness and calmness powerfully demonstrate the confidence they have in God.

To be still and do nothing in a time of crisis is extremely difficult – especially for men. In the Old Testament book of Chronicles, the army of Israel was confronted by the formidable force of the Ammonites and the Moabites at En Gedi. Their leader, King Jehoshaphat, a great general, was afraid. So much so that he declared a fast and sought God's help in prayer. He didn't expect the answer he received.

God spoke through a man called Jahaziel and said, "Do nothing. Be still and know that I am God." They obeyed and the enemy was defeated. Read the story! Jahaziel had also said, "The battle is not yours, but God's."

It took a much braver man to do nothing, to be still, than to act in this situation. Actually, Jehoshaphat did do something: he obeyed God. He had total confidence in God and the victory was won.

The greatest example of being still, and one that amazes and humbles me after all these years, is Jesus Himself. At Eastertime I often perform my one-man-drama where I am a Roman Centurion. At the moment when I am driving the nails into Jesus' hands and feet, I get overcome by the fact that He was silent. Acts 8:32 (NKJV) says, "He was led as a sheep to the slaughter; and as a lamb before its shearer is silent, so He opened not His mouth."

"Be still and know that I am God." And another victory was won – the greatest of all time.

What is the Lord saying to you today?

264

Be silent before the LORD, all humanity, for he is springing into action from his holy dwelling.

Zechariah 2:13 (NLT)

We are considering the Bible phrase, "Be still, and know that I am God." I have been walking with Jesus now for nearly fifty years. I can't understand it when people say to me that God doesn't exist. Whom have I been talking to all my life? Well, I guess they would say I've been talking to myself. But the bigger question is, who has been answering? They would say it's just coincidence, to which I would answer and say, "Funny isn't it – the more I pray, the more coincidences happen!"

When we pray, God answers. When Jesus prayed, the Bible says He went away to a quiet place; He went to be still. When we pray, we need to do the same: be still; relax in His presence and quietly hand over our worries and concerns to Him. And that's what most people do – tell God about their troubles and ask Him for His help. But what happens next really sorts the sheep out from the goats. You were 'being still' in His presence, you might have felt a lovely calmness come over you, but then you say, "Amen!" and the stillness is gone. You walk away with the same worries and cares playing on your mind, losing you sleep and peace.

God is not just a heavenly confidante. With confidantes a trouble shared is a trouble halved. With God a trouble shared is a trouble banned. Peter talks about "casting all your care upon Him, for He cares for you" (1.Pet.5:7, NKJV). Give Him your cares in the stillness of His presence and leave them with Him. Take the stillness with you, not the cares. That's the whole point. Be still and know that He is God. Have confidence in His greatness!

If I tell God my troubles and then go back trying to fix things, what am I saying? He needs my help. "It was nice to talk but I don't think You are going to do anything." Let Him do it – stand back, be still, wait.

When the burden is lifted and then the solution comes, it will strengthen your faith because it had to be Him!

265

Sow for yourselves righteousness; reap in mercy; break up your fallow ground, for it is time to seek the LORD, till He comes and rains righteousness on you.

Hosea 10:12 (NKJV)

I have been in some powerful meetings over the years; meetings where God moved in mighty ways, but the most awesome thing of all is when the Holy Spirit brings silence. We tend to call it a holy hush. A stillness descends on the congregation and nobody moves or speaks. The atmosphere is charged, filled with the presence of God.

"Be still, and know that I am God." Most of our services and our personal devotions are about communication – communication with God – but the next level is communion – communion with God. I don't mean breaking bread; I'm talking communing, connecting, being so aware of His presence that all other communication is unnecessary. To do this you have to be still and wait.

Yesterday, someone reminded me of today's verse in Hosea which talks of this very thing. "For it is time to seek the LORD, till He comes." We don't usually do that. We don't usually seek the Lord till He comes. Just recently I have had several things happen that have been a real worry – the sort of things that keep you awake at night. I have, of course, prayed about them and even given them to the Lord – casting my cares upon Him. But something new has happened. The Lord has taught me to stay there, to wait, to cast until I know that He has caught! To be still and know that He is God. And then I can walk away, as we said yesterday, with the stillness not the cares.

When I read my favourite books, the ones about great Christians through the ages, I come across this time after time: waiting on God, staying in His presence till the peace comes. Sometimes it comes as a 'word from God', a Bible verse; sometimes as a feeling, a lifting of the burden; but it does come. Try it.

266

...be still, and know that I am God.

Psalm 46:10 (NIV)

We have seen how this statement from Psalm 46 speaks about our confidence in God, that we can leave things in His hands. We also saw that there is a time to be silent and just commune with God. Today I want to take you right back to the beginning of your Christian walk and talk about the stillness of salvation.

Religion says that you must earn your salvation, you have to do something worthy, be good, atone for your sins. That is where our faith differs. It is not religion. The New Testament shows us that there is absolutely no way we can earn or deserve salvation. We cannot make ourselves better. In fact, trying to do that simply compounds the problem.

I knew someone who was a winchman on a rescue helicopter. His job was to rescue people at sea and often they were drowning. When he reached them, hanging on the end of the wire, they would struggle; they would try to save themselves and that would exacerbate the situation. He told me that sometimes he would have to headbutt them with his helmet and knock them out so that they would be still enough for him to rescue them!

To be saved we need to be still and know (acknowledge) that He is God – or maybe in this case, know that He is God and be still. Jesus has done it all. Everyone has a price on his head and Jesus has paid it. He has Himself atoned for our sins, He has taken the punishment that we deserved, He has shed His blood that we might be forgiven and made acceptable to God. What do we have to do? Just accept it. Surrender! Be still and just say thank you.

Maybe there is someone reading this who does not know Jesus, hasn't been saved. Maybe you are trying to be good and hoping that you will be accepted by God. That will never work. Surrender. Give in. Be still.

Pray this: *"Lord God, I know that I could never be good enough to deserve salvation, but I thank you that You accept me as I am. I believe that Jesus has done everything necessary by dying on the cross for me and rising from the dead. I surrender to you, Lord. Make me a new person. Cleanse me of all my sin and come and live in me. Amen."*

267

...be still, and know that I am God.

Psalm 46:10 (NIV)

This week we have been considering what the phrase "be still, and know that I am God" from Psalm 46 means. If we look at the psalm and its background, we find some interesting things.

This psalm has been an inspiration to millions, from Bach to Obama. It is believed that even Shakespeare left his mark on this psalm. The King James Bible was completed in 1611 and Shakespeare was forty-six that year and in the employ of King James. If you take the forty-sixth word from the beginning and the forty-sixth word from the end and put them together, it makes Shakespeare.

Remember, on Tuesday I said that there is a similar phrase in 2 Chronicles that contains the command given by God to King Jehoshaphat: "...stand still and see the salvation of the LORD, who is with you..." (2.Chron.20:17, NKJV) Well, this psalm was written by the Sons of Korah at that very time when the armies of Ammon and Moab were amassed against the army of Jehoshaphat. So this psalm was based on a word from God from the prophet Jahaziel.

This word from God and the song that came from it have been a great comfort to many people in times of trouble. Part of it is read at almost every Christian funeral, it has been quoted by many leaders in times of war and it is part of the liturgy in many denominations.

But it is more than a comfort, it is a declaration. Spurgeon called it a "song of holy confidence" because it demonstrated the greatness of God, His supremacy and His triumph. Can you imagine what it was like for the leaders of the army of Judah as they looked out and saw a vast force that they knew could easily annihilate them? Can you then imagine this word being given to them – "God has got this, just stand still and watch"? And before their eyes God won the victory for them.

Now, look at your own situation. Maybe you are facing insurmountable problems. The odds are stacked against you. Like Jehoshaphat you go to God in prayer. Then you declare this word, this psalm, over your problems. "Stay still and watch," God says, "I've got this!"

268

...far above all principality and power and might and dominion, and every name that is named, not only in this age but also in that which is to come.

Ephesians 1:21 (NKJV)

The first chapter of Ephesians is one of my favourite chapters in the whole Bible; there is such magnificent majesty in it and reading it makes your spirit soar! You are going to read it now, aren't you? I hope so.

One of the ways this chapter lifts us is through the use of the word "all". This little word leaves no room for debate, does not tolerate exclusions and makes what follows it a firm declaration. All means all.

Also, verses 15 to 21 are all one sentence – one hundred and sixty-six words! That must be one of the longest sentences in the Bible! But it builds triumphantly and brings us to the peak when it declares that the Lord Jesus Christ is "far above all principality and power and might and dominion, and every name that is named, not only in this age but also in that which is to come".

I just found myself singing Charles Wesley's wonderful little hymn, "This, this is the Christ we adore, our faithful unchangeable friend, whose love is as great as His power and neither knows measure nor end!" This is the Christ we adore – the God we know. This is our friend – Jesus!

It's nice to have an important or famous friend. How good it makes us feel to introduce them to someone. "This is my friend Professor Roy Peacock," I remember saying with a smile from ear to ear. What about, "This is my friend the Lord Jesus Christ, who is seated 'far above all principality and power and might and dominion, and every name that is named, not only in this age but also in that which is to come'"? The highest position in the universe! A greater name than any other! A position that will not change for all eternity! My friend, you know! Oh yes, I know Him personally.

What could be greater than this?

Don't be beaten down by your worries and cares and fears for the future. You have a friend who is master of all things. Don't be deceived into thinking that the devil is almost as powerful as Him. Jesus is *far above* all others! His power and authority is *far above* all others'. There is no comparison.

This, this is the Christ we adore! And may He bless you today!

303

TUESDAY, 16TH FEBRUARY, 2021

...He raised Him from the dead and seated Him at His right hand in the heavenly places, far above all principality and power and might and dominion, and every name that is named, not only in this age but also in that which is to come. And He put all things under His feet.

Ephesians 1:20-22 (NKJV)

Yesterday we saw how Jesus is described in Ephesians 1. In ancient times the phrase 'all things under one's feet' meant that everything was subject to the person – something like master of all he surveys but even stronger. It meant that you had total authority. It conjures up a picture of a monarch on a throne, the throne being on a dais and everybody else being at ground level – literally under the level of the ruler's feet.

This is speaking of the Lord Jesus Christ and the position of honour and authority that the Father has given Him; not just the authority of an earthly monarch but authority over every spiritual entity – principality, power, might and dominion.

Now let's go back to the earthly throne room. You are there among the courtiers bowing low before the king. Then the king extends his sceptre in your direction and says, "Come here." You tentatively approach. He is smiling. You hesitate. Then he says, "Come up and sit with me." Everyone gasps. You climb the steps and sit down next to him. What does that mean?

In the next chapter of Ephesians it says, "But because of his great love for us, God, who is rich in mercy, made us alive with Christ even when we were dead in transgressions – it is by grace you have been saved. And God raised us up with Christ and seated us with him in the heavenly realms in Christ Jesus..." (Eph.2:4-6, NIV)

God has raised us up and made us sit together with Jesus! Can it be true? Yes, that is what the Bible says. The tense that it is written in means it is a done deal.

So, what do you notice when you are sitting with someone? Depending on how tall you are, your heads might be on a different level but your feet are on the same level. Therefore whatever is under their feet is also under your feet. If you are in Christ Jesus then you too have authority in His name.

Charles Wesley's wonderful hymn says, "Jesus, the Name high over all, in hell or earth or sky; angels and mortals prostrate fall, and devils fear and fly. Jesus, the Name to sinners dear, the Name to sinners giv'n; it scatters all their guilty fear, it turns their hell to heav'n."

But Jesus looked at them and said, "With man this is impossible, but with God all things are possible."

Matthew 19:26 (NIV)

Today I want us to consider our future and how to shape it in Christ. After the pandemic is over, we will be able to hug people again. But wouldn't it be sad if some people retained the fear that Coronavirus caused and never hugged anyone again?

When we become a Christian, "all things are made new" – we are free to live without the limitations, fears and failures that we experienced in our former lives. As far as God is concerned, those things are over and done with – they are 'under the blood' as we used to say. Unfortunately, sometimes these things raise their ugly heads again.

The devil likes to make out that nothing has really happened to us and so he brings up our past and tries to colour our future with it. Don't allow this to happen. You are free. Jesus always used scripture to counter the devil's attacks, and so if he comes to you with suggestions like, "You can't speak in public; remember what a mess you got in when you tried at school," respond with, "I can do all things through Christ who strengthens me."

We are not the same person any more and we have resources that we did not have before. Even after nearly fifty years of public ministry the devil still tries it on with me. "You can't do that," he says. Philippians 4:13 has been my watchword all my life.

It is not only the devil who raises the past. Stupidly, we go fishing around in it and drag things into our new lives. We cannot fully find a future unless we fully lose the past. I would not have got far with my international ministry if I had dragged my youthful fear of heights into my new life – I have spent half my life at thirty-five thousand feet!

Our new life in Christ is a life of potential, a life free from natural limitations, a life of the possible not the impossible. I heard of a mission organisation called 'Mission Possible'. Jesus said, "…with God all things are possible."

As I have mentioned before, a friend of mine wrote a song called 'He broke all my limitations'. I have often thought of that line when I feel that I'm not good enough or that something is beyond me. In Christ I can!